THESE

PRECIOUS

DAYS

THESE PRECIOUS DAYS

· ESSAYS ·

Ann Patchett

HARPER  PERENNIAL

NEW YORK · LONDON · TORONTO · SYDNEY · NEW DELHI · AUCKLAND

HARPER ● PERENNIAL

FIRST HARPER PERENNIAL EDITION PUBLISHED 2022.

Designed by Elina Cohen

Library of Congress Cataloging-in-Publication Data has been applied for.

ISBN 978-0-06-309279-2 (pbk.)

22 23 24 25 26 LSC 10 9 8 7 6 5 4 3 2 1

to Maile Meloy

Contents

CONTENTS

Essays Don't Die

The first time I remember seriously thinking about my own death, I was twenty-six years old and working on my first novel, *The Patron Saint of Liars*. No matter where I went, I carried the entire cast of characters with me—the heroines and heroes and supporting players, as well as the towns they lived in, their houses and cars, all the streets and all the trees and the color of the light. Every day a little bit more of their story was committed to paper, but everything that was still to come existed only in my head. Remembering things is how I work. I didn't have outlines or notes, and because of that, I was hounded by the thought of stepping off a curb at the wrong moment, or drowning in the ocean (this second scenario seemed more likely, as I was living in Provincetown, Massachusetts, where I swam in the freezing water and was prone to cramps).

Were I to die, I'd be taking the entire world of my novel with me—no significant loss to literature, sure, but the thought of losing all the souls inside me was unbearable. Those people were my responsibility. I'd made them up, and I wanted them to have their chance. The specter of my death stayed with me until the novel was finished, and when it was finished, death lit out for a holiday.

No luck lasts. A few chapters into my second novel, there death was, picking up the conversation exactly where we'd left off. I was living in Montana by then, a state full of potential deaths I'd never thought to worry about: falling off a hiking trail and down the side of a mountain, being hit by a runaway logging truck, being eaten by a mountain lion or a bear. Every trip outside was a meditation on mortality. But when I wrote the last page of that novel, death packed up without a word. Through editing, copyediting, page proofs, book tour, it never crossed my mind that I might break through the solid ice that had formed over the river and be swept away.

When death came back for the third time it was, as always, without fanfare. I was deep into my third novel then, and had been at the job long enough to recognize the pattern.

My professional life has continued to be marked by this on-again, off-again relationship, and, weird as it is, the problem isn't unique to me. Before she boards a plane, one friend sends me instructions as to where in her house she's hidden a thumb drive with the files for her uncompleted novel; another friend asks me if I could just finish her book for her if she dies. "I left a Post-it on my computer," she tells me, "saying you'll write the end."

According to my small, unscientific study, writers who were already deep into a project when the pandemic hit were okay going forward, while those of us who had yet to start, or had barely started, froze in our tracks. Death had gotten the jump on me this time; I was worrying about it before I'd even come up with a fully formed idea for a novel. What was the point of starting if I wasn't going to be around to finish? This didn't necessarily mean I believed I was going to die of the coronavirus, any more than I believed I was going to drown in the Atlantic or be eaten by a bear, but all those scenarios were possible. The year 2020 didn't seem like a great time to start a family, or a business, or a novel.

Of course I was still writing essays. I'm always writing essays—eight hundred words on owning a bookstore for a newspaper in London, my ten favorite books of the year for a magazine in Australia, an introduction for a newly reissued classic, maybe a little piece about dogs. Essays never filled my days, but they reminded me that I was still a writer when I wasn't writing a novel.

That was how I found my loophole: death has no interest in essays.

Why hadn't I noticed this before? When I wrote my first essay collection, *This Is the Story of a Happy Marriage*, death didn't even bother to rattle the windows. The book felt so ridiculously personal that I worried only about whose feelings I might hurt, and gave no consideration as to whether I might step on a snake. I realized that for all the essays I'd written in my life, I'd never once heard the ethereal *shush* of a scythe being sharpened nearby. Had death wandered off because no immense cast of imagined characters could be obliterated? Or was it because the things I wrote about in essays were true, verifiable? Were I to abruptly exit in the middle of writing an essay, there would be someone around who, with a certain amount of research, could bring it to conclusion. They might not write it the way I would have, but the same facts would be available to them. Or maybe the facts themselves were the problem. Imagination can be killed but facts are infinitely harder to snuff out. I know it might not seem this way. Time works tirelessly to erase facts—this country works tirelessly—but facts have a way of popping up, their buoyant truth shining all the more brightly with time. Maybe that was why death wasn't interested in essays; essays don't die. I decided to go all in.

I began to write longer essays, and I wrote them for myself: Why the sudden desire to get rid of things? What did it mean at this point in my life not to have children? Other essays came out of conversations I had with friends, most notably the piece about my three fathers. After my friend Kate's father died, she told me she was going to write about him. I'd been thinking of writing about my own three fathers for fifteen years but had never found the courage to follow through. I asked her if I could tag along. Writing is such solitary work, but in this case her companionship made me brave.

It wasn't until I wrote the title essay, "These Precious Days," that I realized I would have to put a book together. That essay was so important to me that I wanted to build a solid shelter for it. I started writing more essays. I went back and looked at other pieces I'd written in the past few years. Most of them I ignored, but those that were strongest I took apart and wrote again. It's a wonderful thing to be able to go back to something that's a couple of years old, see the flaws in the fullness of time, and then have the chance to make corrections and polish it up—or in some cases, throw the whole thing out and write a better version. *That's* something I never get to do with novels. Through these essays, I could watch myself grappling with the same themes in my writing and in my life: what I needed, whom I loved, what I could let go, and how much energy the letting go would take.

Again and again, I was asking what mattered most in this precarious and precious life.

As for death, I have remained lucky. Its indifference has never waned, though surely it will circle back for me later. Death always thinks of us eventually. The trick is to find the joy in the interim, and make good use of the days we have.

Darrell Ray, Ann Patchett, Frank Patchett, and Mike Glasscock.

September 2005

· Three Fathers ·

Marriage has always proven irresistible to my family. We try and fail and try again, somehow maintaining our belief in an institution that has made fools of us all. I've married twice; so has my sister. Our mother married three times. None of us set out for this. We meant to stick our landing on the first try, but we stumbled. My parents divorced when I was five. My mother and my stepfather Mike had their final parting when I was twenty-four. She married Darrell when I was twenty-seven, and they stayed together until he died in 2018, when I was fifty-four.

My problems were never ones of scarcity. I suffered from abundance, too much and too many. There are worse problems to have.

The second time my sister, Heather, married, she wanted a real wedding. Heather and her new husband, Bill, threw a terrific party in a fancied-up barn that had been turned into an event space.

They'd hired a swing band with a handsome front man—Heather and I both had a terrible crush on him, and now neither of us can remember his name. Karl and I had eloped a few months before, and those beautiful words of love and commitment were still fresh. We drank the champagne, danced in a line, blew soap bubbles into the night sky above the bride and groom. Only my stepfather Mike was sullen. His third marriage was nearing its end, and he was in love with my mother again. But my mother was happy with Darrell, and so Mike danced with me for most of the night.

My father, who had always hated my stepfather, hated him less now that he too had lost my mother. At my sister's wedding, my father contented himself with simply hating my mother, even though she had left him for my stepfather in 1969. Beneath the glow of the little white lights draped over the ceiling's crossbeams, my stepfather's love for my mother and my father's hatred of her looked remarkably similar.

Darrell noticed none of this. He had fallen down the brick stairs that led to the back door of their house eight weeks before and fractured several vertebrae. He was wearing a brace beneath his suit, beneath his clerical gown. He was a retired Presbyterian minister and he officiated my sister's wedding, despite the pain it caused him to walk and stand and breathe. He hung on through the dinner and then got a ride home.

But the story I want to tell begins just after the wedding was over and before the reception began, while the photographs were being taken. Or it happened months before that, when I first realized all three of the fathers were going to be at Heather's wedding—the family equivalent of a total solar eclipse. I wanted a picture of that.

I called my father first, as I pegged him to be the one most likely to say no, but he surprised me. Sure, he said, fine. He didn't care. Then I asked Mike, who would have found a way to get me the North Star had I wanted it. He hesitated but then said yes as well. He didn't like the idea, but as far as I was concerned he didn't have to like it. It would take two minutes. Darrell had never met my father before, and had met my stepfather only once in passing. Unlike my father and stepfather, Darrell owed me nothing, but he said he'd do it.

The wedding took place in late September on a day that was clear and bright and still a little warm. After Heather and Bill had been photographed with every possible configuration of family and friends, I lined my mother's husbands up together. In one picture it's just the three of them in their dark suits, and in the other I am with them in my garnet bridesmaid's dress. Darrell holds up one of my hands, Mike holds the other, and my father in the middle has his hand on my waist. They look like they're trying to steady me. My father is the handsome one, the one whose face registers genuine happiness for the day. Darrell is smiling bravely, very straight in his back brace. And Mike looks like he's going to leap out of the frame the second I let go of his hand.

"We were all standing there waiting on the photographer," my father told me later on the phone. "And Mike said, 'You know what she's doing, don't you? She's going to wait until the three of us are dead and then she's going to write about us. This is the picture that will run with the piece.' " My father said the idea hadn't occurred to him, and it wouldn't have occurred to Darrell, but as soon as Mike said it, they knew he was right.

He was right. That was exactly what I meant to do. That is exactly what I'm doing now.

THE THREE FATHERS died in the order in which my mother had married them, and they died in the inverse order of their health. My father went first, even though he had made a religion of the elliptical trainer, the treadmill, the NordicTrack. He spent four slow years dying of a neurological disease called progressive supranuclear palsy, which in the end confined him to a wheelchair. My stepmother took care of him at home, a Herculean task that allowed him to die in the comfort of their bed.

Mike didn't have a fourth wife. He spent his last two years living with his older daughter, Tina, who gave him all the love and attention he had denied her as a child. Mike made death look easy. He had some dementia, and six weeks after he was diagnosed with kidney failure he went gently in his sleep.

Darrell made death hard. He hadn't been well for decades. After his broken back there was a series of splintering falls, a terrible car accident, a shunt for hydrocephalus, and two kinds of cancer. But he kept on living. When I was sitting by Darrell's bed in the assisted-living center where he spent his last, excruciating years, I thought again about the photograph. He was the last, and the one who had played the smallest role in my life. I held his skeletal hand and thought about what I would write after he died.

But when death finally came I found I didn't want to think about Darrell anymore. I didn't want to think about any of them. I had—along with my sister and my stepsisters, my mother and stepmother—spent so many years seeing them through and then seeing them out. I went back to the assisted-living center to empty Darrell's room the night he died, to drag the unopened cases of Depends and Ensure to the community room for anyone who wanted them, and then I carted off his paperbacks and impossibly large shoes to Goodwill. When I was done, I was done with all of it. That remained the case for a long time.

IN 1974 MY father signed up for the "100 Greatest Books of All Time" from the Franklin Library. He went for the full leather option— silk-moiré endpapers, sewn-in satin-ribbon bookmarks, every edge of every page gilded in twenty-two-karat gold. When the people at the Franklin Library came up with this monthly subscription service, my father was the sort of customer they had in mind. He didn't intend just to buy the books, he intended to read them. He intended to be the kind of person who sat in his home library of leather-bound books with embossed spines reading *The Return of the Native*. Month after month, year after year, he spent a significant amount of money to be that person.

My father had grown up the third of seven children. He was born in 1931, the first of the Patchetts to have been born in this country. His parents left England to find work in California, and after a long stretch of nothing—it was the Depression—his father landed a job as a machinist at Columbia Pictures. But when the set builders went on strike he went with them in solidarity, and all of them were blackballed from working in the studio system again. My grandfather became a janitor at the *Los Angeles Times*, a filthy job because of the ink that got on everyone's hands. Later he was able to get my grandmother a job in the cafeteria there. The family of nine shared a three-bedroom house on Council Street near Echo Park in Los Angeles. My father slept in a narrow bed on the back porch.

When my father got out of the navy, he moved back to Council Street and worked in a liquor store for a couple of years while he applied to the Los Angeles Police Department. He kept being rejected because a doctor said something was wrong with his heart, until finally another doctor said nothing was wrong with his heart. He became a police officer. He married my mother, a beautiful nurse. They had two daughters and bought a house on Rossmoyne Avenue in Glendale. Then my mother fell in love with Mike, who was a doctor at the hospital where she worked, and when Mike moved to Tennessee she packed us up and followed him there.

Without us, my father rented out the house on Rossmoyne and returned to Council Street. He lived with his father and his sister Cece, who worked for the phone company. When Heather and I flew from Nashville to visit for a week every summer, we slept in Cece's bed and Cece slept on the couch, somehow convincing us that the couch was where she'd wanted to sleep all along. Our father was back in his bed on the porch. After the yearly purchase of two plane tickets, he used what was left of his savings to take us to Disneyland or Knott's Berry Farm, but the place we all liked best was Forest Lawn. Forest Lawn was free. We would bring a lunch and walk the paths through the exemplary grass to see where the movie stars were buried, then we would go and stand in the crisp, cold air of the flower shop, which looked like a summer retreat for hobbits. The place smelled overwhelmingly of carnations, a scent I still associate with those happy afternoons spent in the cemetery.

Our father moved back to the Rossmoyne house when he married our stepmother. She made the place a loving home where we were always welcome. The Franklin Library extended its offering beyond a hundred, and my father bought those latecomers as well. After that he subscribed to the presidential series.

Every book arrived with a slim pamphlet that included an overview of the text and some study questions to consider. It soon became clear that my father was not going to get through the *Oresteia* one month and *The Decameron* the next, but he faithfully read the pamphlets and kept them stored in the small box that had been sent for this purpose. He believed he would catch up eventually, if not on vacation then once he retired. He wanted to read the books and he wanted the books to be read. He was all too happy when I sat down with *The Red Badge of Courage* or *Pride and Prejudice* when we came to visit in the summer. He let me take his copy of *Anna Karenina* to the condo he and my stepmother had bought in Port Hueneme up the coast from Los Angeles. I sat in the living room reading day after day and wouldn't go to the beach.

This father, you might think, is the perfect father for a writer. To which I would say, yes and no.

For all his love of books, my father believed that childhood development rested on the ability to play volleyball. Even on the beaches of Southern California, I doubted this was true, but in the Catholic girls' school my sister and I attended in Nashville, I was sure he was wrong. From the other side of the country, my father wanted to shape us. He had better luck with my sister. Heather was three and a half years older. She'd had three and a half more years to spend with him. When he gave her instruction on what classes to take and what clubs to sign up for and how many sit-ups to do every night, she listened. I didn't listen. When I was nine he sent Heather a volleyball net and a ball and $10, which was her payment for forcing me to play. She was to be his emissary and my coach, but we fought like wolves in those days. She strung the net up from the carport to the fence and then took it down, because you can lead your sister to the volleyball net but you cannot make her spike.

My father wanted me to be athletic. He wanted me to be on teams, join clubs, start clubs. He wanted me to run for office in any organization that held elections. He wanted me to audition, volunteer, be a part of something, submit. When I claimed to have no interest in a high school sorority he was pushing, he told me to become a member of that organization, rise through the ranks, and then change the system from within. He wanted me to infiltrate.

What mattered, he told me, was being well-rounded, but there was nothing well-rounded about me. I found another book and slunk into a corner. I told him I was going to be a writer. My father didn't mind my reading—he was a reader—but he told me he didn't see how I was going to be a writer.

I'm sure it's a common state to feel unseen by one's father, but the fact that I saw my father only one week a year made my condition literal. My father and I didn't see each other, and so we didn't understand. It was clear that he didn't know me, but it took a long time for me to realize that I didn't know him either.

"Someday you'll get divorced," he told me when I was in high school. "You'll have a couple of kids to support. You're not going to be able to do that writing." I couldn't be so selfish, he was saying. I had to think about what was best for those kids. It doesn't take a bucket of insight to figure out where this was coming from. My mother hadn't listened to him either. She thought my becoming a writer was an admirable plan.

My father wanted me to be a dental hygienist, though whenever he came back from vacation, he would tell me how much fun I'd have working on a cruise ship. I might have killed him had we lived in the same house, he might have killed me, but long-distance phone calls were expensive in those days and we talked only once a month. My sister took his instructions to heart—he wanted her to go to law school. She was the smart one, my sister, an excellent student. But when he gave me advice, I held the phone away from my ear. You are a duck, I would tell myself. This is rain.

I'm older now than my father was then, and I think about these conversations differently in the aftermath of time. Maybe he was trying to save me from suffering. He remembered his father walking through Los Angeles all day looking for work with a sandwich in his pocket, a wife and seven children back on Council Street. He remembered moving home after the navy, working in a liquor store, sleeping on the porch again. Wouldn't he try to spare me that? I wasn't much of a student when I was young, and my career plans were pretentious—I dreamed of making a very small living from my art. Maybe all he could do was operate within the world he knew: Catholicism, the navy, the police department. Captains gave orders and sailors went to sea. Who was I but a swabbie? He'd taken orders and I would take orders. No one exists on paper and pens, alone in a room without anyone to tell them when to get up and what to eat and where to go and when to sleep.

But I was a writer and nothing else, and to miss seeing me as such was to miss me altogether. I wrote and read and read and wrote. I stacked every egg I was ever given into a single basket. I can see how that would be unnerving for a parent.

Did I tell you I loved my father, that he loved me? Contrary to popular belief, love does not need understanding to thrive. My father made me laugh more often than he made me want to strangle him. We hashed out articles we read in the *New Yorker*. We listened to arias and tried to guess the composers. Our very happiest times were spent on the two linen sofas that faced each other in the Rossmoyne house, drinking gin and tonics and reading Yeats aloud, passing the leather-bound volume back and forth. "Who will go drive with Fergus now, / And pierce the deep wood's woven shade, / And dance upon the level shore?" "This one," he would say, and read me "The Lake Isle of Innisfree." Then he would hand me back the book and I would say, "This one."

But he also dragged us to the alley behind the grocery store at 6:00 a.m. so that we could hit tennis balls against the back wall of Ralph's. I was no better at tennis than I was at volleyball, but my sister would hit and hit and hit. Every time he sent me down the alley to retrieve the scattered balls I thought, I'll show you. I will not hit or play or join or score but I will write and I will show you.

It turns out that having a hard wall to hit your tennis balls against is what gives them bounce. Having someone who believed in my failure more than my success kept me alert. It made me fierce. Without ever meaning to, my father taught me at a very early age to give up on the idea of approval. I wish I could bottle that freedom now and give it to every young writer I meet, with an extra bottle for the women. I would give them the ability both to love and not to care.

"I'm not saying you can't have a hobby," he would say. "Writing is a perfectly fine hobby. Just don't think it's your job." With the buffer of two time zones between us, his disapproval began to feel more like a joke over the years. I got an MFA from Iowa, a handful of fellowships, a smattering of prizes. I published stories, articles, three novels, and still he sent me notices for summer work on cruise ships. I had no money and never asked for money. I lived in a tiny apartment and drove an old car. I had neither children nor debt.

My father read my stories, and then my books in manuscript. He helped me with research. He gave me notes. He was proud of me and good to me, he just didn't think this thing I was doing was actually a job.

What finally tipped the balance in my favor was something I'd never imagined: I became rich. *Rich* is a useless word, since everyone has her own definition, but in this case use mine: I had so much money I no longer knew exactly down to the last dollar how much I had. I could give money away without needing it back. I had written a book about opera and terrorism in South America that became very successful, and after that, my father changed. He now thought my being a writer was the perfect plan.

"I used to tell her she should be a dental hygienist," he would say, dropping his arm over my shoulder when I gave readings in Los Angeles, when all the Patchetts and all their friends and families were in attendance. "Good thing she never listens to me."

MY STEPFATHER MIKE had four children with his first wife. He left them in Los Angeles and took my mother and sister and me to Nashville. "Six kids," he would say when we were alone, "and you're the only one I'll never have to worry about." The first time he said that I was probably eight, and he continued to repeat the message in one way or another for the rest of his life. Did he actually see something in me when I was straw-haired and spindly? Or did I become successful because he repeated it with the certainty of an oracle: You Will Be the Winner?

The way I would be the winner, and Mike was positive about this, was by being a writer. "One of these days I'm going to open up one of your books and it's going to say, 'To Mike Glasscock.'"

But that could never happen. It would kill my father if I dedicated a book to Mike. These were the issues I wrestled with in middle school.

You might think there's a beautiful sort of justice in this—my father and my stepfather equally certain of their opposing views of my future. My reward for having one father who knew I would fail was having another father who was certain I'd succeed. A good theory, except for the fact that my stepfather was crazy, and my father was utterly sane.

Crazy is another sloppy word, like *rich*. It's all a matter of reference. My stepfather was by any measure a successful man, a surgeon who lectured all over the world and was sent the most difficult cases in the specialized field of neurotology. He flew a helicopter, rode motorcycles. He bought a farm thirty miles outside of town with a gate and a long gravel driveway. He had a water system installed and sank a gas tank, by which I mean we had a gas pump next to the carport in case the filling stations were abruptly closed. He buried gold coins beneath the marigolds and lugged cartons of dehydrated food and jugs of water up to the attic. Every house we lived in was filled with guns: guns holstered under chairs, in nightstand drawers, behind clock faces, in air-conditioning vents. The *Playboy* magazines stayed out on the coffee table in the living room while the hard stuff smoldered on the top shelf of the bedroom closet, where all the children found it. My stepfather broke plates and put his fist through the hollow doors and thought I was the second coming of Christ.

Mike liked to take me to the hospital with him on the weekends. He would leave me in the doctors' lounge while he went to see his patients. I would spend the morning reading books and eating powdered-sugar doughnuts and drinking Orange Crush. He would leave me in the car for an hour while he stopped at the apartment where his scrub nurse lived. Driving home, he would tell me the sad stories of his childhood, his teenage parents who shipped him off to live with his grandparents, the love he desired and never received. He spent his days slicing tumors out of people's brains. He would come home with bruises under his eyes from leaning into a microscope for twelve or fourteen hours at a stretch. He was financially responsible for two wives and six children. He bought racehorses and dug oil wells with no knowledge of how either of those enterprises worked. He took up sculpture and fencing. He rebuilt a houseboat in the driveway. He spent five mornings a week in analysis for more years than should be legal. All he wanted was to be a writer.

I remember being home from college and Mike and I watching Olivier's *King Lear*. When the credits rolled, one read "By William Shakespeare."

"That's all I want," Mike said to me, pointing at the television set. "That three or four hundred years from now people will watch something on television that says, 'By Michael Glasscock.'"

Mike subscribed to the monthly book series from the Easton Press, and like my father he went for the full leather option. Mike liked sets—sets of Shakespeare, of Dickens, the cunning little set of hardback Chekhov stories that sat on his desk while he read Ian Fleming and James Clavell. If my father was a man who meant to read the 100 Greatest Books of All Time but never did, my stepfather was a man who'd tell you he'd read them already. He taught me how to play chess, drive a car, throw a knife, develop black-and-white photographs (first in the bathtub and then later in the darkroom he built off the den). He taught all of us how to shoot—rifles, shotguns, handguns of every stripe—then how to take those guns apart to clean them. He made us practice grabbing the gun from beneath the chair in the living room in case we were kidnapped.

A woman once wrote me a letter that said she and her husband had a beloved daughter, and the girl showed a real talent for writing. "What can we do," the woman asked me, "to help her grow up to be like you?"

To be a writer, you have to like your own company. Ours was an easy house in which to be alone. We did not congregate in central locations. We left our rooms to eat our meals, and went back to our rooms. My sister had the full approval of our father, but that was like having a suitcase full of francs after France joined the eurozone. They were worthless, except to remind you that you used to be rich. She spent a couple of summers sleeping on the floor of the walk-in linen closet to avoid having to share her room with my stepfather's children. Finally she moved down to the basement. The basement was not a nice place, even with the dehumidifier running twenty-four hours a day. There were silverfish and centipedes down there but no bathroom, no interior access to the house, no window. It didn't matter. She went to the basement to get the hell away from us. I stayed in my room. I read and I wrote. I climbed through the woods, and when we moved into town the summer before I turned thirteen, I circled the block on my bicycle, waiting for dark. It was good to be outside.

"Don't ever have children," my stepfather told me again and again. "Biggest mistake I ever made in my life. Promise me you won't ever have children."

Mike started getting serious about writing short stories when we left the farm. He worked on them endlessly, by which I mean he wrote many, many stories but almost never wrote a second draft. He would scrawl them out on yellow legal pads as fast as a court reporter, give them to his secretary to type, and then give them to me to read. Even at thirteen I knew they were awful, but how was I supposed to tell him that?

I learned how to tell him that. Through time and volume he wore my manners away. "You can't have eight pages of someone getting into the shower!" I said without screaming. "Undressing, pulling back the shower curtain, turning the water on, waiting for the water to get hot. Nobody cares! It doesn't move your story along." And so he would cross out the shower scene, have his secretary retype it, and then give it back to me to read again.

I started reading Mike's stories in junior high. He took me to New York when I was eleven. He took me to England when I was fourteen. I started reading his novels when I was in college. He paid for me to go to college. One of the only real fights I remember us having was when I told him he couldn't pay for me to go to graduate school. I had gotten a financial aid package to teach literature but he didn't want me teaching. He didn't want me to have any sort of job. He wanted to believe that we were sharing the education, that I would go and learn and bring the wisdom back because he was too busy to go to Iowa himself. Mike worked so hard at everything he did. He believed that writing was something to be mastered by brute force. He would bludgeon it into submission. He started writing novels on the weekends. They were huge. Sometimes he dictated them, had them typed, and sent them to me without ever reading them himself.

Mike believed in me completely, and in return I read his novels. How many of them were there? Thirty? Forty? I have no idea. Some went as long as five hundred pages, printed out on creamy résumé paper and bound at Kinko's. I cannot begin to calculate how much of my reading life was lost to those books. It was a world populated with big-breasted blondes and long-haired brunettes, men with guns and helicopters and piles of cash. When bodies were mutilated, his writing slowed to ensure medical accuracy. The books were rife with sex and car crashes. Over the years I tried every tack: I did line edits. I did no line edits. I told him he couldn't waste my time like this. I tried to be encouraging. I stuffed them into trash cans in airports and said nothing. For years I would refuse to read them, and then I would relent because he was so certain the one he had just finished was different. It wasn't different. The novels would start coming again. Of course it wasn't only me. Some of these bricks landed on my sister, my stepsisters, maybe one or two on my stepbrothers, but the crushing majority found their way to my doorstep (FedEx First Overnight) because I was the writer. I found him a couple of editors for hire over the years, and they earned every dollar of the huge amount of money he paid them. In the end, when the money was gone, I paid for one myself.

"This would be child abuse," I said to my husband one night as I sat on the couch with a manuscript in my lap. "Except I'm fifty-two."

Mike never stopped writing, and he never stopped trying to get a real agent and a real contract. He paid to have four of his books published. They were the better ones, and still, they were awful. He commissioned artwork for the covers. They were good-looking books. He asked if he could do a reading at the bookstore I co-own in Nashville and I said yes. All his friends and old patients came, all the doctors he had trained, but still, he wasn't happy. He wanted what I had.

I first met Mike when I was five. He and my mother were together most of the time, not all of the time, until I was twenty-four. He and I remained close until he died at eighty-four. He settled as he aged. He became kinder, easier, a better listener. "Who is this wonderful man?" my stepsister Tina would say of him then. "And what have you done with my father?" His writing never improved.

I grew up in the weather of his insanity, and yet the gifts he gave me are legion. Not only did he make me believe I was going to be a writer, he made me believe that this was the prize that topped all other prizes. Through his own strange example, he taught me about work. If this man with an all-consuming job, six children, endless hobbies and endless affairs could find the time to write so many books, even horrible books, I should be able to organize myself for productivity. He taught me that to ask someone to read my work was to ask them to give me their time, and so I resolved to never ask anyone to read anything I'd written until I had done every last thing I could to make it better. Eudora Welty can show us what perfection looks like, but twenty thousand pages of bad fiction read over the course of a life can teach you what not to do. Dialogue, character development, pacing, setting, plot—I had seen every element of the novel run through a meat grinder. By burying me in piles of manuscripts throughout my life, Mike made me careful. What a time saver that turned out to be!

I WAS TWENTY-SEVEN when my mother married for the third time. The very idea of it exhausted me. She didn't see either of her first two husbands anymore, but both men were central in my life: my father wanting me to be more like him, my stepfather wanting to be more like me. I didn't want to find my place in the new family landscape. After all, I was grown and gone, married and divorced myself. I wanted my mother to be happy, that's all. I loved her and I wished her well. However trying her first two marriages had been for me, they had been devastating for her. I put on my best dress and went to the wedding.

Darrell was easy. That was evident right from the start. He knew how to cook. He liked to garden. He had good relationships with his three grown children. He brought very little into the marriage: a clock that had belonged to his grandfather, the clock's own shelf, a few framed pictures. He unpacked several boxes of books, most of them theological in nature, all of them read, many annotated in pencil, none bound in leather. Darrell was not a Franklin Library sort of guy, and he didn't care about my writing at all.

Or he did care, but in the same way he cared about Heather's job as a development officer for a small liberal-arts college. He had a son who was the editor of a newspaper, a son who was a doctor, a daughter who was a real estate agent. He seemed to be equally impressed with all of us. When he read one of my books or came to a reading, he would give me a hug afterwards and say "Aren't you a wonder," which is also what he said when I picked up Italian food for dinner or helped clean out the garage. I heard him say it to his children and to his grandchildren and to my mother. "Aren't you a wonder." It was a statement, not a question, and as many times as he said it, it never sounded like a stock phrase. It was as if he saw us, separately, equally, and found the wonder in each of us. I cannot imagine Darrell being interested in how much money I made or where I went or whom I knew, and yet I always believed he cared about my happiness. If he had any gaping holes in his life, I was never for an instant made to feel they were mine to fill. I knew Darrell for thirty years. He had a wealth of practical knowledge that I admired deeply. He knew how to solve problems, how to talk things through. And it wasn't just ministry he was good at. He was the person I called the morning I came downstairs and found the first floor of my house covered in two inches of water, with water pouring through the light fixtures of the basement ceiling.

Darrell and I occasionally went to the movies together after he retired, when my mother was still working. When he stopped driving, I would drive him around. In all the time I knew him, I can remember him raising his voice to me only twice, once when we were sorting through the contents of the basement before a move and I told him he had to get rid of his lifetime collection of *Mother Jones* magazines, which filled a series of giant, weighty, vinyl-covered binders. He told me the magazines were none of my business, and he was right, none of my business. The second time, we had gone to wait out a tornado in that same basement, and I finally said enough, I was going home. We have a lot of tornado warnings in Tennessee. It would be easy to spend all of spring in the basement. But he yelled at me and told me I wasn't going upstairs. Again, he was right. That was the full extent of our conflict.

I sat by Darrell's hospital bed many times over the years, as he had been at the intersection of bad health and bad luck for as long as I'd known him, but on the whole I didn't do much for him. His sons lived in other states, but his good daughter showed up for the things that daughters are called on to do. He had my mother. There was little need for me.

I don't know how my life might have gone if Darrell had been my father, or if he had been the stepfather I grew up with. It's hard for me to imagine he would have opposed my writing or been zealously in favor of it. But coming in as the third father at a point in my life when I most decidedly did not need a third father, he gave me a wonderful gift: he didn't see me as my work, nor did he see me as an extension of my mother. He let me be just one more person around a crowded table, a valued addition.

Darrell was forever falling. His son-in-law would come to pick him up off the floor. The fire department would come. He broke ribs; he had compression fractures in his spine. He wouldn't eat and dwindled to a pile of bones that made us question how life was sustained. The story went on like this for years, and much of his sweetness was worn away by terrible pain. When my mother could no longer care for him on her own, she put him into assisted living. She went to see him every day. He believed his neighbor came into his room at night and filled his coffee maker with spiders. He lived and lived and lived, and then he died.

It can be hard to remember what someone once meant to you in the wake of so much suffering. Our father died when my sister and I were on the plane going out to California to say goodbye to him. How many times had we flown out to say goodbye? He was there in the bed when we arrived, and we kissed him.

All six of the children got to see Mike in his last week. The book I had dedicated to him was printed just in time, and I showed him the page that read "To Mike Glasscock." He wanted a green burial, and when he died we took his body to a stretch of woods set aside for that purpose. We rolled a cart that carried the pine box my step-brother had made, and we buried him ourselves, shoveling dirt for hours, taking breaks, singing all the songs he liked. *As I walked out on the streets of Laredo, as I walked out in Laredo one day.*

What's so easy for me to see now that all of them are gone, what was so impossible for me to see at the time, was that they were only occasionally thinking of me, and I was only occasionally thinking of them. From each of the fathers I took the things I needed, and then I turned them into stories—my father gave me strength, Mike gave me adoration, Darrell gave me acceptance—and while those stories are true, so many thousands of other stories are equally true, like all the nights in the kitchen of the Rossmoyne house when my father came home from work, a gun holstered on the back of his belt beneath his suit jacket, and I stood on his shoes so we could dance, my father singing and swaying us back and forth, *Embrace me, my sweet embraceable you*. Dear God, how I loved him. How he loved me! How proud he was of what I did, how grateful I was for his help.

And there is Mike, taking me to a nearby farm to pick out a pig for my ninth birthday. I had read *Charlotte's Web* a dozen times and begged to have a pig of my own. He sat me up on a fence and all the piglets ran by and I pointed to the runt. The farmer dropped the small pig in a burlap sack and knotted it and Mike put the thrashing, squealing sack in the back seat of the car and drove us home. I had never been so happy, because now I was a girl like Fern, and Mike had never been so happy, because he had never made anyone this happy before in all his life.

Then I think of Darrell with his family, his children and their spouses and their children, my mother, my sister Heather and her children, our husbands, all of us around the dining room table in the house he shared with my mother, everyone laughing. There had never been so many people in that house before, and the chaos and conversations turned into a kind of light, and I, who was always looking to slip away, wanted to stay with them.

· The First Thanksgiving ·

I was so homesick my freshman year of college that my cousins bought me a plane ticket to come home to Nashville for Halloween. Halloween! It was a fantastic extravagance, the unintended consequence of which was that I really couldn't come home three weeks later for Thanksgiving and then turn right back around and come home for Christmas. I would have to spend Thanksgiving at school. Though I had some budding college friendships, none of them were close enough that first semester to rate an invitation to someone else's house for the holidays. I went to Sarah Lawrence, a half hour north of Manhattan. I lived in a nice dorm that had once been someone's house. The kitchen was still downstairs. I could just sit tight and wait out the long weekend.

Were I to put a pin in the map of my life and say, Here, this is where adulthood began, I would stick it on that Thanksgiving weekend in 1981. I was seventeen years old. While my roommate packed her bag to take the train home to Boston on Wednesday, I walked to the A&P in Bronxville with a shopping list. I had checked a copy of *The Joy of Cooking* out of the library when I realized I would have to stay. I made a list: butter and sugar, onions and celery, various potatoes, a turkey. There was money from babysitting and my weekly shift in the dean's office. I was a girl who always had some money in her pocket. I found five other kids who lived in other dorms who also had no way of getting home and invited them to dinner. When I went to the cafeteria for lunch, I put a lot of silverware in my purse. The house where I lived had plates and cups, a few basic pans, but very little silverware.

It never occurred to me to ask someone if I could stay in my room. It was my room, after all. But on Wednesday night, when the radiators in the house were turned down to whatever temperature was needed to keep water from freezing in the pipes, I wondered if maybe I'd been expected to vacate along with all the other girls in the dorm. Too late now. Buildings and Grounds was closed until Monday morning. In those happy dark ages before cell phones and the internet, such miscalculations were solved not by changing the situation but by changing yourself. I put on another sweater and my coat.

I suppose before I went to college I had been very modestly helpful to my mother on Thanksgiving. When she asked me to peel something, I peeled it, then went away to watch the Macy's parade on television until she called me back to peel something else. I showed no initiative and made no effort until 1981, when the Thanksgiving dinner that people were coming to was mine. That was when I started cutting frozen butter into pea-sized chunks with a frozen knife in my frozen hands to make a pie crust.

Aspects of this story seem mildly shocking in retrospect—the haphazard aloneness of it all, the wrongheaded decision masquerading as moxie. But most stunning is the unquestioned belief that every single thing I cooked had to be made from scratch. I made yeast rolls, for heaven's sake! I cooked down fresh cranberries into sauce! I, who had never touched a raw turkey, washed out the cavity and patted it dry. I cooked the neck and the giblets (along with a little chicken broth) and made a stock from which I would later make the gravy. Why would someone who didn't know how to cook think that this was what Thanksgiving required? I didn't know any better. All those years my mother had made a beautiful dinner I hadn't been paying attention, and now that I needed her guidance I had only enough quarters to call home from the pay phone once. I wanted to call when dinner was over. I wanted to tell her how well it had all turned out.

What I had that day was self-reliance and a book, which, as I would later learn, was all I really needed. When you look up dressing in *The Joy of Cooking* you will not find a footnote that says "Pepperidge Farm is perfectly fine if you're tight on time." No, you will get a recipe for dressing, and if you follow it, step by step, you'll wind up with something delicious. On that freezing holiday weekend when my adult life began, I not only learned to cook, I learned to read. I didn't improvise. If the recipe said "Two teaspoons of chopped fresh sage," that's what went in the pot. Beat the egg whites for seven minutes? I looked at my watch and went to work. I did not glance at the instructions, I followed them, so that even now when someone claims they don't know how to cook, I find myself snapping, "Do you know how to read?" Paying close attention to the text, and realizing that books can save you, those were the lessons I learned my freshman year of college when school was closed. I then went on to use this newfound understanding to great advantage for the rest of my life. Books were not just my education and my entertainment, they were my partners. They told me what I was capable of. They let me stare a long way down the path of various possibilities so that I could make decisions.

And Thanksgiving dinner? It was okay. The baking sheets were cheap and I should have moved up the racks in the oven. I burned the rolls. The mashed potatoes were cold by the time we sat down, and the green beans were still crunchy little twigs. Or to put it another way, dinner was brilliant, the other kids brought wine, and we left the oven door open and the gas burners on and treated the stove as a fireplace. They thought I was amazing because I knew how to make a Thanksgiving dinner, and I thought I was amazing because I'd pulled it off. We were all such grown-ups that night! A bunch of strays mimicking the patterns we'd brought from home. We laughed and drank and stuffed ourselves in fulfillment of the tradition. I wish I could remember whether we had the sense to be grateful then, for food, for the comfort of one another, for the luxury of our education. We were—we are—so insanely fortunate, and much too cool to bow our heads to anything, but in our hearts I hope we recognized the bounty that lay before us.

The year after that, my friend Erica Buchsbaum invited me to come home with her for Thanksgiving. Her parents then invited me for the next two Thanksgivings as well, and they invited me long after we had graduated because I made excellent gravy and they had never learned how. Erica and her mother were with me in the kitchen while I browned the flour in the roasting pan, but they never seemed to get it. And I never taught them because I loved them. I wanted to be invited back.

· The Paris Tattoo ·

A room with two beds usually meant a room with a bed and a cot.
Marti and I were diplomatic about trading off—if I had the bed in
Copenhagen, she got the bed in Strasbourg. I remember that she
had the bed in Paris, but that was a small victory. It was a terrible
bed, a terrible cot, a terrible fourth-floor walk-up in the only pension we could afford. The bathroom was not just down the hall but
down the hall and down a flight of stairs. On the bright side, the
location was good (the location was Paris), and we were nineteen,
so our standards were still breathtakingly low. Marti and I scarcely
knew one another before we embarked on our three-month summer
adventure, but by the end of the first week we had become a single
unit. We shared our toothpaste, our guidebooks, our croissants. We
had one mass-market copy of *One Hundred Years of Solitude*, and
when I finished a chapter I ripped it out and handed it to her, unless
she was a chapter ahead and so ripped it out for me.

By the time we got to Paris, we had been traveling for more than six weeks. We were tired and in want of a laundromat. Even though the city was beyond our modest budget, we wanted to stay in Paris. We could pretend our nasty pension wasn't too far removed from an artist's garret. *Mi chiamano Mimi!* We walked along the soft, straight paths of the Tuileries, we stood in line for half the day to join the masses in the Centre Pompidou, we wandered from one arrondissement to the next, blissfully lost, until we saw the head of a giraffe poking up over the horizon. Then, because we weren't much older than children, we went to the Paris Zoo.

Where to eat, what to eat, and how much we could afford to spend on a single meal were our favorite topics of conversation that summer. Given the size and the culinary significance of the city, it had been our plan never to step into the same café or boulangerie twice. So much for plans. Wandering through the Latin Quarter on our first night, we found a crêpe restaurant whose interior was constructed entirely from bright chunky pieces of broken tile. The walls, the floor, and the booths that pushed up from that floor like concrete eruptions were all covered in haphazard mosaic. Bulky strips of neon tubing pulsed light around the room. Enough of looking at art! We were *inside* the art now. A waitress, who was tall enough and bony enough to call to mind the giraffe we had seen earlier in the day, led us to our booth, handed us our menus, and loped away without a word. She wore a black tank top and extra-long toothpick jeans, a starched white dish towel tied around her narrow hips. It was impossible to comprehend that she was a human in the same way that two American girls grown chubby on pastry were human. Over by the bar, we watched her talking to another waitress every bit as tall and pale and angular as she.

"They must be artists," Marti said.

"Or philosophers," I said, because the second one was wearing glasses with thick black frames propped atop her delicate ears. The glasses made her look serious. We both knew without speaking that we wanted to lose weight, grow tall, move to Paris, and become waitresses. In an instant we saw the beauty of that life stretch out before us.

The second waitress, the intellectual, came to our table and held up her pad and pen, her arms so long and thin and white there should have been a museum built to honor them. In broken high school French, we ordered crêpes. She turned away from us without a word of acknowledgment, and that was when we saw the delicate clutch of flowers inked onto the sharp wing of her shoulder blade.

The year was 1983. We were two nineteen-year-old American girls in Europe. I had won a writing prize that stipulated the money be used for the enrichment of my work, and travel was the most enriching thing I could think of. Marti was living off money she'd saved working in a clothing store near school, with some additional support from her parents. We had no idea where we were going, and so no one in our families knew where we were. Half the time we didn't know where we were. We had train passes, and sometimes boarded a train without checking to see where it was going. We occasionally sent postcards but did not receive any mail. Once, in the middle of July, we called home from a phone center and talked for exactly five minutes because it was so expensive. It was a time before cell phones, before internet cafés, before women with tattoos. Or women with tattoos existed, but until that night in Paris we had never seen one. The other waitress, the one in the tank top who walked us to our table, had one too.

Back in our lumpy bed and lumpy cot, we didn't even try to read Garcia Márquez. The drunken French shouted from the street was easily heard four flights up, and we didn't notice it. In the dark, I asked Marti if she would ever get a tattoo.

"I don't know," she said, but because we were one person, I knew she was thinking about it.

We are not the girls you knew before, is what our tattoos would indicate to the world.

The next day we went to the Musée de l'Orangerie to see the water lilies, and then for lunch we ate couscous near the Gare du Nord. At Notre-Dame, I spent two francs to light a votive candle. We worked out our day from the guidebook, but we knew where we were going at night.

We never considered that the waitresses might not be working. We expected them to be there the way a tourist expects the Mona Lisa to be there. We were not disappointed. The philosopher led us to a different table without a flicker of recognition, her tank top purple.

"I think a fish," Marti said after the waitress had given us our menus and turned away. "A little fish on my shoulder blade."

"I want a black-and-white cow, maybe the size of a quarter, right here—" I touched my arm below my shoulder. (A cow? Why a cow? Why not the Arc de Triomphe? Youth is its own mystery.)

The next day we hiked up to Montmartre to find the grave of Degas and see the Sacré-Cœur, but they made no impression. Our heads were full of nothing but tattoos. I'd never had my ears pierced and was worried about how much the tattoo would hurt, but it wouldn't matter. The tattoos would establish us as free thinkers, sufferers for art, or at least sufferers for a fish and a tiny cow. With our

French/English dictionary, we hammered out the phrase, "Where did you get your tattoo?" We practiced saying it to one another.

That night in the crêpe restaurant, the neon tubing blinking around us, a cheap bottle of wine consumed, we summoned our courage. It was really Marti's courage, since her French was better than mine. "Qui vous a donné ce tatouage?" she asked.

The waitress—it was the first one, the artist—had never actually looked at us before. She was probably only two or three years older than we were, but her excruciatingly angular beauty, her fundamental Frenchness, made her in every sense our senior. She looked at us without comprehension at first, and I was sure that Marti had botched the pronunciation. Then she touched the edge of her tattoo. It was a decorative scroll of flowers and curled lines that ran in a half circle around the side of her arm. She made a little back-and-forth movement with the pad of her finger. "Rub-on?" she said, with a heavy, questioning accent, as if those were the only two words in English that she knew and we shouldn't try to ask her anything else.

And so it came to pass that Marti did not wind up with a small fish on her shoulder, and I, all these years later, do not have a cow loitering on my upper arm.

But that is not exactly where the story ends. In the early part of August, with our Eurail passes expired, our language skills exhausted, and our funds badly depleted, we decided to spend the weeks we had left hitchhiking through the UK and Ireland. One day in Donegal, we got a ride with a vacationing family who were on their way home to Londonderry. Would we like to go to Londonderry?

Which was how we ended our summer vacation in a war zone.

We rode to Northern Ireland in the back of the family station wagon. It was raining the first time we were pulled out of the car at a checkpoint by boys who looked younger than we were, boys with automatic weapons slung across their backs and pistols shoved into their belts, boys with tattoos that started at the wrist and disappeared up the sleeve, tattoos inching up their necks and spreading out across the tops of their fingers. I had seen boys with tattoos before, but none as wrathful as these. I had seen boys with guns before, but had never thought it possible that one of them might shoot me. We were told to get out of many cars in Northern Ireland, our passports checked, our backpacks poked through with rifle tips. I can hardly remember seeing a boy without a tattoo in Northern Ireland that summer, or, for that matter, a boy without a gun. When I didn't see the tattoos and the guns it was easy to imagine they were there, waiting. They were in Coleraine and in Bangor. In Belfast we had lunch at the once-bombed White Horse Inn. We bought Irish fisherman sweaters at a store whose windows had been bombed out days before and gingerly picked the slivers of glass out of the wool. The sign that hung where the window had been read "Bomb Sale."

MARTI AND I flew home two weeks before school started. We tended to study together, in her room or in mine. I took comfort in the sound of her breathing and maybe my breathing was a comfort to her as well. We were never able to keep each other from making bad decisions, not completely, but at least when we made those bad decisions, we were together.

· My Year of No Shopping ·

The idea began in February 2009 over lunch with my friend Elissa, someone I like but rarely see. She walked into the restaurant wearing a fitted black coat with a high collar.

"Wow," I said admiringly. "Some coat."

She stroked the sleeve. "Yeah. I bought it at the end of my no-shopping year. I still feel a little bad about it."

Elissa told me the story: After leaving India the year before, she decided she had enough stuff, or too much stuff. She made a pledge that for a year she wouldn't buy shoes, clothes, purses, or jewelry.

I was impressed by her conviction, but she shrugged it off. "It wasn't hard."

After that, I did some small-scale experiments of my own, giving up shopping for Lent for a few years. I was always surprised by how much better it made me feel. But it wasn't until New Year's Day 2017 that I decided to follow my friend's example.

At the end of 2016, our country had swung in the direction of gold leaf, an ecstatic celebration of unfeeling billionairedom that kept me up at night. I couldn't settle down to read or write, and in my anxiety I found myself mindlessly scrolling through two particular shopping websites, numbing out with images of shoes, clothes, purses and jewelry. I was trying to distract myself, but the distraction left me feeling worse, the way a late night in a bar smoking Winstons and drinking gin leaves you feeling worse. The unspoken question of shopping is *What do I need?*, but I didn't need anything. What I needed was less than what I had.

And so I decided to follow my friend's example. My plan had been to give up what Elissa gave up—things to wear—but a week into my no-shopping year I bought a portable speaker that resembled a very large button. Then I realized my mistake: a no-shopping year should definitely include whimsical electronics, and so I came up with my own arbitrary set of rules. I wanted a plan that was serious but not so draconian that I'd bail out in February, so while I couldn't buy clothing or speakers, I could buy anything in the grocery store, including flowers. I could buy shampoo and printer cartridges and batteries, but only after I'd run out of what I had. I could buy plane tickets and eat out in restaurants. I could buy books because I write books and I co-own a bookstore and books are my business. Could I have made it a full year without buying books? Absolutely. I could have used the library or read the books that were already in my house, but I didn't, I bought books.

Gifts were the tough one for me. I'm a gift giver, and I could see how gift shopping could become an easy loophole. I decided to give books as gifts, but I didn't always stick to it. My editor got married in 2017, and I wasn't about to give him a book as a wedding present.

Still, the frantic shopping for others needed to come to a halt. The idea that our affection and esteem must manifest itself in yet another sweater is reductive. Elissa said she gave people time, a certificate to watch their kids or clean their house. *"That,"* she told me, "turned out to be the hardest thing. Time is so valuable."

I was raised Catholic, and in the same way a child who grows up going to the symphony is more likely to enjoy classical music, and a child raised in a bilingual household is probably going to speak two languages, many people raised Catholic develop a talent for self-denial. Even now my sister and I plan for Lent the way other people plan family vacations: What will we let go of? What good can we add?

My first few months of no-shopping were full of gleeful discoveries. I ran out of lip balm early on and before making a decision as to whether lip balm constituted a need, I looked in my desk drawers and coat pockets. I found five lip balms. Once I started digging around under the bathroom sink I realized I could probably run this experiment for another three years before using up all the lotion, soap and dental floss. It turned out I hadn't thrown away the hair products and face creams I'd bought over the years and didn't like; I'd just tossed them all under the sink.

I started using them again, and they were fine.

In March I wished I had a FitBit, the new one that looked like a bracelet and didn't need to be connected to a smartphone. For four days I really wanted a FitBit. And then—*poof!*—I didn't want one. I remembered my parents trying to teach me this lesson when I was a child: If you want something, wait a while. Chances are the feeling will pass.

The trick of no-shopping wasn't just to stop buying things. The trick was to stop *shopping*. That meant no trawling the sale section of the J.Crew website in idle moments. It meant the catalogues went into the recycle bin unopened, on the theory that if I didn't see it, I didn't want it. Halfway through the year, I could go to a store with my mother and sister if they asked me. I could tell them if the dress they were trying on looked good without wishing I could try it on myself.

Not shopping saves an astonishing amount of time. In October, I interviewed a famous actor in front of 1,700 people in a Washington, D.C., theater. Previously I would have believed that such an occasion demanded a new dress, and lost two days of my life looking for one, when in fact the famous actor had never seen any of my dresses, nor had the people in the audience. I went to my closet, picked out something seasonally appropriate, and stuck it in my suitcase. Done.

I did a favor for a friend over the summer and she bought me a pair of tennis shoes. Her simple act of kindness thrilled me. Once I stopped looking for things to buy, I became tremendously grateful for the things I received. Had I been shopping that summer I would have told my friend, "You shouldn't have," and I would have meant it.

It doesn't take so long for craving to subside. Once I got the hang of giving something up, it wasn't much of a trick. The much harder part was living with the startling abundance that had been illuminated when I stopped trying to get more. Once I could see what I already had, and what actually mattered, I was left with a feeling that was somewhere between sickened and humbled. When did I amass so many things, and did someone else need them?

If you stop thinking about what you might want, it's a whole lot easier to see what other people don't have. There's a reason that just about every religion regards material belongings as an impediment to peace. This is why Siddhartha had to leave his palace to become the Buddha. This is why Jesus said, "Blessed are the poor." It's why my friend Sister Nena, a Catholic nun well into her eighties, took a vow of poverty when she entered the convent at eighteen. Sister Nena was my reading teacher when I was in the first grade, and in the decades since she's taught me considerably more. When I ask her if there's anything she needs me to get for her, she shakes her head. "It's all just stuff," she says, meaning all of the things that aren't God. (If you're in the market for genuine inspiration on this front, I urge you to read Gregory Boyle's *Barking at the Choir: The Power of Radical Kinship*, a book that shows what the platitudes of faith look like when they're put into action.)

Once the year had ended, the question then became: How does the experiment end? Should I just start shopping again? Shop less? I called Elissa. I hadn't seen her in years. She told me that after she bought the black coat she decided to re-up for another year.

"I realized I had too many decisions to make that were actually important," she said. "There were people to help, things to do. Not shopping frees up a lot of space in your brain."

I left my pledge in place for a while, but over time I drifted away—not because I wanted to start shopping again, but because I rarely thought about it anymore. Much to my surprise, not shopping for a year had inadvertently killed my interest in shopping, in much the same way not smoking for a year (so many years ago) had killed my interest in cigarettes. I used to smoke? When I stopped mindlessly scooping up the things I thought I wanted, I had a better understanding of all the ridiculous things people were trying to sell me, like dresses and shirts with the shoulders cut out (though I like to think I wouldn't have fallen for that one even if I had been shopping).

The things we buy and buy and buy are like a thick coat of Vaseline smeared on glass: we can see some shapes out there, light and dark, but in our constant craving for what we may still want, we miss too many of life's details. It's not as if I kept a ledger and took the money I didn't spend on perfume and gave that money to the poor, but I came to a better understanding of money as something we earn and spend and save for the things we want and need. Once I was able to get past the want and be honest about the need, it was easier to let the money go. It was like Elissa had told me when she first explained the benefits of not shopping: "Our capacity for giving is huge."

For the record, I still have more than plenty. I know the vast difference between not buying things and not being able to buy things. Not shopping for a year hardly makes me one with the poor, but it's put me on the path of figuring out what I can do to help. I understand that buying things is the backbone of the economy and job growth. I appreciate all the people who shop in the bookstore. But taking some time off from consumerism isn't going to collapse the financial markets. If you're ever looking for a New Year's resolution, I have to tell you: this one's great.

· The Worthless Servant ·

I'd been asked to write an essay about a saint for a saint anthology but passed on the assignment. I had nothing new to say about Thérèse of Lisieux.

"Some other saint then?" the editor asked.

By the rules of actual sainthood, saints were dead. That was my problem. I didn't think I had much to add to the hagiography of any dead saint. Of course, were I allowed to canonize someone, I'd do it. I knew a priest in Nashville whom I regarded as a saint, even as he'd roll his eyes to hear me say it. If a living saint would meet the criteria, I'd take the job.

"Sure," the editor said. "A living saint would be fine."

Which was how I came to be in Charlie Strobel's car in the middle of June, a few days before summer became unbearably hot. I'd told him I was going to write about him. I didn't mention the saint part.

To grow up Catholic in Nashville is to know at least some of the members of the Strobel family, and long before Charlie and I became friends, I knew the stories of what he had accomplished and what he had lost. We were on our way to the Stadium Inn to visit some homeless men who were about to get their own apartment, and while he drove, Charlie told me a story about Father Dan Richardson. Father Dan was the priest at Assumption, the North Nashville parish in the poor neighborhood where Charlie grew up. It wasn't too far from where we were headed now.

"Father Dan was a father figure to me," Charlie said, his own father having died when he was four. "We lived down the street from the church, and by the time I was in the third or fourth grade, I was an acolyte."

Assumption was a parish with an older congregation, and Charlie remembered the funerals coming one after the other. For every funeral, Father Dan gave the exact same homily. "We knew it word for word. We could mouth it along behind him," Charlie said, and though he is in his seventies now, a good distance from his altar-boy self, he began the recitation: "Father Dan would say, 'We're on this earth to get ready to die. And when we die, God's not going to say, "Charlie (Ann, Sally, John, fill-in-the-blank), what did you do for a living? How much money did you make? How many houses did you have?" God is only going to ask us two questions: "Did you love Me?" and "Did you love your neighbor?" And we can imagine that Charlie (Ann, Sally, John, fill-in-the-blank) will answer truthfully, saying, "Yes, Lord, You know I loved You. You know I loved my neighbor." And then God will say, "Well done, good and faithful servant. Now enter into the kingdom of heaven." ' " Charlie smiled at the thought of it. "He nailed it every single time. He had this soft voice, and his cadence was perfect. Even though I knew exactly what was coming, it never failed to grab me. It was sad, especially if I knew the person who had died, but I never heard it as anything but a positive and hopeful message. We come from God, we return to God, so death was never frightening."

Charlie missed the exit. Neither of us had been paying attention to the interstate, and neither of us was sorry. It gave him time to finish the story.

"Even after I grew up and became a priest, I could never call him Dan. It was always Father Dan. I'd always say to him, What are you going to get me for Christmas this year? And he'd say, 'A bridge,' because the homeless lived under bridges." Father Dan, who was Irish, was always one for a joke. "When I went to see him for the last time before he died, we had a personal talk, a father-son talk, and I told him how much I loved him. Then I said, now I'm going to be your priest, and I did his whole routine—We are on this earth to get ready to die, and when we die, God's not going to ask, 'Dan, how much money did you make?' He's going to ask two questions: 'Did you love Me?' and 'Did you love your neighbor?' And I know you'll say, 'Yes, Lord, You know I loved You. You know I loved my neighbor.' And God will say, 'Enter, good and faithful servant.' "

I was struck by how often the lessons we learn when we're young, the things we could never imagine needing, make it possible to meet what life will ask of us later. "I've grown to be who I am," Charlie said, "because of those life experiences each of us has."

IN ITS FINEST hour, the Stadium Inn must have been a cheap motel where fans of the opposing teams could spend the night before a Titans game. But any football fan who booked a room there now would realize the error of his ways without getting out of the car. When we pulled up to the front, Charlie stopped and looked at the men sitting on the steps, then he looked at me. "I'll leave the car running," he said, trying to calculate how long he might be inside. "You lock the doors and wait."

When I told him I'd go with him, he gave me an enormous smile. "Oh, that's wonderful," he said. He reached in the back seat and pulled out a two-burner hot plate. The Stadium Inn was what my policeman father would have called a flophouse, a pay-by-the-week motel of the lowest possible order. Charlie greeted every man and woman who leaned by the door or sprawled in the lobby. He announced our plans to visit Ron and Sid to the woman at the front desk, who claimed to have no idea who they were. Then he told her he was Charlie Strobel, and that he was expected. "Oh!" she said, smiling and nodding. She gave us the room number and directed us to the elevator. Ron and Sid would soon be moving into their own apartment, an apartment that had no stove. They would be needing a hot plate. We took the one we'd brought upstairs.

Every human catastrophe the carpet in the hallway had endured over the years had been solved with a splash of bleach, which rendered it a long, abstract painting. Beneath the low yellow light, each closed door along the corridor thumped out a distinct musical beat, including the one we were standing in front of. I saw an eye study us at the peephole and then pull away. I stepped to the side, thinking I probably looked like a parole officer. "Sid," Charlie called out in the tone of a cheerful and persistent relative who had dropped in for a visit. "It's Charlie. Open up the door." He waited, and then he knocked again.

It was a long wait, but finally the door cracked open and a single dark eye peered out of a cloud of cigarette smoke, then the door opened wider. "Father!" the man said, and gave Charlie a hug. (Charlie can do without the honorific, as he thinks it creates a distance between people. Still, if using "Father" makes anyone feel better, he accepts it.)

Ron and Sid were salt and pepper shakers, Ron with faded red hair and a graying beard going halfway down his chest, Sid with dark brown hair and a heavy brown beard. Both men wore loose jeans, tank tops, baseball caps. Neither could have weighed much more than a hundred pounds, their upper arms no bigger than their wrists. Introductions were made and they shook my hand. For all their reticence about opening the door, they were clearly pleased we had come. The room contained two unmade beds with a heaping ashtray between them, a console television playing the country music station. A shopping cart was parked against the wall, neatly packed, its contents tarped over and tied. "We're ready to go," Ron said, giving the cart a pat. "We've got somebody coming tomorrow to help us move."

"Are you staying sober?" Charlie asked, his voice making it clear that he would be proud of them if they were, and love them still if they were not.

"We are, Father," Sid said. "Four days, Father," Ron said.

Charlie tried to lead them in a conversation about how much better it was to be clean, and though they clearly wished to please him, their hearts weren't in it. They planned to find jobs once they settled, maybe dishwashing. Ron took off his baseball cap and pushed back his hair to reveal a long scar running across his forehead. "I don't know though," he said. "I don't think so clear since I got hit."

Charlie gave them the hot plate and they marveled at the newness of the thing, still in the box. They talked about the move, and Charlie said he'd get them bus passes. When we were finally ready to leave, both men hugged him again and promised good behavior for the future. They told us about a man five doors down the hall, someone who wasn't doing as well at staying out of trouble, and so we went and knocked on that door for a long time, but despite the music blaring from the other side, no amount of calling could draw him out.

"That's the best I've seen them look in a long time," Charlie said cheerfully as the shuddering elevator dropped to the ground floor. "Their eyes looked good, didn't you think?"

I hadn't seen their eyes before, but I was struck by the sweetness of both men, and how more than anything they looked tired. Homelessness is an exhausting and dangerous state of being. How's that for an understatement?

I've got a card on my desk from Charlie's ordination as a priest in 1970. It's the size of a holy card, but it's plain—no prayer, no saint— just a quote by Robert F. Kennedy. I used to pick it up once or twice a year and read it, but recently I've been reading it every day. It goes like this: "Few will have the greatness to bend history itself, but each of us can work to change a small portion of events, and in the total of all those acts will be written the history of this generation. Each time a man stands up for an ideal, or acts to improve the lots of others or strikes out against injustice, he sends forth a tiny ripple of hope, and crossing each other from a million different centers of energy and daring, those ripples build a current that can sweep down the mightiest walls of oppression and resistance."

The hot plate sweeps down the walls of oppression. The embrace turns the walls of oppression into dust.

CHARLIE HAS A good story that he likes to bring out for fundraisers—that his career with people who have nowhere to live can all be traced back to a single peanut butter and jelly sandwich that he made for a man who'd knocked on the rectory door when he was a young priest at Holy Name. The next step came soon after that, as he explained in a lecture he gave at the local Unitarian church. "They were in the church parking lot, sleeping under my window, and the temperature that evening was dropping below freezing. I didn't think too long about it, probably because I knew I would talk myself out of it. As a pastor, I knew the consequences of such a decision were far greater than simply giving a dozen men one night's lodging. What do you do tomorrow night when they return? And the next night and the next night and on and on? One simple decision could be parlayed into a lifetime commitment. What would the parishioners say? Or the bishop? Or the neighbors? For the moment, I decided that it was the thing to do. Like Scarlett O'Hara, I found myself saying, 'I'll worry about that tomorrow.' So I invited them to spend the night, and they've been with me ever since."

It was while he was trying to meet those immediate needs that Doy Abbott arrived.

"He was my terrorist," Charlie said. "Every morning he woke me up to demand breakfast. He was a regular back at Holy Name. He kicked in the screen door. We had to have that door replaced three times. He cussed out everyone in the parish. He expected everything to be done for him. My mother used to say to me, 'Doy is your ticket to heaven.' And I'd tell her, if he's my ticket to heaven I don't want to go. Everyone in the parish was afraid of him."

Everyone except Mary Hopwood. She was the housekeeper and the secretary and the bookkeeper for the parish. She'd come to work at the age of fifty-five, after raising twelve children of her own. With Doy her tone was always quiet and respectful, and he was respectful in return. They listened to one another.

"About that time I read something Dorothy Day had said. She said what she wanted to do was love the poor, not analyze them, not rehabilitate them. When I read that it was like a light clicking on. I thought about Mrs. Hopwood. I realized that Doy was not my problem to solve but my brother to love. I decided on the spot that I was going to love him and not expect anything from him, and overnight he changed. He stopped the cussing, stopped the violence. I feel we became brothers. I was his servant and he was my master. I was there with him when he died."

CHARLES STROBEL FOUNDED the Room in the Inn and its Campus for Human Development in 1986 as a center of learning, respite, shelter and relief for people living on the streets. Like them, he can pretty much be found there seven days a week. Originally it was formed as an organization of local congregations of all denominations that welcomed people in for a meal and to spend the night once the cold weather set in. The first building they had was typically dismal, with some classrooms for AA meetings and art projects, a place to pray. Charlie's primary gift may be his ability to serve the poor, but he possesses the equally necessary gifts of being able to work with a board, local government, the police, religious organizations of every stripe, and the people who have the means to underwrite his vision. His radical idea was that people who had nowhere to live need not be served in low, dark places, and that people with nothing should be able to stand beside people with everything and hold up their heads. The Campus building looked as new and stylishly modern in its glass and steel construction as the expensive condominiums that sprawl through Nashville a few blocks away. The dignity with which Charlie had always treated all people was reflected in their surroundings. The mission statement of the Campus reads: "Emphasizing the scriptural ideals of love and community through service to the homeless, our Campus provides faithful people of Nashville an opportunity to respond directly to the broken and the disenfranchised among us. The fellowship with the poor is at the heart of our purpose."

What that means is that I am the person the Campus is serving. Part of its mission is to give me the chance to experience what has been the enormous joy of Charlie's life—the opportunity to respond directly to the broken and disenfranchised among us.

"All you have to do," he tells me, "is give a little bit of understanding to the possibility that life might not have been fair."

The trouble with good fortune is that we tend to equate it with personal goodness, so that if things are going well for us and less well for others, it's assumed they must have done something to have brought that misfortune on themselves while we must have worked harder to avoid it. We speak of ourselves as being blessed, but what can that mean except that others are not blessed, and that God has picked out a few of us to love more? It is our responsibility to care for one another, to create fairness in the face of unfairness and find equality where none may have existed in the past. Despite his own experiences with unfairness, this is what Charlie has accomplished.

When Charlie's father died of a heart attack at the age of forty-six, he left behind four children between the ages of eight years and four months. Afterwards, Charlie's mother, Mary Catherine Strobel—who had lost her own mother in a house fire when she was an infant and her much-loved father when she was sixteen—took a job working as a clerk for the fire department for $185 a month. She also took care of two great-aunts, Mollie, who was eighty-one at the time, and Kate, who was seventy-eight. The way Mary Catherine interpreted her husband's death and their subsequent hardships was that none of it was God's fault. God, along with her husband, would be right there watching over them.

And while God, in the newfound company of Martin Strobel, watched the children from heaven, Aunt Kate and Aunt Mollie watched them during the day while Mary Catherine worked. "They were the reason it was so easy for me to believe Jesus' words, 'I am among you as one who serves,'" he said of his aunts. "And that led me to the next step in logic, to believe that God loves us and provides for all our needs—just as any devoted servant would—because I had experienced it so lovingly from Aunt Mollie and Aunt Kate."

He told me a story from Luke 17, in which the servant who does everything that is asked of him and then, joyfully, does more, is called "a worthless servant" (or "an unprofitable servant," or "a servant who deserves no credit," depending on the translation). It is a state of loving service so deep, so all-encompassing, that the servant loses himself, so that the worthlessness becomes a kind of transcendence. "They were worthless servants," Charlie said, remembering his aunts, his mother. "They wanted nothing more than to serve us, which means that we were their masters. They did everything they could for us. They never disciplined us. I never remember their asking me to help them around the house." Charlie asked if I was following him, because the concept of the achievement to be found in worthlessness can be a murky one. It is not the stuff of Sunday sermons. Certainly I could think of many instances in which people who had been served were not then inspired to go and serve others, but if being profoundly loved enabled us to love profoundly then, yes, I understood.

"Wouldn't that be a wonderful thing to have on your tombstone?" he said to me. "'Worthless Servant'?"

I told him I wasn't there yet, but that I could see it as something to aspire to.

"I hesitate to say this," he said, and then paused for so long that I wondered if he did in fact plan to proceed. "So many people have struggles with their faith, but God has never been a struggle for me. *I've* been a struggle for me, but I could never honestly believe in the nonexistence of God."

It was the only thing he hesitated to tell me the entire day. He felt it might be cavalier to admit that something that was so difficult for so many had come to him, and stayed with him, without effort.

In the main lobby of the Room in the Inn there is a wall sculpture of a tree with over a thousand leaves. Every leaf bears the name of a homeless man or woman who has died in Nashville, and the presence of God did not waver any time a new leaf was added. It did not waver in December of 1986, when Charlie's mother, Mary Catherine, then seventy-four, was kidnapped from the parking lot of Sears in Nashville and murdered by an escaped convict from Michigan, the first victim in a spree that ultimately took six lives.

But the way the story was remembered over the years was that she had been working at the Room in the Inn at the time, and that she was killed by a homeless man. People said that Mary Catherine had started the Room in the Inn, and that Charlie took up her work as a penance. By making her murder a consequence of her own associations, people could safely distance themselves from such a random act of violence. Charlie was often asked if he would continue his work after his mother's death. "If it was worth doing before," he would say, "why wouldn't it be worth doing now?"

"Many have said that she did not deserve to die the way that she did," her son said at his mother's funeral Mass. "Yet for years, we have heard it said that 'God did not spare his only Son but delivered him up, and the Son emptied himself and humbled himself, obediently accepting even death, death on a cross.' In Mama's death, our family believes that the viciousness inflicted on such gentleness and kindness, as was her way, brings about a great communion with Jesus. So how can we question its course? It seems to run true to the form of Jesus' own death. And why speak of anger and revenge? Those words are not compatible with the very thought of our mother."

"Of course her death changed all of us," he told me that afternoon after we had left Ron and Sid, while we were on our way to visit a formerly homeless woman in the hospital who was struggling to care for her grandchildren as her health declined sharply. "But maybe not the way people thought it did. Our mother's death helped me focus on what was important. After that I became more single-minded about what I should be doing with my life."

Throughout the course of life there is a long line of fathers and sons, parents and children, servants and masters, forgiven and forgivers, and at different moments we are called on to take up one role and then the other. When we do it right, we are bearing Christ's example in mind.

Charlie is doing it right.

I'VE BEEN THE host of the fundraising breakfast for the Campus a couple of times, one of those giant hotel ballroom situations with bitter coffee and cool scrambled eggs. Charlie finds it painful to ask his friends for money, and I don't mind at all. Is this my spiritual strength? My ability is to stand on a stage and explain to people why they should sign the pledge card next to the basket of cinnamon rolls.

After the videos and the testimonials, after the people who serve and the people who have been served tell their stories, I'm on. The room is full of professional types checking their phones. We've promised to get them out the door by eight, so I make it quick. I tell them I will never work in the foot clinic. I won't serve lunches, cut hair, distribute ice water on summer days. But I will write a check, because even while it isn't much, it's something, which has got to be better than doing nothing at all. I tell them not to let greatness be the enemy of goodness.

Maybe instead of doing the work, I'll ride in the car beside the person who's doing the work. Maybe it will be enough that I listen and tell the story.

When the breakfast is finished, people gather in a large, loose circle around Charlie, wanting a moment of his attention before they go, wanting to make sure he knows they came. After all, he serves these people as well. He hugs them in the same way he hugged Ron and Sid, with gladness and acceptance. *You are four days sober and I love you. You're about to get in your BMW and I love you. You are not my problem to solve but my brother to love, all of you.* We want to get close so we can convince ourselves that he is made of some rare and superior material that hasn't been given to us, but it isn't true. Calling him a saint is just a way of letting ourselves off the hook. After riding around with Charlie, I find it shocking to realize how simple it would be to see myself as a worthless servant, to find joy in the service of others, to open my heart and let it remain open to everyone, *everyone*, all the time. The trick is in the decision to wake up every morning and meet the world again with love. I have to think the pyrotechnics of sainthood—crucifixion and Catherine wheels, the fire and stake—would be easier than this tireless, unconditional love. Standing in the ballroom of the Renaissance Hotel is somehow harder than waiting in the bleach-splattered hallway of the Stadium Inn, because here we don't know enough to ask for forgiveness, nor do we realize that we're the ones being served. Once the crowd has finally dispersed, the person who has mastered the calling of human decency finds his valet ticket and, after shaking the hand of the man who parked his car, heads back to work.

· How to Practice ·

I started thinking about getting our house in order when Tavia's father died. Tavia, my friend from early childhood (and youth, and middle age, and these years on the downhill slalom), grew up in unit 24-S of the Georgetown condominiums in Nashville. Her father, Kent, had moved there from Los Angeles after his divorce in the 1970s and stayed. Over the years we had borne witness to every phase of his personal style: Kent as sea captain (navy peacoat, beard, pipe), Kent as the lost child of Studio 54 (purple), Kent as Gordon Gekko (Armani suits, cuff links, tie bar), Kent as Jane Fonda (track suits, matching trainers), Kent as urban cowboy (fifteen pairs of boots, custom-made), and finally, his last iteration, which had in fact underlain all previous iterations, Kent as cosmic monk (loose cotton shirts, cotton drawstring pants—he'd put on weight).

Each new stage in his evolution brought about a new set of interests: new art, new cooking utensils, new reading material, new bathroom tile. Kent taught drama at a public high school, and on his schoolteacher's salary, in the years before the internet, he shopped the world from home—mala prayer beads carved in the shape of miniature human skulls, an assortment of Buddhas to mix in with the wooden statues of saints (Padre Pio in his black cassock, as tall as any five-year-old). He laminated the receipts and letters of authenticity that came with his purchases and filed them away in zippered leather pouches.

I grew up in 24-S, in the same way that Tavia grew up in my family's house. We knew the contents of each other's pantries and the efficacy of each other's shampoo. And while our house was much larger (it was a house, after all), the domain of the Cathcarts—Kent and Tavia and Tavia's older sister Therese—had a glamour and exoticism that far exceeded anything most Catholic schoolgirls had ever seen. Candles were lit at all hours of the day. The walk-in closet in Kent's bedroom had been converted into a shrine for meditation and prayer. A round, footed machine that looked like a plate-sized UFO burped out cascades of fog from the kitchen counter. The dining room chairs were spring green, with backs carved to mimic the signs of the Paris Métro—a flourish of art nouveau transplanted to Nashville. Kent had the seats of those chairs reupholstered in hot-pink patent leather. Tavia and I spent many happy hours of childhood standing between the two giant mirrors (eight feet by six, crowned with gold-tipped pagodas) that faced each other from either end of the tiny living room. We watched ourselves as we fluttered our arms up and down, two swans in an infinity of swans.

After his daughters were grown and gone, Kent amassed an enormous collection of Tibetan singing bowls that crowded into what had once been Therese's room, each on its own riser, each riser topped

with a pouf made of Indian silk. He played them daily, turning sideways to move among them. When Tavia came home from Kentucky
to visit, she slept at my house, as there was no longer an inch of
space for her in 24-S.

"Can you imagine what he could have done if he'd had money?"
I said to her. We were standing beside stacked cases of Gerolsteiner
mineral water in Kent's galley kitchen. Despite his chronic lack of
space, Kent was a disciple of bulk purchasing. This was in April
of 2020, during the early days after his death, and we were sick
with missing him. The dresser drawers had not yet been opened,
the overburdened shelves in the highest reaches of the closets were
undisturbed. Still, Tavia and Therese had already found more than
thirty power strips. Always a director, Kent saw every room as a
stage. Lighting was just one of his many forms of genius.

Tavia wanted to show me the painting of the goddess Kali riding
a white ox, her six blue arms reaching out in every direction, that
Kent had left me in his will. The painting was in his bedroom on
an elaborate wrought-iron easel with a portrait light. She told me the
easel and the light were mine as well.

"I don't want to seem ungrateful," I said after careful study. I liked
the painting, and was touched that he would think of me in relation
to the destroyer of evil forces, but it was really big.

Neighbors, caregivers, former students, friends: he had chosen a
remembrance for each of us. Kent's will was remarkably specific:
Tavia got the fourteen-inch All-Clad covered sauté pan; Therese got
the extensive collection of light bulbs; Tavia got the blue wool blanket; Therese got the midsize dehumidifier. The list went on and on:
art, artifacts, household supplies. Tavia and Therese decided to pool
what they'd been given and split the proceeds equally, since most

of their inheritance would have to be sold. Neither of them had the space to keep more than a few mementos. I added the blue goddess to the sale.

"Take something else then," Tavia said. "He'd want you to have something."

In the end, I took a blue quartz egg held upright by a silver napkin ring. I took a case of Lance peanut butter cheese crackers and a gross of Gin Gins ginger candy for the staff at the bookstore. I claimed six boxes of vegetable broth for myself.

For the rest of the summer Tavia drove down from Louisville on the weekends to work on the cleanout with her sister. I, too, kept going back to 24-S, both to see my friend and to bear witness to the closing down of a world that had helped to shape me. "He made everything magic when he was alive," Therese said sadly one day. "Now it's all just stuff." Friends and acquaintances filed in before the estate sale, wanting to pick through the bounty. I bought the painting of a floating house that had hung in Tavia's bedroom throughout our childhood, the very first painting I ever loved. I bought the green-and-pink dining room chairs and gave them to my mother. Tavia was hugely relieved to know that she could still come and sit in them.

The deeper 24-S was excavated, the more it yielded. Unit 24-S became the site of an archaeological dig, cordoned off from the rest of the Georgetown condominiums, where the two sisters chipped into the past with little picks.

How had one man acquired so many extension cords, so many batteries and rosary beads? Holding hands in the parking lot, Tavia and I swore a quiet oath: we would not do this to anyone. We would not leave the contents of our lives for someone else to sort through, because who would that mythical sorter be anyway? My stepchildren? Her niece? Neither of us had children of our own. Could we assume that our husbands would make order out of what we left behind? According to the actuarial tables, we would outlive them.

Tavia's father died when she and I were fifty-six years old. At any other time, we might have been able to enjoy a few more years ignoring the fact that we, too, were going to die, but thanks to the pandemic, such blithe disregard was out of the question. I put Kent's egg and its silver napkin ring on the windowsill in my office, where it ceased to be blue and took on an inexplicable warm, orange glow—Kent's favorite color. Every day I looked at it and thought about all the work to be done.

My friend Rick is a real estate agent who lives in our neighborhood. We run into each other most mornings when we're out walking our dogs. He'd been after me for a while to look at a house that was for sale down the street. "Just look," he said. "You're going to love it." I didn't want a different house, but months after Kent's death, his legacy still nagged. Maybe by moving I could force myself to contend with all the boxed-up stuff in my own closets.

Walking down the street to see a house that we passed every day, Karl and I convinced ourselves that this was exactly the change we needed, so we were disappointed and relieved to find that we didn't like this other house nearly as much as we liked the one we already lived in.

"I wonder if we could just pretend to move," I said to Karl that night over dinner. "Would that be possible? Go through everything we own and then stay where we are?"

I could have said, "I wonder if we could just pretend to die?" but that pulled up a different set of images entirely. Could we at least prepare? Wasn't that what Kent had failed to do? To imagine his own death part of his spiritual practice, to look around 24-S and try to envision the world without him?

Karl had been living in our house for twenty-five years. I'd been there for sixteen—the longest I'd ever lived anywhere by more than a decade. Ours was a marriage of like-minded neatness. Karl's suit jacket went directly onto a hanger. I wiped down the kitchen counters before going to bed. Our never-ending stream of houseguests frequently commented on the tranquility of our surroundings, and I told them that the secret was not having much stuff.

But we had plenty of stuff. It's a big house, and over time, the closets and drawers had filled with things we never touched, didn't want, and in many cases had completely forgotten we owned. Karl said that he was game for a deep excavation. He was working from home. I had stopped traveling. If we were ever going to do this, now was the time.

I started in the kitchen, a room that's friendly and overly familiar, sitting on the floor to address the lower cabinets first. The plastic soup containers were easy—I'd held on to too many of those. At some point I'd bought new bread pans without letting the old ones go. I had four colanders. Cabinet by cabinet, I pulled out the contents, assessed, divided, wiped down, replaced. I filled the laundry basket with the things I didn't want or need and carried those discards to the basement. I made the decision to wait until we'd finished with the entire house before trying to find a place for the things we were getting rid of. This is a lesson I picked up from my work: writing must be separate from editing, and if you try to do both things at the same time, nothing will get done. I would not stop the work at hand to imagine who might want the square green serving dish I'd bought fifteen years before and never put on the table.

What I owned didn't surprise me half as much as how I felt about it: the unexpected shame that came from having seven mixing bowls, the guilt over never having made good use of the electric juicer my mother had given me, and, strangest of all, my consistent anthropomorphizing of inanimate objects—how would those plastic plates with pictures of chickadees on them feel when they realized they were on their way to the basement? It was as if I'd run my fingers across some unexpected lump in my psyche. Jesus, what was *that*?

My willingness to idly spin out a narrative for the actual chickadees that pecked at the bricks outside my window was one thing, but where did this quick stab of sympathy for tableware come from? I shook it off, refilled the laundry basket, and headed downstairs, wondering if this was a human condition or some disorder specific to novelists. My ability to animate the people who exist solely in my imagination is a time-honed skill, not unlike a ventriloquist's ability to throw her voice into a sock puppet, a ventriloquist who eventually becomes so good at her job that she can make her hand speak convincingly without the sock, until finally there's just the empty sock singing "O mio babbino caro" from the bottom of the hamper. Of course, it might not be a problem of humans *or* writers but something specific to me, though I doubt it. If this were my problem alone, more people would be cleaning out their kitchens.

To end day one on a positive note, I struggled to open a drawer with about thirty-five dish towels crammed inside. They were charming dish towels, many unused, patterned with dogs, birds, koalas, the great state of Tennessee. I decided that ten would be plenty.

I washed and folded them all, then took the excess down to the basement. I reveled in the ease with which the drawer now opened and shut.

That was the warm-up, the stretch.

THE NEXT NIGHT after dinner, I hauled out a ladder to confront the upper half of the kitchen cabinets. A dozen etched crystal champagne flutes sat on the very top shelf, so tall I could just barely ease them out. A dozen? I had collected them through my thirties, one at time. Some I'd bought for myself, others I'd received as gifts, a single glass for my birthday, wrapped in tissue paper, as if I were a bride for an entire decade in which I married no one. Had I imagined that at some point twelve people would be in my house wanting champagne? Everything about the glasses disappointed me: their number, their ridiculous height, the idea of them sitting up there all these years, waiting for me to throw a party. (See, there, I'm doing it again: *the glasses were waiting.* I had disappointed the glasses by failing to throw a party at which their existence would have been justified.) But it wasn't just the champagne flutes. One shelf down, I found four Waterford brandy snifters behind a fleet of wineglasses. In high school I had asked my parents for brandy snifters, and I had received them at the rate of one a year. In high school I had also scored six tiny liqueur glasses and a set of white espresso cups that came with saucers the thickness of Communion wafers. The espresso cups were still in their original cardboard box, the corner of which had, at some point, been nibbled away. I had never made a cup of espresso because I don't actually like espresso.

"Dad changed his look every year for the kiddos," Tavia had told me, "kiddos" being what Kent called his students. "They loved it. They were always waiting to see who he was going to be next."

Who did I think I was going to be next? Scott Fitzgerald? Jay Gatsby? Would I drink champagne while standing in a fountain? Would I throw a brandy snifter into the fireplace at the end of an affair? I laid the glasses in the laundry basket, the tall and the small, separating them into layers with a towel. Downstairs, I set them up on the concrete floor near the hot-water heater, where they made a battalion both ridiculous and dazzling.

I had miscalculated the tools of adulthood when I was young, or I had miscalculated the kind of adult I would be. I had taken my cues from Edith Wharton novels and Merchant Ivory films. I had taken my cues from my best friend's father.

I had missed the mark on whom I would become, but in doing so had created a record of who I was at the time, a strange kid with strange expectations, because it wasn't just the glasses—I'd bought flatware as well. When I was eight and my sister, Heather, was eleven, we were in a car accident along with our stepfather. We each received an insurance settlement—$5,000 for me and $10,000 for her, because her injuries were easily twice as bad as mine. The money, after the lawyer's cut, was placed in a low-interest trust that we would access at eighteen. When Heather got her money, I petitioned the court for mine as well. I told the lawyer that the silver market was going up, up, up, and if I had to wait another three and a half years I'd never be able to afford flatware.

They gave me the money, maybe because they realized that any fourteen-year-old who referenced the silver market was a kid you wanted to get off your docket. I bought place settings for eight, along with serving pieces, in Gorham's Chantilly. I bought salad forks, which I deemed essential, but held off on cream-soup spoons, which I did not. With the money I had left, I bought five South African Krugerrands—heavy gold coins I kept in the refrigerator of the doll house that was still in my bedroom—then sold them two years later for a neat profit.

"KEEP EVERYTHING YOU want," I said to Karl. "I don't want you to feel like you have to get rid of things just because I'm doing this."

"I'm doing this, too." He was working through closets of his own.

I found a giant plastic bin of silver trays and silver vases and silver chafing dishes in a hidden cupboard under the kitchen bar. Serving utensils, bowls, tea services, a chocolate pot. I won't say I had completely forgotten them, but they were out of sight and therefore out of mind. The bin hadn't been opened since I'd wrapped the pieces and stored them, maybe fifteen years before. I spread the contents out on the dining room table. These things were all Karl's, and, like my glasses, predated our marriage.

He idly reunited a dish with its lid. "Let's get rid of it," he said.

"Maybe you want to hold on to some of it?"

"Ten years ago I would have said yes," he said.

I waited for the second half of that sentence to arrive, but nothing came. Karl started to pile the silver back in the bin without a hint of nostalgia. I was worried that he would regret this later and hold it against me. I said as much, and he told me I was nuts. That I was nuts was becoming increasingly evident. Once full, the bin of silver was as heavy as a pirate's chest, and we struggled to get it down to the basement together. He then called Leslie, the nurse at his medical practice who steers him through his long, hard days with good sense and good cheer, and told her to come over with her daughter to check out what was available.

I was mercifully able to keep myself from saying, *We were going to wait*. Of course this would be Karl's favorite part, the part he would never be able to wait for: he got to give these things away. The first time I ever met Karl, he tried to give me his car.

An hour later we were in the basement with Leslie and her daughter. Leslie came from work and was wearing scrubs. Her daughter, Kerrie, also a nurse, was wearing hiking sandals and what appeared to be a hiking dress. She had recently returned from a journey down the Colorado Trail—Denver to Durango—logging in five hundred miles alone. She came down with COVID along the way and waited it out in her tent.

"She just got engaged," Leslie told me. Kerrie smiled.

"You're going to need things," Karl said.

Leslie laughed and told us that her daughter could still fit everything she owned in her car.

I believed it. Kerrie was the embodiment of fresh air and sunshine, her only adornment a mass of spectacular curls. Clearly, she had chosen to pursue a completely different model of adulthood. I watched as she took careful steps around the glasses and the cups laid out across the concrete floor. She lifted a single oversized champagne flute and held it up. "You really don't want these?" she asked.

I told her I didn't want any of it. I didn't tell her that she shouldn't want any of it either. She took the champagne flutes. She took the brandy snifters, the decanter. She took the set of demitasse cups, but not the espresso cups. She took the stack of glass plates and the large assortment of mismatched wineglasses that had multiplied like rabbits over the years. Whenever she appeared to have reached her limit, Karl picked up something else and handed it to her. She accepted a few silver serving pieces, the square green serving dish. With every acquisition she asked me again. "Are you sure?"

I went through the motions of reassurance without being especially reassuring. The truth was, I felt oddly sick—not that I was going to miss these things but that somehow I was tricking her. I was passing off my burden to an unsuspecting sprite, and in doing so was perpetuating the myths of adult life that I had so wholeheartedly embraced. I pictured all those champagne flutes tied to her backpack as she and her mother wrapped them tenderly in dish towels. When they were finished, I helped them carry their load out to their car. There they stood in the light of the late afternoon, thanking me, thanking me, saying they couldn't believe it, so many beautiful things.

I had laid out my burden on the basement floor and Kerrie had borne it away. Or at least a chunk of it. There was still so much of the house to sort.

"Don't feel bad," Karl said as we watched them back out of the driveway. "If we hadn't given it to her she would have registered for it."

I did feel bad, but not for very long. The feeling that came to take its place was lightness. This was the practice: I was starting to get rid of my possessions, at least the useless ones, because possessions stood between me and death. They didn't protect me from death, but they created a barrier in my understanding, like many layers of bubble wrap, so that instead of thinking about what was coming and the beauty that was here now, I was thinking about the piles of shiny trinkets I'd accumulated. I had begun the journey of digging out.

Later that evening, Karl called his son and daughter-in-law and they came over to look through the basement stash. After great deliberation, they agreed to take a Pyrex measuring cup and a tulip auger. Karl's daughter came the next morning and took the teacups, the industrial mixer, and every bit of the remaining silver. She was a woman who threw enormous parties for no reason on random Tuesdays. She was thrilled, and I was thrilled for her. It had all changed that fast. The point was no longer making sure that the right person got the right things. The point was that those things were gone.

NIGHT AFTER NIGHT, I opened a closet or a drawer or a cupboard and began again. The laundry room was surprisingly depressing, with that gallon container of a concentrated household cleaner called "Tuff Stuff" which I had bought so many years ago from a Russian kid who was selling it door to door. He told me to mix it with water and put it in a spray bottle. When he saw that I was about to decline, he unscrewed the cap and took a slug straight from the bottle. "Nontoxic," he said, wiping his mouth with his hand. "You try?" I found a half dozen bottles of insect repellent dated for use in the early 2000s, an inch of petrified Gorilla Glue, the collar and bowl of a beloved dog long passed. The laundry room was where things went to die.

Every table had a drawer and every drawer had a story—none of them interesting. I scouted them out room by room and sifted through the manuals and remotes and packets of flower food. I found the burned-down ends of candles, campaign buttons, photographs, nickels, a shocking quantity of pencils, more decks of cards than two people could shuffle through in a lifetime. I gathered together the paper clips, made a ball out of rubber bands, and threw the rest away.

I never considered getting rid of the things that were beautiful—the brass cage with its mechanical singing bird that I'd given Karl for our anniversary, the painting of the little black dog that hangs in the front hall. Nor did I care about the things we used—the green sofa in the living room, the table and chairs. After all, if Karl and I were to disappear tomorrow, someone would want all of that. I wanted all that. I was no ascetic, though I say that with some regret—I grew up with the Sisters of Mercy and attended twelve years of Catholic school. (Kent, who loved his worldly goods, had studied at the Trappist monastery at Gethsemani in his early years.)

I was aiming for something much smaller than a vow of poverty, and was finding that small thing hard enough. I turned out the lights on the first floor and went upstairs.

The closer I got to the places where I slept and worked, the more complicated my choices became. The sandwich-size Ziploc of my grandmother's costume jewelry nearly sank me, all those missing beads and broken clasps. I have no memory of her wearing any of it, but she liked to sort it now and then, and she let my sister and me play with it. Somehow the tangle of cheap necklaces and bracelets and vicious clip-on earrings had managed to follow her all the way to the dementia ward. I scooped it out of the nightstand in her room after she died, not because I wanted it but because I didn't know how to leave it there.

In the end I decided to let it go, because who in the world would understand its significance once I was gone? I had my grandmother's heart locket with pictures of my mother and grandfather inside. I had the ring with the two ovals of green glass that her brother Roy gave her when she graduated from eighth grade. I had her wedding ring, thin as a thread, which I wore on my left hand now.

I found little things that had become important over time for no reason other than that I'd kept them for so long: a small wooden rocking horse that a high school friend had brought me from Japan, two teeth that had been extracted from my head before I got braces at thirteen, a smooth green stone that looked like a scarab—I couldn't remember where it had come from. I got rid of them all. I found the tall Madame Alexander dolls of my youth wrapped together in a single bag on the highest shelf of the closet in my office. They were what was known as fashion dolls, which meant that they were beautifully dressed and not meant to be played with, but I had slept with the black-haired girl for years. She had neither stockings nor shoes, and her hair was disheveled, her crinoline wilted. I had buried my whole heart into her. The other doll, a Nordic blonde, was still perfect down to the ribbons on her straw hat because I'd never wanted a second doll. I had loved only the black-haired one. I loved her still. The blonde I only admired. I hadn't thought about those dolls from one decade to the next, and still they were there, waiting. Maybe, like the sock in the hamper, they'd been singing all that time.

I could see that even after childhood's long and sticky embrace, followed by more than forty years in a sack, both dolls were resplendent in their beauty, lit from within. I took them to my mother, who said she could freshen them up. She washed and ironed their dresses, restitched the snaps, put new elastic in the waistbands of their underskirts. She artfully reconfigured the messy black hair in a way that made the doll look older and more introspective. I wrote to my friend Sandy, attaching pictures, and asked if her grandchildren would like to know the true friends of my youth. She wrote back immediately to say yes. Yes.

Champagne flutes by dolls by teeth, I felt the space opening around me. Unfortunately, the people closest to me could also feel it opening. Having heard that I was cleaning out, my mother gave me a large box of letters and stories I'd written in school. She'd been quietly saving them, and even as I balked (I didn't want to see those stories again), my sister, also cleaning out, dropped off a strikingly similar stack of my early work. They had sensed a vacuum in my house and rushed in to fill it.

MY SISTER'S FRIEND Megan and her eight-year-old daughter, Charlotte, came to visit as I was nearing the end of my project. Megan and Charlotte were driving a loop from Minneapolis to the Great Smoky Mountains and back, hiking and camping along the way. They were spending the night with my sister, and Heather brought them over to see me. At that point I had only a little bit of the basement to go.

"I told Charlotte I'd show her your bathroom," Heather said.

"She loves seeing other people's bathrooms," Megan said.

And so we went upstairs, the four of us. As Megan was walking by my office, she stopped. "Oh, Charlotte," she said. "Come look at this. Come see what she has." The child walked into my office and immediately clapped her hands over her mouth to keep from screaming. I switched on the light. She was staring at my typewriter, a cheap electric Brother I used for envelopes and short notes.

"*You have a typewriter!*" Charlotte started hopping up and down.

"What she really wants is a manual," Megan said. "We've looked at a bunch of them but they never work. Once they get old, the keys stick."

There were two manual typewriters in the closet right behind us. One was my grandmother's little Adler, a Tippa 7 that typed in cursive. She used it for everything, so much so that I could type a note on it now and feel as if I were reading her handwriting. I wasn't giving the Adler away. I also owned an Hermes 3000 that my mother and stepfather had bought for me when I was in college, the most gorgeous typewriter I could have imagined. I wrote every college paper on it, every story. In graduate school, I typed at my kitchen table in a straight-backed chair that my friend Lucy had bought at the Tuesday-night auction in Iowa City. Draft after draft, I banged away until my back seized, then I would lie flat on the living-room rug for days. A luggage tag was still attached to the Hermes's handle—Piedmont Airlines. I brought the typewriter home with me every Christmas, even though it weighed seventeen pounds. Such was my love for that machine that I hadn't been able to imagine our being separated for an entire holiday vacation. The stories my mother had, the ones my sister returned to me: they were all typed on the Hermes.

My mother and my stepfather, my darling Lucy, college, graduate school, all those stories—they made up the history of that typewriter. It waited on a shelf in the very closet where the dolls had been kept. When I was cleaning out the closet, I never considered giving either of the typewriters away, but I don't think I'd used them once since I got my first computer when I was twenty-three. I took Megan aside. "I've got a manual," I whispered to her.

She looked slightly horrified. "You don't want to give that away."

I told her that I'd sleep on it, that she shouldn't say anything to Charlotte. I told her to come back in the morning.

I didn't need the glasses or the silver, those things that represented who I thought I would be but never became, and I didn't need the dolls, because they represented who I had been and no longer was. The typewriter, on the other hand, represented both the person I had wanted to be and the person I am. Finding the typewriter was like finding the axe I'd used to chop the wood to build the house I lived in. It had been my essential tool. After all it had given me, didn't it deserve something better than to sit on a shelf?

Yes, I accept that this is who I am. I was thinking about what the typewriter deserved for its years of loyal service.

In any practice there will be tests. That's why we call it a practice— so we'll be ready to meet our challenges when the time comes. I had loved a typewriter. I had believed that every good sentence I wrote in my youth had come from the typewriter itself. I had neglected that typewriter all the same.

Kent, the Cosmic Monk, laminated his prayers. He'd laminated pictures of his daughters, his granddaughter, his dog. He'd laminated good reviews of my novels. After he died, Tavia found two laminated cards on which he'd written:

I have everything I need.
All that is
Not Ladder
Falls Away

He had two of them because it was the prayer he needed to say twice. We had tried the world on for size, Kent and I, and one way or another, we would figure out a way to let it go.

I took the Hermes down from the closet shelf and unsnapped the cover, typed *I love you iloveyou*. The keys didn't stick. I looked online to see if replacement ribbons were available. They were. I watched a video of Tom Hanks, that famous champion of manual typewriters, replacing a ribbon on a Hermes 3000. "No typewriter has ever been made that is better than a Hermes," he said in a salesman's voice.

Well, that was the truth.

That night, while Karl and I were walking Sparky, I told him about Charlotte. I told him what I was thinking. "As much as I loved it, it would be wonderful if someone could use it. How many little girls are out there pining for manual typewriters?"

"So give her mine," he said.

I stopped. The dog stopped. "You have a manual typewriter?" There were *three* manual typewriters in the house?

Karl nodded. "You gave it to me."

I had forgotten. I had given Karl an Olivetti for his birthday when we were first dating because I was used to dating writers, not doctors. Because I didn't know him then. Because I saw myself as the kind of woman who dated men with manual typewriters. I'd bought it new. Twenty-six years later it was still new.

Abraham looked up and there in a thicket he saw a ram caught by its horns. He went over and took the ram and sacrificed it as a burnt offering instead of his son.

Okay, it wasn't like that. But I had been ready to let the Hermes go, and now I didn't have to let it go. There was another typewriter caught in the thicket.

When I gave the Olivetti to Charlotte the next morning, she thought I'd given her the moon. She had imagined herself as a girl with a typewriter. And now she was.

· To the Doghouse ·

I first found Snoopy in Paradise, California, the tiny town in the foothills of the Sierra Nevada Mountains that was later erased by fire. As children in the late 1960s and early '70s, my sister and I spent our summers there with our grandparents. We found the place to be perfectly named. "We're on our way to Paradise," we would say, and "We've been in Paradise all summer." After the fire, which swept through some forty-five years after my grandparents left for Nashville to be closer to us, my sister searched the internet to see if their house had been spared, but the street was gone. Everything was gone.

The sharp detail with which I can remember that house is overwhelming to me now—the room where my grandparents slept in twin beds, the room where I shared a bed with my sister. I remember the cherry trees, the line of quail that crossed the back lawn in the morning to the ground-level birdbath my grandmother kept full for them, *Family Affair* and the Watergate hearings on television. Everything about those summer days is tattooed on my brain. I was an introverted kid, and not a strong reader. My grandmother had a stock of mass-market "Peanuts" books she'd bought off a drugstore spinner. Titles like *You've Had It, Charlie Brown* and *All This and Snoopy, Too* were exactly my speed. I memorized those books. I found Snoopy in Paradise the way another kid might have found God.

Influence is a combination of circumstance and luck: what we are shown and what we stumble upon in those brief years when our hearts and minds are fully open. I imagine that for Henry James, the extended European tour of his youth led him to write about American expatriates. I, instead, was in Northern California being imprinted by a comic strip. When the morning newspaper came, my sister and I read the funnies together. Always "Peanuts" was first. I learned the happy dance and it has served me well. My formative years were spent in a Snoopy T-shirt, sleeping on Snoopy sheets with a stuffed Snoopy in my arms. I was not a cool kid, and Snoopy was a very cool dog. I hoped the association would rub off on me.

That was pretty much the whole point of Charlie Brown's relationship with Snoopy: the awkward kid's social value is raised by his glorious dog. Anyone could see what Charlie Brown got out of Snoopy, even when Snoopy was blowing him off—but what did Snoopy get out of it? I'm guessing it was the loyalty, the doglike consistency that people want in a pet, which of course makes Charlie Brown the dog. I had no problem with this. I would have been thrilled to be Snoopy's dog. I was already his student. Snoopy was a writer, and it was my intention to follow in his path.

Did I become a novelist because I was a loser kid who wanted to be more like the cartoon dog I admired, the confident dog I associated with the happiest days of my otherwise haphazard youth? Or did I have some nascent sense that I would be a writer, and so gravitated towards Snoopy, the dog-novelist? It's hard to know how influence works. One thing I'm sure of is that through Snoopy, Charles Schulz raised the value of imagination, not just for me but for everyone who read him.

Snoopy was a famous World War I flying ace who often found himself in dogfights with the Red Baron. He quaffed root beer in the existential loneliness of the French countryside, and then was Joe Cool on campus. He pinched Charlie Brown's white handkerchief to become a volunteer in the French Foreign Legion and was a leader of the Beagle Scouts, a motley flock of little yellow birds. He was a figure skater and hockey player in equal measure, an astronaut, a tennis star, a skateboarder, a pugilist and a suburban pet whose doghouse contained oriental rugs, a pool table, and a van Gogh. This wasn't just a dog who knew how to dream, this was a dog who so fully inhabited his realities that everyone around him saw them, too. Snoopy heard the roar of the approving crowd as clearly as he heard the bullets whizzing past his Sopwith Camel. Having ventured fearlessly into the world, he could come back to the roof of his doghouse and sit straight-backed in front of his typewriter, to tap out the words that began so many of his stories: "It was a dark and stormy night."

Wait, am I seriously discussing Snoopy, a cartoon dog, as a writer? Am I believing in him as he was drawn to believe in himself?

I am. I did. I do.

"Theoretically, my older brother should be my role model," Linus's brother Rerun says. "But that blanket business takes care of that. /

Which forces me to look elsewhere, and maybe ask the question. / Can the neighbor's dog be a role model?"

The answer is yes.

One day Snoopy is sleeping on his back with his head in his water dish. "Psychiatrists will tell you that there's no better way to relax than to lie with your head in your water dish!" his thought bubble says. Two months later, Charlie Brown and Linus and Lucy and Schroeder are all resting blissfully with their heads in water dishes. It's amazing to me that I didn't just roll over and stick my head in the birdbath.

I once published a long essay in the *Atlantic* and found myself at the mercy of a smart, zealous young copy editor who told me that it went against the magazine's style manual to use "it" as a syntactic expletive that has no meaning.

"Are you telling me Dickens wouldn't have been allowed to write, 'It was the best of times, it was the worst of times'?"

"That's what I'm telling you," he said.

"You wouldn't let Snoopy say, 'It was a dark and stormy night'?"

"Not if he was writing for the *Atlantic*."

Why wouldn't Snoopy be writing for the *Atlantic*? The first time I'd ever heard of *War and Peace* was when he performed a six-hour version with hand puppets, just like the first time I heard of Christo was when Snoopy wrapped up his doghouse.

Snoopy works hard up on the roof of the doghouse. He sees his own flaws. He types, "Those years in Paris were to be among the finest of her life. / Looking back, she once remarked, 'Those years in Paris were among the finest of my life.' That was what she said when she looked back upon those years in Paris / where she spent some of the finest years of her life," which is followed by the thought bubble, "I think this is going to need a little editing . . ."

Snoopy didn't just write his novels, he tried to get them published. In those dark days before electronic submissions, he taught me what it would mean to stand in front of a mailbox, waiting to hear from an editor. He taught me—I cannot emphasize this enough—that I would fail. Snoopy got far more rejection letters than he ever got acceptances, and the rejections ranged (as they will) from impersonal to flippant to cruel. Later, I could see we'd been building up to this. It wasn't as if he'd won all those tennis matches. The Sopwith Camel was regularly riddled with bullet holes. He was willing to lose, even in the stories he imagined for himself. He lost, and he continued to be cool, which is to say, he was still himself in the face of both failure and success. I could have skipped those two years at the Iowa Writers' Workshop because the whole writer's life had been mapped out for me.

First, the importance of critical reading:

Charlie Brown to Linus: "I'm sorry . . . Snoopy can't go out to play right now . . . he's reading."

Linus: "Dogs can't read."

Charlie Brown: "Well, he's sitting in there holding a book."

Snoopy in his chair: "There's no way in the world that Anna Karenina and Count Vronsky could ever have been happy."

Then: Imagination, work, rewriting, being alone, realizing that all the good titles had already been taken—*A Tale of Two Cities*, *Of Human Bondage*, *Heart of Darkness*, Snoopy came to all of them too late—sending your work out into the world and facing rejection, which Snoopy internalized and used to his own advantage, he lived through all of it.

Linus rings Charlie Brown's doorbell and says, "Ask your dog to come out and play 'chase the stick.'"

Snoopy comes out and hands him a note: "Thank you for your offer to come out and play. We are busy at this time, however, and cannot accept your offer. We hope you will be successful elsewhere."

Snoopy taught me that I would be hurt and I would get over it. He walked me through the publishing process: being thrilled by acceptance, ignoring reviews, and then having the dream of best-sellerdom dashed: "It's from your publisher," Charlie Brown tells Snoopy. "They've printed one copy of your novel. / It says they haven't been able to sell it. / They say they're sorry. Your book is now out of print."

There was more work to do, other books to write. What mattered was that you knew how to love the job.

"Joe Ceremony was very short," Snoopy types. "When he entered a room, everyone had to be warned not to stand on Ceremony." At which point Snoopy falls off his doghouse backwards, cracking himself up, only to climb up again and look at his typewriter lovingly. "I'm a great admirer of my own writing."

Oh, beagle, isn't it the truth? That moment when you write a single, perfect sentence is worth more than an entire box of biscuits.

When I didn't get into the MacDowell Colony, I remembered Snoopy telling Woodstock, "I think it's an illusion that a writer needs a fancy studio / A writer doesn't need a place by the ocean or in the mountains / some of our best books have been written in very humble places." It was enough to send Woodstock back to his nest to type, and to send me back to the kitchen table.

Snoopy dedicated his first book to Woodstock, "My friend of friends."

I probably would have been a writer without Snoopy. I know without a doubt I would have loved dogs. What I don't know is if my love of writing and my love of dogs would have been so intertwined. Snoopy wasn't just my role model, he was my dream dog. Because he had an inner life, I ascribed an inner life to all the dogs I knew, and they proved me right. I have lived with many dogs I considered to be my equals, and a couple I knew to be my betters. The times I've lived without a dog, the world has not been right, as if the days were out of balance.

"You know what my grandfather says?" Linus tells Sally. "He says every child should have a dog . . . / He says that a child who does not have a dog is like a child deprived." To which Snoopy, lying on the roof of his doghouse, adds, "The actual term is 'Living without benefit of beagle.' "

I've never been able to name a dog Snoopy, in the same way I couldn't name the piglet I got for my ninth birthday Wilbur. It would have been asking too much of the piglet, and would have seemed obvious to the farm girl I'd become. I compulsively reread *Charlotte's Web*, another book with a great set of lessons about writing. To name a dog Snoopy would be to set the dog up for failure, because no matter how great he was, his ears would never turn him into a helicopter. I did, however, name the dog I have now for Charles Schulz, whose nickname was Sparky.

Sparky has exceeded every expectation. A small gray-and-white rescue, he comes with me to the bookstore and stands straight up on his back legs to greet customers. Surely he has the talent and the patience to write a novel of his own; I'm just glad he never wanted to. I've accepted the fact that my dog is cooler than I am, but it would be hard to deal with if he were also a better writer. And anyway, it would take too much time away from our relationship. My happiness is, in fact, a warm puppy.

The girl I was in Paradise could never have imagined what life would look like a half a century later—how much would be lost and how much gained. I learned how to shape myself into who I was going to be with the guidance of a dog in the funny papers. People ask me about my influences but really it was just the one: Snoopy was my aspiration, my role model. I heard the dog whistle, silent to everyone around me, and followed.

· Eudora Welty, an Introduction ·

Not long ago, I decided it was time to reread *To the Lighthouse*, or I should say it was time to read it. So many years had passed since I'd first picked it up that I remembered nothing but Mrs. Ramsay and the boat. The copy I bought had the words "with a foreword by Eudora Welty" at the top of the front cover in tiny white letters that all but disappeared into the skyline above the name Virginia Woolf. I didn't realize the bonus I was getting until I opened the book.

"As it happened," Welty's foreword begins, "I came to discover *To the Lighthouse* for myself. If it seems unbelievable today, this was possible to do in 1930 in Mississippi, when I was young, reading at my own will and as pleasure led me. I might have missed it if it hadn't been for the strong signal in the title. Blessed with luck and innocence, I fell upon the novel that once and forever opened the door of imaginative fiction for me, and read it cold, in all its wonder and magnitude.

"Personal discovery is the direct and, I suspect, the appropriate route to *To the Lighthouse*. Yet discovery, in the reading of a great original work, does not depend on its initial newness to us. No matter how often we begin it again, it seems to expand and expand again ahead of us."

There could be no truer account of my own experience with *The Collected Stories of Eudora Welty*, and since I've come to praise, it seems only fitting to use her praise of Woolf as the place from which to set sail. My introduction to Welty was her story "A Visit of Charity," which I read in a seventh-grade English textbook. I was twelve, slightly younger than the story's Campfire Girl. Marian is an unsympathetic centerpiece, wanting only to deliver her plant to some old lady and get her credit points, but I was terrified for her nevertheless, as she is shoved into the tiny, sick-smelling room with two old ladies and their clawlike hands. They may have been mad or demented, but mostly they are desperate for her company and her ability to disrupt the boredom of their day. By twelve I had lived enough to have met old people who wanted to swallow me up, and so my heart went out to this selfish girl. But reading it again at an age much closer to the crones than the Campfire Girl, I find my sympathies have shifted. God help those old women, stuffed away in a shabby care facility to wait for their deaths. They have no one to turn their frustrations on but each other. I look at Marian in her little red cap and think, Kid, it wouldn't kill you to sit down for a few minutes and brighten their day.

This is why we have to go back, because even as the text stays completely true to the writer's intention, we readers never cease to change. If you've read these stories before, I beg you, read them again. Chances are you'll find them to be completely new.

When *To the Lighthouse* was published in 1927, Virginia Woolf was forty-five. Eudora Welty read it three years later when she was twenty-one. *The Collected Stories of Eudora Welty* was originally published in 1980, when Welty was seventy-one. A year later, she circled back to write the foreword to Woolf's masterpiece. While I fully understand that this is nothing more than time at work, I find it moving to imagine Welty reading *To the Lighthouse* when Woolf was still alive, just as Welty was alive when I first found that story. When I was young, English textbooks were dominated by dead male authors, and Welty distinguished herself in my mind not only for her unsettling tale of charity but for being neither a man nor dead.

The year *The Collected Stories of Eudora Welty* was published, my mother gave me a copy for my birthday. I was seventeen. Not long after, Welty came to Nashville to give a reading at Vanderbilt, and Tavia and I arrived an hour early to secure a front-row seat. It was the first time I'd been to a reading. Welty was child-sized, sitting up on the stage behind a table with whoever it was that introduced her that night. I was a few years older than Marian the Campfire Girl at that point, and the great author seemed very close to the ancient women in the Old Ladies' Home. Before the event began, I walked up onto the stage with my book and asked her to sign it for me. I had no idea of protocol in those days. Someone should have stopped me. I opened the book for her and she shook her head. "No, no, dear," she said. "You always want to sign on the title page." Then she turned the page and signed her name, thereby stopping my heart.

Eudora Welty read "Why I Live at the P.O." that night, and in doing so thrilled the faithful. It was exactly what we were hoping to hear, and yet in reading this collection again so many years later, I have to wonder if she ever felt confined by those anthologized favorites—"Why I Live at the P.O.," "A Worn Path," "Powerhouse," "The Wide Net"—because while those stories are essential, they fall short of representing the darkness and depth of her body of work. Reading the collection now from beginning to end is an experience not unlike going to a retrospective exhibition, walking through room after room of paintings to see the full development of a vision. You might linger for an extra moment in front of the canvas most frequently reproduced on postcards and T-shirts, but what you're seeing over the course of the exhibition is a life played out in art. We have a tendency to lift out those pieces that are most pleasing to us, or that best illustrate a particular point—a collection of stories about place or race or a particular moment in history—but none of that captures Welty's extraordinary dexterity as she steps from comedy to horror to family drama to farce to the retelling of classic mythology. In the same way that her narrative voice is capable of moving from character to character, her style shifts with allegiance to nothing but the compassionate truth. She could accomplish anything because of her complete understanding of the world in which she lived.

When I first read *The Collected Stories of Eudora Welty* I thought she was a fabulist, a writer endowed with a superior imagination and love of tall tales. She was that, of course, but Welty, who spent most of her life in Jackson, Mississippi, in the house her father built when she was a child, was also telling the truth.

"The reason it's so impossible to write about Mississippi," Donna Tartt once told me, "is that everyone thinks you're exaggerating." It had never occurred to me that Welty was accurately representing a culture until I married into that culture myself. In the last quarter century, during which I've been going to Mississippi regularly, I've come to believe that Welty was to her state what Joan Didion was to California or Saul Bellow was to Chicago: the clear eye of verisimilitude. I no longer read "Clytie" as Southern Gothic because I believe in every member of Clytie's family as I believe in her impossible ending. When the man and woman leave Galatoire's in New Orleans and drive south in "No Place for You, My Love," they might as well be going to the end of the earth. They cross their own version of the river Styx on a ferry and reach a place where the road peters out into a strip of crunchy shells. It may be a metaphor, but it's also real. Throughout this book the characters speak of the incessant hell of the heat, of the need to lie down in the middle of the day because of it. "It was like riding a stove," the woman on the ferry thinks. Anyone who's passed a summer in Mississippi will tell you, it may be art but it's also a fact.

No writer I know of tells the truth of the landscape like Welty. The natural world is the rock on which these stories are built, and its overbearing presence informs every sentence. "There were thousands, millions of mosquitos and gnats—a universe of them, and on the increase." I could take this book apart and type it up again, sentence by perfect sentence, to say, *This is exactly what Mississippi is like*: "Once he dived down and down into the dark water, where it was so still that nothing stirred, not even a fish, and so dark that it was no longer the muddy world of the upper river but the dark clear world of deepness, and he must have believed this was the deepest place in the whole Pearl River, and if she was not here she would not be anywhere." Everything exists in layers, from the sun to the scorching sky to the highest leaves of the trees to rooftops and porches and grass and dirt, the muddy water in the river and the fish in the water and the quieter, truer place beneath even the fish.

This is the world into which Welty repeatedly places her characters. They interact first with the landscape and then, if there's any energy left after that, with one another. What's amazing about the stories is how rarely the people speak to one another, or, when they do, how seldom anyone seems to be listening. It's more likely that the dialogue is interior, which is why "The Key," a story about two deaf-mutes waiting in a train station, is particularly deft. Even in that most loquacious favorite, "Why I Live at the P.O.," Sister can't clear her good name despite her passionate monologues because no one in her family will listen.

Eudora Welty died on July 23, 2001. I was in my kitchen in Nashville when I heard the news on the radio. Without much thought, I put a black dress in a bag and drove south to Meridian, where I spent the night with my mother-in-law. The next morning I drove over to Jackson. I arrived hours early, thinking I'd be standing in the street with a throng of the short-story faithful, but I got a seat in the church. Everyone did. A storm of brief and terrible violence had swept through that morning, and instead of making the weather worse, as summer storms are wont to do, it made things better. It was seventy-five degrees as we made our way to the cemetery after the service, something I doubt had ever before happened in Jackson in July. I doubt it will happen again. Greatness had come through once, which is really all that we could hope for, and the world that had been so justly represented took back the one who loved it best.

· Flight Plan ·

Three of us were in a 1947 de Havilland Beaver, floating in the middle of a crater lake in the southwest quadrant of Alaska. The pilot was recounting the toll the Vietnam War had taken on him, while over in the right seat, Karl listened. Due to proximity, I was listening as well, though chances are they'd forgotten I was there. Outside, the water sloshed against the pontoons, rocking the plane gently side to side. No one had asked this man to tell his story in a long time, but Karl had asked, and so the pilot put the plane down in the lake, turned off the ignition, and began.

Karl and I were spending a week at a fly-out lodge outside of Il-iamna, by which I mean nowhere near Iliamna but closer to Iliamna than to anywhere else. Every morning the dozen or so guests wres-tled ourselves into neoprene waders and were divided into groups of three or four or five. Along with thermoses and sandwiches and tackle boxes and a guide, we were loaded into a string of warhorse floatplanes bobbing at the dock. The pilots who flew for the lodge struck me as men who would have had a hard time finding work elsewhere. After a flight of twenty or thirty minutes, we would land on a river or a lake, then pile out of the plane and into a small, waiting boat. The plane would then taxi off while the guide and the boat took us even deeper into nowhere, the idea being that fish congregated in secret locations far from civilization. But there was no civilization, and there were plentiful fish in the lake in front of the lodge. Taking a plane to a boat to find an obscure fishing spot was just a bit of Alaskan theater. After we reached whatever pebbly shoal the guide had in mind for the day, we arranged our flies and waded hipdeep into the freezing water to cast for trout. Despite the significant majesty of the place, standing in a river for eight hours wasn't my idea of a good time. Bears prevented me from wandering off. Rain prevented me from reading on the shore. Mosquitoes prevented everything else.

So when, on the fifth day, Karl suggested we skip the fishing and pay extra to spend the day flying instead, I was in. Flying was what he'd come for anyway: the early-morning trip out to the fish and the later afternoon trip back to the lodge. Karl liked talking to the pilots—who put him in the right seat and let him wear the headset—and they liked talking to him because free medical advice was hard to come by. Karl and I were less than a year into our relationship when we went to Alaska, and I didn't yet fully understand the centrality of airplanes in his life. After Alaska, I got it.

When the talk of war was done, the pilot asked Karl if he'd ever flown a Beaver, if he'd had the experience of taking off from the water and landing on the water. Karl said no, he had not. Even though Karl had been flying since he was a boy, at forty-seven he still didn't have his pilot's license. He was honest about this—he was honest about everything—which should not be confused with being thoughtful about everything.

"You have to tip the nose up when you land," the pilot said. "That's the mistake people make. It's hard to get the depth perception because of the glare, so you wind up hitting with the nose. Then you flip. You want to try?" He was so grateful to Karl, and this was the only gift he had to give.

The day was bright with puffs of clouds and low winds. If the offer to fly the plane was technically illegal—the pilot was not a certified flight instructor and the plane belonged to the lodge—we were well outside the long arm of the FAA. Karl and his new friend put on their headsets.

I was no stranger to the single engine. My stepfather Mike had rented planes when I was growing up, and, with my mother, flew to some of the medical meetings where he gave lectures. Sometimes I was in the back with the luggage. My mother had taken enough flying lessons to know how to land should she be called upon to do so. She went so far as to solo, but then quit before she got her license. When we moved to the country outside of Nashville, Mike bought a tiny bright-red helicopter which he flew for years. He kept it in a hangar in the front of the farm where we lived. My mother had no idea how to land the helicopter.

After a demonstration—up, around, down again—the pilot turned over the controls. This was not Lake Michigan. Getting up to speed required circling, but the take-off had to be straight towards a fixed point on the horizon and into the wind. Karl took off towards the shore and then we lifted off the lake, past the mountains, through the clouds, around the blue sky, back through the clouds, past the mountains, then nose up, plane down, smack into the lake. The pilot was right; it was hard to see it coming. I reminded myself to relax my jaw. The pilot offered Karl some pointers, some praise. There was a quick discussion of how the landing could be improved and then we were off again, a tighter circle, greater speed, straight up, lake-mountain-cloud-blue sky-mountain-lake, the nose up as we came down. The jolt was harder this time—I felt it in my spine—but before I could fully register my relief we were up again: a carnival ride for which no one bothered to take tickets.

I wasn't given to airsickness or seasickness, but the combination of air and water in rapid succession was something new. I turned away from the window to contemplate the floor, a stamped metal rusted at the edges, like a service elevator in a hospital. I stared at it while Karl took off, turned above the lake, then dropped back down onto the surface. Repetition was the key to learning. The only thing I could throw up in were the pilot's waders, which seemed better (better?) than throwing up on the stamped metal floor. I held down my breakfast through sheer force of will. Still, the constant plunge was disorienting. I was angry at both of the men in the front— especially the one I was sharing a bed with back at the lodge—for not considering how seriously unpleasant this might be for someone who didn't live to fly. But despite the rage and the nausea pulsing in the back of my throat, I wasn't afraid. Considering that about half of all small-craft fatalities occur during either takeoff or landing; considering that taking off and landing were all we were doing; considering that the plane was rusted and the pilot had struggled with the aftereffects of Agent Orange and my boyfriend had never landed a plane on water before; considering that this lake was somewhere far from Iliamna and no one knew we were there in the first place;

considering that if the plane flipped, as it had been established these planes could do, I would probably not be able to swim through the freezing water in my rubberized sack of neoprene (which I had stupidly worn against the cold), and if I did make it to the shore, my chances of surviving whatever came next were probably zero—I should have been afraid.

But Karl and I were together, and he was the person slamming the plane onto the lake, so I was not.

"KARL FLIES?" PEOPLE say to me. "Have you ever flown with him?"

I fly with him all the time, and when we're together in the plane I've never been concerned, not about black clouds or lightning, not about turbulence that could knock the fillings from your teeth. The times that I'm afraid are the times when I'm not in the plane, and by "afraid," I mean an emotion closer to terror. Take, for example (there are so many examples), the time that Karl flew a Cessna to Kingston, Ontario, to look at a boat, and on the way home had to land on an airstrip somewhere in Ohio because the weather was so bad. The tiny airport office was locked and he stood under the wing to call and let me know he'd be late. He called again two hours later from Bowling Green, Kentucky, to say that he had landed a second time because the transponder was out, which meant the plane couldn't be tracked. The weather was still bad.

"Stay there," I said. "I'll drive up and get you." Bowling Green was an hour away by car.

He said no. He said, let's wait and see. Maybe he could fix it, or find someone to fix it. It was nine o'clock but the flight was so short.

Two hours later there was still no call, and still no answer when I tried his cell phone. Around midnight, the clock and I had a conversation. I told the clock I wanted to wait another fifteen minutes before my new life began, the life in which Karl had been killed in a plane crash. I requested fifteen minutes more in this world—which I was quickly coming to see as the past—before figuring out who to call, who to wake up. *You'll remember this feeling when the phone rings*, I told myself. *You'll remember how scared you were when he calls to tell you he's fine.* And it was true. As many times as I've been in exactly this situation, I never forget it, and it never fails to shock me, the flood of adrenaline that does not serve for fight or flight but drowns me. At twelve-thirty I shifted my perspective again, from wondering what it would be like if he were dead to the knowledge that he was dead, and I decided I could wait another fifteen minutes. He would be dead forever, so what difference did it make if I gave myself a little more time? I still had no idea what I was supposed to do.

After I had extended the final cutoff two more times, he walked in the door. That's how these stories always end, of course, except for the one time they don't. I saw the headlights against the garage door and went outside in the rain to meet him with my love and my rage and my sick relief. I wanted to kill him because he had not been killed. I wanted to step into his open jacket and stay there for the rest of my life, for the rest of his life. How had he not called?

"I did call. I called you from Kentucky."

"But you never told me you'd left Kentucky."

"It took a long time to get the transponder fixed."

"Then why didn't you call to say you'd landed?"

"It was too late." In the house, he went to the refrigerator and poured himself a glass of orange juice. He was dead tired but not dead. "I didn't want to wake you up."

He might as well have said, *I thought you were sleeping because I have no idea who you are, or who any normal people are.*

I stayed awake for what was left of the night to watch him, just to make sure he was really there, and in the morning I asked who I was supposed to call. Who do I call after midnight to try to find you?

Karl sat with the question before answering. For the first time he seemed to grasp my sadness: past, present, future. "They'll call you," he said.

"Who will call me?"

"There's something called the ELT, the emergency locator transmitter. If the ELT is activated then someone will call you. You're my emergency contact."

"How is it activated?"

"Either manually or on impact." I hadn't considered that scenario, the one in which the phone finally rings and it isn't him.

THIS STORY GOES back to Lindbergh, who flew to Paris when Karl's father, Frank, was nine. Frank was one of a whole country of children, an entire world of children, who could now look up and imagine themselves in the sky. Frank became an oral surgeon. He married Jo and they had two children, Karl and Nancy. Frank started taking flying lessons in a Tri-Pacer with Karl in the back seat. A few weeks after Karl's brother Michael was born, Frank bought his first plane, a 1947 Ercoupe. He asked their minister to come to the house after dinner, after Karl and Nancy were in bed. Jo was in her pajamas, the new baby in her lap. The minister sat on the couch between them while Frank told his wife he'd bought a plane.

The Ercoupe was big enough for two small people. Frank let Karl fly when they were together because the plane was so easy—tricycle landing, no rudder pedals, and it steered like a car. Not only had Frank bought a plane without telling his wife; he let their eight-year-old son fly it.

Meridian, Mississippi, has its own page in aviation history. The Key brothers, Fred and Al, set the world record for endurance flying in 1935 by circling the town in a Curtiss Robin for twenty-seven days without landing. The idea of developing a safer method of aerial refueling (a second plane connected to the Curtiss Robin in midair to pump in fuel) began as a stunt to save their local airfield from being closed. The airfield, later named Key Field, was saved. After the Second World War, Fred and Al opened Key Brothers Flying Service. When Karl was ten, Fred gave him a job after school, sweeping out hangars, cleaning spark plugs, gunking the engines and driving the fuel truck out to gas up the planes. Why not? He was always hanging around the airfield anyway. When someone needed a ride to New Orleans to pick up a plane, Karl would go along with Fred to fly co-pilot on the way home.

"Co-pilot?" I asked. "And you were what, twelve?" Tales grow tall in Mississippi, a byproduct of humidity and heat. Was it possible a twelve-year-old was flying planes? I have learned to ask the same questions multiple times.

"All you had to do was keep the altitude steady. Most of the planes only went eighty-five or ninety miles an hour." The joke was that

"I.F.R." didn't stand for "instrument flight rules" but "I fly railroads." Karl said if he flew over the track for the Southerner it would take him straight back to Meridian.

This gave Fred Key a chance to eat his sandwich.

The past is made of stories that are unlikely to happen now, and Mississippi is made of stories that are unlikely to have happened in the first place, like the time Frank had engine trouble and had to land on the highway. That made the papers. Or the time Frank and Jo flew the Ercoupe to a dental meeting in Vicksburg and got so lost that Jo had to use binoculars to try and figure out where they were. Finally they spotted a water tower with the name of the town painted on the side.

Around the time Karl started flying right seat with Fred Key, he rode his bike to the airfield early on a summer Saturday morning. There was a Piper Super Cub that hadn't been there the day before. The Cubs had always been exactly the same, which is to say you could get it in yellow or you couldn't get it. But this Cub was white with red stripes, which should have been a tip-off. Cubs didn't have ignition keys. All that was required to start them was the turn of a switch and the push of a button. Karl left his bike in the grass alongside the runway, untied the wings and the tail, pulled off the chocks. The cockpit smelled new. He turned the switch and pushed the button. He had never soloed before, and this seemed like the day.

"It wasn't like I was flying to Mexico," Karl said, after I pointed out that had been a stupendously bad idea. "I taxied out, took off, made one turn around the pattern. The whole thing took ten minutes, and I probably wasn't more than six hundred feet off the ground. It would have been fine except that the engine quit."

The engine quit?

"I had to land it in the field. I came down maybe twenty feet short of the runway."

Over time, you come to know the seminal stories of the person you live with. I knew this story, and when I pressed hard against it, Karl came up with every detail he could remember: It was muddy. He pushed the plane back where it had been near the hangar. It wasn't heavy, there was a handle on the side and he leaned against the fuselage to direct it. It was still early and there was no one else at the airfield. He washed the plane and tied it down, replaced the chocks, then rode his bicycle home to tell his father what he'd done. It was Mr. Tony's plane, and Frank sent Karl to Mr. Tony to apologize. Mr. Tony listened, and then asked Karl if he'd switched the gas tank when the engine quit. No horror, no recrimination, just "Did you switch the gas tank?" The Piper Cub had a single tank, but this was a Super Cub. The Super Cub had two tanks and you had to switch them over manually. Sixty years after the fact, Karl pulled up a diagram of a Piper Cub and then a Super Cub on his phone to show me where the tanks were placed. I didn't care where the tanks were placed.

"What were you thinking?" I asked him.

"About what?"

"About taking a plane, about flying by yourself, about the engine quitting. What did you think when the engine quit?"

"Those planes can glide a long way."

We stared at each another—one person who flew planes, one person who believed there was an emotional narrative to flying planes. The two lines did not intersect.

"You weren't scared?"

Karl thought about it. "It was a long time ago."

"I know."

"Well, then, not that I remember."

Not long after Karl borrowed Mr. Tony's plane, his father let him solo in the Ercoupe, maybe so that Karl would get over any bad associations about soloing, or maybe because the kid had already proven he could do it in someone else's plane, so why not?

It wasn't until later that I wondered what I'd say were I pressed to remember how I felt the first time I drove a car by myself, or the first time I ran out of gas. If there were actual feelings associated with those events, I had no access to them, because it was a *car*.

Which was how Karl felt about planes.

KARL WENT TO college on a scholarship. Frank sold the Ercoupe and then bought a Luscombe Silvaire 8a. Years later, he sold the Luscombe and bought a Cessna 150. After he died of head and neck cancer in 1988, the family sold the Cessna 150. Frank's Ercoupe and his 150 both crashed in 2008. Both pilots were killed.

KARL GOT HIS first pilot's logbook when he was twelve. By the time he went to college he had logged almost two hundred hours. He didn't realize the hours didn't count because he hadn't taken a flight physical, but he didn't mind. The logbook made him feel like a real pilot. After college he went to Oxford University, where he got a master's degree in philosophy and theology. He married Kathy, whom he had met as an undergraduate, and they went to Rhodesia to teach for the last year and a half before the country became Zimbabwe, and then they came back to Mississippi. Karl went to medical school. He and Kathy had two children. In all that time, he never flew a plane. In 1984, Karl and his family were living in Nashville, and he bought a 1968 Beechcraft Baron with their next-door neighbor. The neighbor used the plane during the week to go to business meetings and Karl used it on weekends to go back to Mississippi. They hired the same pilot. After they sold that plane, he bought part interest in a Cessna 421. Karl later sold that plane to a friend of his, who ran out of fuel and crashed it in a cornfield in Indiana at Thanksgiving. "He crashed upside down," he told me. "Everyone lived."

"How did he crash it upside down?"

"Well, the weather was terrible, and one of the engines went out, so the plane would have been listing to begin with."

WHEN KARL AND I met in 1994, he was divorced and had a 1967 Beechcraft Bonanza, a model commonly referred to as "the doctor killer" because the plane was so streamlined that it was hard to control. "Doctors have enough money to buy them," Karl said, "but they aren't good enough pilots to fly them." Thanks to the Key Brothers Flying Service, Karl was a good enough pilot. The Bonanza he bought had been on the cover of *American Bonanza Society Magazine*. He loved that plane, then loved it less, then sold it. Later, he bought a 1958 Piper Comanche (loved; loved less; sold), followed by a 1970 Beechcraft Sundowner, and then a 1958 Cessna 175—every one of them a gorgeous piece of junk. They were the kind of planes that compelled other pilots to stride across the tarmac and offer congratulations. The planes Karl had were the planes other men wanted. They would have been real bargains, too, except that the Comanche needed a whole new engine. The 175 needed a custom propeller. The Bonanza needed new gas tanks, which meant the wings had to be taken apart. The new gas tanks and the wing removal and replacement cost as much as he'd paid for the plane. Then it also needed a new engine.

With the exception of the Cessna, Karl owned these planes without having a license, which meant he could fly by himself or he could fly with a passenger so long as he had an instructor along. It meant that for the first ten years of our relationship there was someone else in the plane whenever I was with him, but Karl was always the one flying. He flew alone all the time, mostly to Meridian to see his mother. He would say he put off getting his license because he didn't have enough time to study for the written exam, but in fact he studied for it ceaselessly. He put off getting his license because he wanted to be sure he'd get a perfect score. He got his license, and the perfect score, the year before we married. After that it was just the two of us in the plane. He took more courses. He got his unusual attitudes certification, which teaches pilots what to do if they inadvertently get upside down, how to come out of spins, how to think fast. He got his tailwheel endorsement, which meant he could fly a tailwheel plane.

WHEN I AM in the plane with Karl, I read, I look out the window, I sleep an untroubled sleep, my head against the window.

KARL COULD GO for years without a plane. These intervals usually came after something had happened—once the governor on the propeller went out, making it impossible to control the propeller speed; another time the landing gear wouldn't come up. He would tell me about these things weeks after the fact, a confession of a close call that I had missed entirely. Then he'd sell the plane, as if to punish it. "I'm done flying," he'd tell me. "I did it and I'm glad, but it's out of my system now." Then he would take to bed with a copy of *Trade-a-Plane* to see what was for sale.

During one plane-less stretch before we were married, Karl arrived at my house for dinner, and when I met him at the door and kissed him, I stepped back. I had never encountered anything as cold as his face. "How cold *is* it out there?" I asked. I thought of the line from the Thornton Wilder play *The Skin of Our Teeth*: "It's simply freezing. The dogs are sticking to the sidewalks!" It was December. I remember because it was the day after my birthday. Karl had waited until after my birthday to tell me he'd bought a motorcycle.

I understood he wasn't interested in baking bread, that there would be no Scrabble or yoga in our future as a couple, but couldn't there be a hobby in which death was not a likely outcome? I told him I was going to start smoking again.

"What?"

"You asked me to quit and I quit. I'm starting again." He left quickly after that—no dinner—and rode home. He lived three blocks away. While trying to get the garage-door opener out of his pocket, he slipped on the ice and the bike fell on top of him. He was able to dig out his cellphone and call his son for help. The next day, he sold the motorcycle to one of the managers in his practice for half of what he'd paid for it two days before. The day after that, the manager who had purchased Karl's bike cut the price again and sold it to someone else at the behest of his wife.

Eventually, Karl was going to die. Eventually, we were all going to die. I understood this, but I wanted him to give me the luxury of forgetting. I wanted not to have to contemplate his loss so vividly while he was still here. I would take a plane over a motorcycle any day, maybe because planes were what I was used to and because Karl had cut his permanent teeth in an airplane. Boats seemed safer than planes, until they didn't. In 2003, he was part of a sixteen-person team that raced an eighty-two-foot yacht from Rhode Island to Germany. When the boat sailed away I stood on the dock in Newport and cried, with good reason. In the two weeks they were gone they were hit by eighty-foot waves in eighty-knot winds. There was an electrical fire on the boat. At one point, a rogue wave smashed into the hull and Karl, standing at the helm and tied to a line, was knocked into the side of the cockpit. For three days he couldn't stand. For six months after coming home he had a hematoma on his hip that looked like someone had worked a grapefruit under the skin.

He decided he wanted to fly again. He bought the Sundowner and then got rid of it. Two years later he bought the Cessna 175, then got rid of that. He said it was time to stop flying. He was done with planes.

I like to tell people that Karl would be the perfect person to be stranded with on a desert island—he tells a good story, can fly a plane and sail a boat, and could take out my appendix if he had to. He could entertain me on the island, save my life on the island, get me off the island.

What could be better than that? I wanted him to be the brave and adventuresome person he was. He worked so hard at a job that was often relentless and depressing, and if this was his pleasure, who was I to say it should be otherwise?

I tried not to say it.

The years went on. Karl bought an old lobster boat. He got it cheap because it was hard to steer. He'd go out after work and take it a few miles down the river and a few miles back. He liked the quiet. He said he wished that there could be one more plane.

KARL'S MOTHER, JO, was still in Meridian, still in the same house she and Frank had moved to when Karl was a baby in her arms. We drove down to Mississippi to see her three or four times a year. I enjoyed the five-hour drive, but Karl didn't. "If I had a plane," he said, "I'd go to see my mother once a week for lunch."

Jo was eighty-seven when we started having this conversation. Karl was sixty-one. He felt as though the time for another plane had passed, and then he felt as though there was still a chance. He would say he was finally free of his desire, and then that desire would come over him again like some sort of malarial fever. He showed me pictures of the planes he wanted, including a home-built ultra-light called a STOL CH750 that looked like a sixth-grade art project writ large. Over time I learned to offer no resistance. "Pretty," I would say when he showed me the picture. I didn't want to be the reason he didn't have a plane, the reason he was gripped by fits of misery specific to a man who wants to be in the sky and is stuck on the ground. At some point I'd had a revelation: it would be better for him to die in a plane than to keep talking about whether or not to get a plane. This isn't exactly a joke. At his worst, Karl was like a sad parakeet sitting on a swing in a cage year after year. It was unnatural.

When I told him to get another plane, he said the matter deserved more thought. He gave it a few more years. His choices narrowed, then shifted. He reorganized his priorities. I recently found the list of pros and cons I'd written out one night after dinner in an attempt to move the process along. Karl dictated.

Diamond: 2013—PRO: Almost new. Two engines. Eco-friendly (fuel savings). Holds eight hundred pounds. Flies a hundred and sixty knots. Air conditioning. Deicing. CON: Lands fast. Not licensed to fly a twin engine.

Cirrus: 2015—PRO: Seventy-five hours on the engine. Flies at a hundred and eighty knots. Holds eight hundred pounds. Full warranty. Air conditioning. Deicing. Parachute. (Parachute?) CON: Lands fast.

de Havilland Beaver: 1952 (no floats)—PRO: New engine. Flies at one hundred and twenty knots. Lands slow. Holds two thousand pounds. Six seats. Excellent guy factor [see: pilots crossing the tarmac to congratulate you on your plane]. CON: no air conditioning or deicing. Primitive instruments. Can't fly long distances.

While Karl pondered his choices, I thought about what could and could not be controlled. In flying, three factors obtain: the skill of the pilot, the reliability of the equipment, and the X factor— the lightning, the flock of starlings sucked into the engine. Because Karl's skills as a pilot were impeccable, and there wasn't a damn thing I could do about birds, that left the plane as the one thing I could control.

"The Cirrus," I said. "But not that Cirrus. A new Cirrus. A Cirrus right off the showroom floor." The Cirrus lacked the guy factor, but was the safest and most reliable plane on the market—the Toyota Corolla of aviation.

Karl was genuinely horrified by my suggestion. He was tormented by the expense of his hobby to begin with. (Though as hobbies go, there are many that are costlier, deadlier, and a hundred-percent illegal. Find the good and praise it.) He believed that planes should always be bought on the cheap, and that hunting for deals was an essential part of the mission statement. But after years of conversation and analysis, test flights and looking at pictures on his iPad, I had finally achieved clarity.

He shook his head. "Too much money."

"I don't care if we have to sell the house. I'm not going to enjoy having extra money if you're killed in a cheap plane."

He was the pilot and I was the plane and the birds were the birds and this was our marriage. It was the best we could do.

Karl was seventy-one when we bought the Cirrus. The plane had fixed landing gear. Karl told me that pilots over seventy couldn't be insured for planes with retractable landing gear because pilots over seventy had a poor record of remembering to put the landing gear down. The Cirrus came with a training course and an impressive maintenance package. It came with a parachute—not individual parachutes for the pilot and passengers, but a single super-sized one for the plane itself. Karl talked me through this. If something were to happen, I should pull the throttle back to idle and turn the fuel selector off. "Turn the ignition off if you think about it," he said, "but chances are you won't have to worry about that. If you're deploying the parachute, the engine is presumably dead."

I looked at him. "The engine isn't dead. *You're* dead. If I'm the one doing this, it's because you're no longer flying the plane." There it was again, the inevitable future I was forever hedging against.

"Okay," he said. "That makes sense. So reach around and turn the key, then pull down the red handle above your head. It takes about forty pounds of pressure so pull hard, both hands." He mimed how the pulling should go, a C-curve and then straight. "Then the parachute opens and you'll just waft down. It only works if you're above six hundred feet or more, so don't spend too much time making up your mind."

I would not picture the trip down after the parachute had opened, or calculate what it meant for our chances. I didn't want to know.

By the time Karl got the Cirrus, his mother was ninety-seven, though ninety-seven in Meridian is about eighty-four everywhere else. Women last longer in Mississippi. I packed lunch in a large box and a cooler and loaded it into the hold. Karl was so happy to be flying again, and I was happy because we were together in the plane. I understood I had no influence on the safety of the flight, but I was with him, and when I was with him I didn't worry about it. If something happened, it would happen to both of us. I looked down at the green quilt of the South, all those small plots of land stitched tight, the snaking rivers and lines of trees, the beautiful earth as seen from a clear sky.

We landed at Key Field, where Karl had learned to fly. Karl's brother-in-law, Steve, picked us up and drove us out to the lake, where we met Karl's mother and brother and sister, and ate our lunch at a picnic table. Three hours later we were back at the airport. It seemed like the best use of a plane I could imagine.

Steve waited to watch us take off. There were two runways, and ours was the only plane departing. As with everything else in

Meridian, it wasn't hard to imagine that what you were looking at was pretty much what Karl had been looking at when he worked there sixty years before. In that way, the plane was a time machine that took us back to the past, to his past. We buckled up and waved to Steve. Karl did his flight check. I put on my headphones, the music-listening kind instead of the flight kind, and tapped on Philip Glass. Taxiing down the runway, I was thinking about how it had all worked out so well. After so much deliberation and perseveration, the right choice had been made, and, in our own strange way, we had made it together. As the wheels lifted off the tarmac, my door opened. I hadn't latched the door.

The pilot's headset does not communicate with noise-canceling headphones playing piano music. With my right hand I used everything I had to hold the door closed, and with my left hand I was hitting Karl in the chest and frantically pointing down, down. We were ten feet off the ground, twenty feet, it goes very fast—planes, life. I tried to communicate with all available urgency and no words that he should *PUT THE PLANE DOWN NOW.* And he did. With very little runway left, he landed. He did not go into the field beyond the pavement. He stopped. He took off his headset.

"I didn't latch the door!" I cried. Karl was beaming.

For him, this was not a story about my mistake. It was a story about his ability to rectify my mistake. "They taught us how to do that in the safety course. We had to practice this exact thing, how to land right after you've taken off." Flight school! He had shown up, paid attention, simulated the emergency again and again until his response was ingrained.

We were parked at the end of the runway. We were parked at the very place Karl had been unable to reach when he'd lifted the

Super Cub as a boy. "It would have been me that killed us," I said. "It would have been me, and no one would have known."

"You wouldn't have killed us."

"I could barely hold the door closed."

"That was my fault," he said. "I should have checked it before we took off."

"I should at least be able to close my own door." I imagined the door flying off, the plane tipping forward, nose down.

"I would have just circled around and landed."

He would have figured it out on the fly—isn't that where the expression comes from? He would have landed the plane with the door open, closed the door, and taken off again. He would have done it without acrimony or blame. Later, when we were safely back in Nashville, in the car heading home from the airport, he tried to explain Bernoulli's principle as it relates to air pressure as a means of explaining why the door was trying to open instead of being pushed closed. I understood none of it. What I understood was that there was no keeping anyone safe—one person remembers to tip the nose up for the landing while the other person forgets to latch the door— and, in the end, it probably won't be the nose tip or the door. It will be something infinitely more mundane. It will be life and time, the things that come for us all.

Which doesn't mean I'll be able to keep myself from saying, *Careful, call me, come right back.* I will always be reaching for his hand.

How Knitting Saved My Life. Twice.

My grandmother was my role model, with her knitting and the stuff of her knitting: the flat fake-leather folder of colored aluminum needles that zipped up the side. The needles were all numbered and stayed in their designated slots, except for the mystery needles that gravitated to the middle of the case—the loose ones with points on either end, the circular ones that were held together by thin plastic cables that called mitten strings to mind. The balls of brightly colored dime-store yarn lived in a yarn bowl (essentially a wooden salad bowl on a waist-high pedestal that my grandfather had made). Stacks of tatty pattern books were nearby, along with tiny plastic stitch markers in white and yellow and blue, a hand-cranked ball winder, a metal needle gauge, a stitch counter that was also good for keeping track of how many times we walked around the block.

My grandmother sat in her chair in the evenings knitting sweaters, sporty doll dresses, slippers. The whole business was magic as far as I was concerned. Yarn into sweaters was straw into gold.

My grandmother waited for me to ask her for lessons, and when I did, she taught me. When I was a child, I cast on as a child, wrapping the yarn twice around my index finger and dipping the needle through. "This is the wrong way to do it," she said. "I'll show you the right way later." What she wouldn't let me do wrong even for a minute was to hold my yarn in a two-fingered pinch up by the needles. My aunt Rae was a master knitter, by which I mean argyle socks and gloves with cables down the fingers, and she held her yarn like an unschooled six-year-old her entire life, refusing to change. My grandmother saw this as a failure of her parenting. She would not make the same mistake with me. She started me off knitting squares, which she referred to as "Knitting knitting." I knit octagons, then trapezoids, then rectangles. I dropped as many stitches as made it onto the opposing needle. My grandmother, radiant in her patience, picked them up for me, then gave me back my knitting.

PATTERN.

Knitting was something I had played at over the years, and only in the presence of my grandmother. I'd gone beyond the square but had not progressed past the scarf and simple slippers. The summer Marti and I went to Europe, I was struck by the desire to progress. In Denmark and Belgium, in the countryside of France, we watched women knitting. They knit in parks, in cafés, on trains. They made it seem like a task that was essential to adulthood. "I don't know how to knit," Marti said, looking over her shoulder at the women we passed. Marti was from a family of intellectuals. I said I would teach her.

I was qualified to teach her how to knit a square. We bought some needles and yarn in Cherbourg, then boarded a ship to Rosslare. After a few days in Dublin, we started hitchhiking without any sort of plan. We wound up wherever people dropped us, in towns that saw few tourists but contained endless rivers of yarn. While Marti went in search of art or meaningful architecture (she was dreaming), I went to yarn stores and sat on the floor and knit. Because I wanted to stay ahead of my friend, I finally learned how to read patterns, how to work with different colors, how to use the funny little double-pointed needles. When I dropped a stitch, I simply walked up to any female person who was older than I was and handed her my knitting. I did not limit myself to women in yarn shops. If there was a woman in Ireland or the British Isles in the summer of 1983 who didn't know her way around a dropped stitch, I never met her. In retrospect, this seems sexist and reductive on my part, but at the time it was just luck. "I've made a mistake," I would say by way of explanation, and hold out my needles.

"Oh, dear," the woman would say, and then she would fix it for me, and sometimes, if nothing else was going on (it seemed that very little was going on), she'd teach me how to fix it myself. That was how I learned to knit.

Marti, who had an excellent grasp of art history, struggled with the burden of knitting. She said this was because she was left-handed, but I never cut her any slack. One day we hitched a ride in an eighteen-wheeler heading north through Scotland. The wide windows and high seats offered a panoramic view of the countryside. Marti and I shared the single front passenger seat. I was churning out an Icelandic sweater on circular needles while she struggled with her square. I gave her a hard time, I admit that, and did not mention the ten years I'd spent on the square myself. I was sticking my fingers through the gaping holes of her little practice square, a slice of wool Swiss cheese. Marti never addressed her problems as they arose. She ignored her dropped stitches, thinking they would in time find their way back to the needle. When we came to a gas station, she went inside to get a Coke, and when she was gone the rig driver, who wasn't much older than we were, began to scold me in a burr so thick I had almost no idea what he was saying. I kept asking him to repeat himself.

"You can't pick at her," is what he was saying, or it was something close to that. *Yee cun peek atur.* Scottish mystifies me, but finally I got the gist: "You shouldn't be cruel. She isn't right."

Marti, he was telling me, was handicapped, the proof of which was that she was a woman who didn't know how to knit, and I was cruel to continually point out that which should have been gently overlooked.

That night, Marti and I rented a room in a house on the desolate north coast of Scotland, where we watched in horror as the owner sat and pulled apart the most beautiful sweater I'd ever seen, winding the yarn back into balls. "I wanted a new sweater," she said while we sat there aghast, unable to save it. "I've had this one for years."

CABLES.

I taught Marti how to knit, and in return she taught me how to smoke. After college, she became a runner, stopped smoking, married, and had two children. She knit them tiny sweaters. My life took a different path. Try to knit a sweater and write a novel at the same time. It doesn't work. No one pushes back from her desk to knit a few rows and contemplate the sentence on the page, but a cigarette, with its two-minute burn, is the perfect vehicle for reflection. It's not as if I made a conscious choice to smoke instead of knit, but when I came to realize that the smoking had to stop, I decided to use knitting as my means of cessation.

This had to do in part with the woman we had watched unraveling that sweater in Scotland all those years before. When she started to knit it up again, she did so with a cigarette clamped in the far right corner of her mouth, her right cheek raised, her right eye closed tight against the rising smoke. She wasn't just parking the cigarette there while she knit, she was actually smoking it, with an aggressive puffing that did not require that the cigarette ever be removed from her mouth. The ash grew overlong and was unacknowledged when, at last, it fell. It created a picture so starkly unattractive that I knew I would never knit and smoke at the same time, even if I were alone with the doors locked and blankets thrown over every mirror and window. Knitting and smoking were two things that must never coexist. Because my hands were needed to smoke, I used knitting to occupy my hands. When I craved a cigarette, I reached for my needles instead. I promised myself I had to hold on for only five more rows, after which the impulse had usually passed. Still, I found the desire to smoke could not be completely thwarted by simple Icelandics on circular needles. I needed something more complicated. I started knitting cables. I counted stitches and adhered to rigorous patterns. I couldn't put my knitting down because I'd never be able to figure out how to pick it up again.

It took me more than a single try to quit. I would finish a sweater, go to a party, and the next thing I knew I was smoking again. The next thing I knew I was knitting again. Should I have taken a half-finished sweater to every party I went to? It's not as if I ever stubbed out a cigarette and someone pressed a ball of yarn into my hand, but the two things became connected in my mind. I wanted to smoke, and so I knit. When I quit smoking for good, I was knitting compulsively. Chain knitting.

Knitting, we may remember, did nothing for my writing. Smoking did nothing for my health. In the end, I had to quit them both.

CAST OFF.

Or I did until Lucy died. Lucy was a terrible knitter. She never finished anything. She'd leave her knitting on the subway a dozen rows in. When she died we were both thirty-nine. She'd been my beloved friend for seventeen years. I got into bed, not having any idea what I would do with the day or the next day or all the weeks and months that would follow. I got a pack of cigarettes, my first in years, and smoked them in bed. That was when my friend Erica sent me a box of yarn, skeins and skeins of chunky pink wool—not a loud pink, not a girlish pink, but a pink that called to mind a sunset in winter, dusky and tinged with blue. It was late December and cold. She sent me thick wooden needles and cursory directions—*knit two, purl two*. Forever. Until you run out. I looped the skeins over my feet and rolled them into balls. They were the kinds of yarn and needles children start with so that they can feel the heft of their accomplishment. It was a good yarn for the grieving because even on the days I did nothing, I could point to my knitting and say to myself, *Look at all I've done*. Several times I ripped it back and started again. I cast on. I wanted something wider, a little looser. I got out my grandmother's needles, which I had inherited, and experimented with the gauge. Like Penelope, I never wanted to finish that scarf, and so I made it last a long, long time.

Erica is the best knitter I've ever known. She can make a cardigan with elegant buttonholes that lie flat. She's made me fingerless gloves to write in and lacy shawls to throw over my shoulders. And when I was at the bottom of the well, she threw down a length of yarn and told me to knit myself back up. She didn't care how long it took. She would be waiting at the top, holding on to her end.

All these years later I still wear that scarf, though only on very cold days. It's enormous, like Japanese high fashion, an entire sheep's worth of wool. Sometimes I think I'll take it apart and make something more practical, two smaller scarves, but then I think about all the people this scarf has to hold—my grandmother, who taught me to knit, and Marti, whom I taught to knit, and Lucy and all the things she didn't get to finish, and Erica, who made sure I got it done, and all of our collective love and hope and disappointment. When I think about it that way, I'm amazed I was able to knit it all in.

· Tavia ·

As I was hiking alone in Utah one recent summer, a chicken crossed my path. I was two miles in on the trail and had yet to see another living soul, so she was my first interaction of the day. The chicken stopped and turned her head away, pretending not to notice me. I'd never spent much time in Utah before, and I didn't know if loose chickens were common at high altitudes. I pulled out my cell phone and called Tavia back in Kentucky. The chicken waited.

"You can't take a picture, can you?" she asked, knowing full well my fifteen-year-old flip phone didn't take pictures. I was, however, perfectly capable of description. The chicken and I remained motionless while I gave Tavia the details: mottled brown, full-size, with some white spots around the neck.

"Prairie chicken?" I guessed, although the chicken and I were a long way from any sort of prairie.

"Almost impossible," she said. "Prairie chickens are extremely rare." After a few more questions—what was my altitude? What did her head look like?—Tavia told me it was a grouse, maybe a sharp-tailed, maybe a sage. Then, since we were on the phone anyway, she asked how my mother was doing.

Insofar as life is a game show, Tavia Cathcart is my lifeline. She exists as one with the natural world. She's hunted for wildflowers in Patagonia and led groups of people straight up the side of a mountain in Mexico to witness the migration of millions of monarch butterflies. She runs a nature preserve in Kentucky, writes plant identification guides, and has a gardening show on Kentucky Public Television that was nominated for an Emmy. She is a polymath of plant life, of insect life, of chicken life. We've been friends since we were seven.

Tavia says the first time she saw me, we were in a dance class and I was trying to hide behind my mother. I don't remember this, but that doesn't matter. Tavia and I operate off a common hard drive: she remembers half and I remember half. We were both born in Los Angeles in December 1963. We each have one older sister. Our parents divorced around the same time—my mother getting custody and moving us to Nashville, her father getting custody and moving them to Nashville. It was enough to make a person wonder if my mother and her father were having an affair, but they weren't. The Cathcarts and the Patchetts met for the first time in Nashville, at the Catholic school where Tavia and I were enrolled in second grade.

All that would be a significant set of coincidences for an adult, but for two little girls it was a directive from the universe to inter-twine our lives, a fact that pleased our parents, since they relied on

each other for pickups, drop-offs, sleepovers. Either we were together at Tavia's apartment or at my house, or we were in the houses
of our respective grandmothers, who lived a few blocks away from
one another and very near our school. In the summers, the Cathcart
sisters and Patchett sisters would fly back to Los Angeles together
to each visit our missing parents. Of all our friends in Nashville, I
alone knew Tavia's mother, and she alone knew my father. I have
pictures my father took of the two of us at fifteen, our pants rolled
to our knees, wading into the Pacific Ocean. We believed that if life
had gone another way and we had stayed in California, we would
have found each other there.

In many ways we were an unlikely match. Tavia, the most beautiful child in the world, grew into the most beautiful girl. She was
the captain of the cheerleading team.

"Do you have to say that?" she asks me.

I do. Historical accuracy is important.

She was the sweetheart queen, sorority president. Boys trailed
her like a tail on a kite, discomfited by desire. Girls stuck by her
because Tavia's idea of fun was outsize. When she laughed, she bent
at the waist, her auburn curls sweeping the floor. Once when we
were shoe shopping, my mother told Tavia that if she laughed and
bent over one more time she was going to kill the poor guy who was
sitting on a low stool, waiting to slide her foot into the shoe he held
in his trembling hand.

As for me, well, I wasn't that girl. Not only did I pale beside her
(of course I did, everyone did) but I lacked her buoyancy and ease as
well. I was a serious kid. No boys were standing outside my window.

"You were too busy making art," she tells me, as if boys were kept
away by the force field of my poetry, my ceramics.

This is where the reader might be tempted to think that she was "the pretty one" and I was "the smart one," but that would be a fairy tale. Tavia is scorching smart.

People like to believe that women like Tavia will be punished eventually, that, having been given too much in the way of luster, they must lack the intelligence or depth that would bring them true happiness. We are all but promised that such women will make some horrible mistake early on, usually one involving a man who pays them too much attention, or they'll take what the world offers them and burn up quickly. Beauty ensures there will be no close friendships to see them through. How could they have friends when other women are hobbled by jealousy, when men only want to sleep with them? Somehow Tavia failed to acknowledge any of this. She worked hard. She went about her life with what I can only describe as glee. As far as I could tell, everybody loved her.

We graduated from high school and moved away. We married too young and then got divorced, though Tavia held on longer than I did. Neither of us had children. For a while we lived in different parts of California.

"I don't remember a single bad word between us," she said. "But that would be my selective memory, so who knows?"

I do remember her expressing sadness when I lit a cigarette while we were walking on the beach in our twenties. "All this beauty," she said, gesturing out to the ocean, "and you're smoking?"

Eventually I stopped smoking. I found success as a writer. Tavia had some luck as an actress, which was her father's dream. She played Cherie in a production of *Bus Stop*. For years I had the theater poster pinned on my closet door, Tavia perched on a bar stool wearing fishnets, her hair bleached platinum, putting Marilyn

Monroe to shame. She went to a lot of auditions, landed a little part in the movie *Mrs. Doubtfire*.

Somewhere along the way, acting became less important. She moved to San Francisco and made money in the early days of tech. Then the money became less important too. No one saw it coming when she stepped away. My bombshell best friend moved to the Sierra Nevada Mountains, went off the grid, and began to teach herself about the natural world. She studied field guides, committed herself to learning the habits and patterns of what was in front of her. She memorized all the Latin names, genus and species. She then went on to learn the names and habits of plants and animals she had never personally met. This was no small task. She worked on this for years and then decided she would work on it for the rest of her life. Not only could she tell me it was a grouse I was looking at that day in Utah, she knew that the tiny piece of lichen that appeared to be walking across my computer screen was an aphid lion, and that the birds that came out of nowhere one morning and covered my house and my neighbor's house and every branch on every tree were cedar waxwings. For her it was all about taking a giant step backwards, back to her childhood and her happiest memories of following her grandmother in the garden, back to sitting in the dirt surrounded by zinnias. She had managed to peel off other people's expectations in order to see what a life that was entirely her own would look like. It looked like the natural world.

I read an article recently about how friendships can die over time. We shouldn't feel bad about it, the article said. People change after all, grow in different directions: nothing lasts forever. It's true, of course, that we have changed, but Tavia and I are in this life together. We found each other as little girls, and through everything, we've held on. Some years all we've managed to do is exchange birthday cards, while other years we've talked on the phone every week, usually when she's driving to work. In the best years we see each other all the time. It really doesn't matter. Ours is a friendship full of elasticity and trust. For fifty years we've adjusted our bond to fit the times. Fifty years! Somewhere buried inside us are the selves who left school early to go back to my mother's and listen to Keith Jarrett records.

"It felt so cosmopolitan," Tavia says.

I had played Piglet to her Winnie-the-Pooh in the school play. We sat together on the stairs of my cousin's basement, drinking wine, waiting out a tornado. I remember in our thirties when we were both living in Nashville again and Tavia's mediocre boyfriend gave her a Valentine's card he hadn't signed—not his name, not hers, not "love." When she called, she could hardly tell me what had happened, she was laughing so hard.

"Did he think I was going to save it and give it to someone else next year?"

She helped me with every plant in my novel *State of Wonder*. She helped me with the birds and snakes and biting ants. She has a key to our house and would stay here when she came down from Kentucky to visit her father. We are both happily married now, another marvel. Our husbands talk while we slip away to walk our dogs. We always have dogs, Tavia and I. We always have each other.

"We became friends because we were the lucky ones," she told me once. "Everything turned out so well for us, it's almost embarrassing."

And maybe that's true, except that of all the myriad and conflicting words I could use to describe Tavia, lucky isn't one of them. At every turn, happiness was her decision. She started working after school at fourteen, finishing her homework while the rest of us were in bed asleep. She has spent her life saddled with Type 1 diabetes and has dealt with all the attending health problems. Not only did she take care of herself, she took care of everyone else. She didn't complain. But it was more than that—no matter the hand she was dealt, it always looked like she was winning. Even in hard times, she made her life look effortless, glamorous. Born on New Year's Eve, she seemed to exist in a perpetual fizz of golden champagne bubbles. That was her choice. Working at the nature preserve, she puts on a little lip gloss before firing up the chain saw.

Last winter, she told me how to rescue the enormous beetle that had tried to hibernate by stuffing half his body into the window sash outside the room where I write. It was twenty degrees when the bug was blown loose by a storm and caught in a tangle of dried-out leaves and abandoned spiderwebs. "He may be dead already," I said when I called her.

"Bring him inside," she said. "Let him warm up a little."

Following her instructions, I carefully removed the web with a Q-tip and then left him alone on my dresser. A few hours later, he tentatively stretched a few legs. Tavia told me to build him a cave, to put a mason jar on its side and then fill it halfway with dirt. She told me to cover it with leaves. I followed her directions and then nudged him into his new home in a planter by the back door. He seemed to take to it.

I saw him again in the spring, or I saw his close relation, sitting on the mat at the front door, antennae waving. It was a robust beetle. You might think I'm overstating the coincidence, but this wasn't an insect species I'd seen before or would ever see again—as long as my little finger, twice as wide, half as thick. It was the kind of bug you remember.

"The next time you see Tavia . . . ," is what I imagined him saying to me.

"I know," I tell him. "I know. She saved you. You're grateful. Get in line."

There Are No Children Here

I was late. My itinerary said the event started at two thirty when in fact it started at two o'clock. I was speaking at an Important Book Festival with an author I admired but had never met, and when I arrived early, or what I thought was early, he was already on the stage chatting away, an empty stool beside him. I ran down the center aisle, apologizing to everyone I passed, and took my place.

"I'm so sorry," I said, by way of introduction.

The author, let's call him Q, could not have been nicer. He was charming, gracious, very tall. He handled the situation easily, and certainly no one in that packed house had been troubled by my absence. Q was that rarest of birds—a commercially successful literary author. I was on tour for my second novel, which would go on to make even less of a ripple than my first, if such a thing were possible. Our books, Q's and mine, had come out around the same time from the same publisher, which is why I was allowed to ride his coattails at the book festival. "We were just talking about what it takes to be a real writer." Q gestured to the audience who had served as his conversational partner in my absence.

I covered my nervousness with enthusiasm. "Terrific!" I said, because truly, who wouldn't want to know? "What does it take to be a real writer?"

"Well, the first thing is, you have to treat writing as your job." Now he was talking to me. "I rent an office. Five days a week I get up and go to work. I put on a jacket, kiss my wife goodbye, and leave the house. I go every day at the same time. I stay a minimum of six hours. Writing is a job, and you have to treat it that way because if it isn't your job, it's your hobby."

"This is wonderful!" I said. "This is why it's so great to listen to writers talk about how they work, because it just goes to show that everyone has their own way." I gave a quick sketch of my life, which included writing in my dining room, in my pajamas, without a schedule. For me, the pleasure of being a writer came from the fact that writing felt nothing like a job. I took my work seriously, but if my grandmother got lonely or needed me to take her to the doctor, or a friend needed a ride to the airport in the middle of the day, I was the person to call. Flexibility was what writers got instead of health insurance.

Q looked at me. He looked at the audience. "You should get an office."

"I live alone."

"It doesn't matter. It's a mindset."

"What else?" I asked. I could barely afford my apartment.

"A visual dictionary," he said.

"A what?"

"You can't call yourself a writer if you don't have a visual dictionary."

"Are you serious?"

He was.

"I'm a writer, and I have no idea what a visual dictionary is." I was oddly thrilled by this exchange. Our disagreement made a gentle spectacle. No harm done by being late.

He looked at me, puzzled. How could I not know this? He patiently explained that a visual dictionary had pictures of things in which all the parts were labeled—airplanes, human bodies, dogs—so if you were writing a story with, say, a lawn mower in it, you could look up the picture of the lawn mower and reference the parts so that you would come across as someone who really knew his way around a lawn mower. "You might need to know the difference between a Doric column and an Ionic column," he added for good measure.

"To think I've come this far without one."

"You should get one," Q said. "They're great."

I told him I would do exactly that while the audience busily wrote the words *visual dictionary* on the back of their programs. And then, because we were on a stage with time still on the clock, I asked him if there was anything else a person needed in order to be a real writer.

"Children," he said.

"Children," I repeated back, though I hadn't misunderstood him.

He nodded solemnly, for now he was imparting his deepest wisdom. "You can't be a real writer if you don't have children."

"Why not?"

"Because until you have children, you don't know what it means to love."

I told him I didn't have children. What I didn't tell him was that I would never have children, and that I had known this for a very long time. I was thirty years old.

"Well—" He stopped. He unfolded his enormous hands. What else could he say?

It struck me very clearly that I could reach into this man's chest and pull out his heart in front of the audience. "Emily Dickinson," I said to him. "Flannery O'Connor, James Baldwin, Eudora Welty, Henry James."

He shook his head sadly. "All I can tell you is that you don't know what's missing until it's there."

"And when you wrote your first book?" I asked. I could pull out his heart. I wanted to.

"I wasn't a real writer then," he admitted. "I didn't know."

"We've had a friendly disagreement up until now," I said. I was the new kid, the ingénue. "But I have to tell you, people without children have known love, and we are writers."

A few nervous audience questions popped up after that. They were trying to smooth things over for us, save what could not be saved. When the merciful clock told us our time was up, we walked off the stage in opposite directions and never laid eyes on one another again.

2.

I once got a letter from an editor I'd never met praising me for the work I do on behalf of authors and books and bookstores, the gist of which went something like this: You know how people will say of someone who's selfish and stupid that they should be forcibly sterilized? Well, you do so much good in the world, you should be forcibly impregnated.

It took me a minute to realize he meant this as a compliment.

3.

Upon the publication of my first essay collection, *This Is the Story of a Happy Marriage*, I landed a spot on a national radio talk show I'd never been on before. As I sat in the recording studio in Nashville, before we started, the host spoke to me through headphones from another state. She told me how much she liked the book. She reminded me that the interview was taped, and said that if any questions made me uncomfortable, all I needed to do was tell her and we could stop. I told her I couldn't imagine what she could ask that would make me uncomfortable, and so we began. She wanted to know how I felt about not having had children.

"I feel fine about it."

"Do you regret your decision?"

"No," I said. "I don't regret it."

"Do you feel that as a woman you were forced to choose between your work as a writer and having children?"

"No," I said. "No one forced me to do anything. I just didn't want children."

"Male writers can have children and careers and it isn't as hard for them."

"They probably have wives."

"But is that fair? Your husband is considerably older than you are.

Chances are you'll be alone at the end of your life. Don't you worry about that?"

I sat in the booth and stared at the microphone hanging in front of my face. Ben, who owned the studio, Ben, whom I'd known for years, looked up at me through the glass. I was there to talk about a book I'd written, a book that had nothing to do with not having children.

"I bought long-term care insurance," I said.

It wasn't the answer she was looking for. She pressed on, as if my childless life were a matter for investigative reporting. "But doesn't that make you sad? The thought of being old and alone?"

"I don't mind talking about this," I said. "I don't have children. It's not a secret. But I wonder, would you ask Jonathan Franzen the same questions? He doesn't have children."

When the interview aired, all the questions about my childlessness had been edited out.

4.

I like to say that I was raised by nuns. My sister and I were dropped off at the convent in the morning, an hour before school started, and we often stayed an hour after the other children went home because our mother was working. Those were the best parts of the day, when the kids were gone. I liked washing the blackboards and putting books away. We went back to the nuns' private kitchen and the sisters would give us little jobs to do, like folding napkins or putting the silverware into its assigned spots in the silverware drawer. If the nuns were strict during the school day, they struck me as a very comfortable lot once the students had gone. They were considerate to one another, they made jokes. They paid minimal attention to our presence. Most of the time they seemed to forget we were there at all. As long as I asked for nothing, I could spy on them, not by hiding behind a curtain but by being unobtrusive and listening. The nuns worked with children and were happier once those children had gone home. After all, none of them had children of their own. They had made that choice, and from my vantage point, they didn't appear to have any regrets.

People used to ask me if I ever thought about being a nun when I was young, and the answer was no, I always wanted to be a writer. But still, I found certain nonreligious aspects of religious life inspiring.

5.

On book tour in Seattle, a different book tour, yet another book tour, I had lunch with my old friend Debra, whom I hadn't seen in years. Debra and her partner were trying to decide whether to have a child.

"I don't know," she told me. "I'm on the fence. We make lists of all the pros and cons. We go back and forth." Debra was in her early forties but her partner was younger. Her partner would carry the child. "Don't you wrestle with this?" she asked me.

I told her I did not.

"But you must have, at some point."

When I was a child, my bed was covered in stuffed animals. I slept with my head propped up on the edge of a giant green frog. My sister wanted only baby dolls, the more realistic the better—dolls whose hinged eyelids came down like shutters when you leaned them back. She practiced changing their empty diapers. She swaddled them and carried them in her arms. Even the memory of those dolls makes me shiver.

"All my life people have been telling me I must want a baby, or that I'm going to want a baby later on," I said. "It's like someone telling me the car keys are in the drawer in the kitchen. 'Go get the car keys out of the drawer.' So I go and I open the drawer and the car keys aren't in there. In fact, nothing's in there. The drawer is empty. I go back and tell them, the keys aren't in the drawer, and this person says to me, 'No, they are, you just need to try harder. Go back and look again.' It doesn't make any sense, but I do it. I go back and look, and the drawer is still empty. People are always telling me I'm wrong. Total strangers have told me that I'm wrong, that I need to go back and check one more time, but there's never anything in the drawer, and there's never going to be anything in the drawer."

My friend thinks about this for a while, and then she nods. "That must be really nice to know," she said.

And I tell her yes, it's wonderful.

6.

The day after I saw Debra, I left Seattle and flew to Portland. That's the way book tours work. The woman who picked me up at the airport was a probation officer. She liked books and authors, so she moonlighted as a media escort every now and then when her schedule allowed. After lunch, she took me to the International Rose Test Garden, home to more than ten thousand plants. I don't remember how the subject came up, but as we followed the gravel pathways through the dizzying blossoms, she told me she had always known she didn't want to have children. When she was twenty-five, she decided to have a tubal ligation.

"No one would do it," she said. "Every doctor I went to see told me to wait, that I'd change my mind later on and be sorry for what I'd done. When I pressed them, they said I had to have a psychiatric evaluation, and I did it because I wanted the surgery. And they still wouldn't do it."

"What happened?" I asked. So many roses.

"It took me two years," she said. "But I got it. They think we don't know our own mind when we decide to have an abortion, but we also don't know our own mind when we decide to put ourselves in a position where we'll never have to have an abortion."

"That's because we're fools," I said. "We can't be trusted."

I was still thinking about that woman when I finished the tour a few weeks later and flew home. I was thirty-seven years old and I knew my mind. I told Karl I was going to have a tubal ligation. It would still be another four years before we married.

He shook his head. He told me no.

"A valid opinion," I said, "but they aren't your tubes."

"Never have a surgery you don't need to have," he said to me.

"Having surgery has to be better than taking birth control pills."

"It's not. You've done fine on the pill and you never know when a surgery will go wrong. If nothing's broke, don't fix it."

I thanked him for his input and went to see my gynecologist, who was also a friend. I told her I wanted a tubal ligation.

"No," she said.

"I'm not conducting a poll. I'm asking you to tie my tubes."

"Things can always go wrong, and you're doing well on birth control. If a woman is doing well on birth control, and she goes off it to have a tubal ligation, nine times out of ten she goes back on the pill."

"Even though she can't get pregnant?"

My doctor nodded, explaining that the pill had benefits that extended beyond contraception. "Just go home," she told me. "You're fine."

I thought about the probation officer back in Portland having this same conversation for two years, having it at twenty-five instead of thirty-seven, and my heart was full of admiration. And exhaustion.

7.

I saw the sister of a friend at a Christmas party. I knew from my friend that her sister had tried to get pregnant for a very long time without success, and that she and her husband were finally able to adopt a child. There she was, a champagne glass in one hand, a beautiful baby girl up against her shoulder. It was Christmas, but this was the reason we were celebrating. I admired the baby. I congratulated her.

"Imagine how selfish a person would have to be to not have a child," she said to me.

8.

Karl asked me if I was pregnant.

I laughed and shook my head. "No, why? Do I look pregnant?"

"You do, actually." Because he's a doctor his opinion on such matters carries extra weight.

I was forty years old at the time, and he was fifty-six. I shrugged. "Well, no reason to think so." Was I unnerved? I wasn't sure. I had been fortunate. Birth control, used as directed, had worked my entire life. "I'll keep you posted."

The next day we were in the car. Karl was driving. "If I were pregnant," I said to him, "and there's no reason to think that I am, but if I were, what would you say?"

"That it would be your decision."

"I know it would be my decision, but what would you say?"

There was not a beat before his answer, not a flicker of hesitation. "I would say that I'm thrilled. I would say that this is the best thing that could ever happen to us."

I was floored by this answer, and also surprisingly touched. "Really?"

"When a woman tells you she's pregnant, the answer is always 'I'm thrilled,' or you're a complete idiot."

9.

I once saw a woman with six small children in a store: a baby strapped to her chest, a child barely walking holding her finger, the other four stair-steps. They hung together, a small flotilla, as she guided them forward. I watched in admiration and something like gratitude. *Thank you for keeping the species alive,* I could have said to her. *You're doing such good work.*

10.

The only time in my life I can remember thinking I might want children, or could imagine possibly wanting them in the future, was when I went to the Todds' house. Dick Todd was the editor for my first two books. He worked at Houghton Mifflin, which was still in Boston then. Dick lived two hours away in the Berkshires and came in to the office once a month, if that. He and his wife Susan lived in an old farmhouse in a wide field. They had raised their three daughters there, Emily, Maisie, and Nell. On several occasions I was invited to their house for the weekend. Emily was in school in Scotland then, Maisie was off at college, and Nell, at least at first, was still in high school. They had a Chesapeake Bay retriever named Coco, who was, according to her vet, the largest dog in Franklin County. Coco slept in the middle of whatever room the people happened to be in. There were always friends coming over, big dinner parties, spectacular Thanksgivings, lots of writers. The dishwasher had been broken for years and they used it as a drying rack after washing the dishes by hand. I was colder in that house than I can ever remember being anywhere else in my life. I slept in Emily's bed upstairs, spreading my coat over the bedspread, and watched the constellation of glow-in-the-dark planets and stars she'd stuck on the sloping ceiling.

Susan and Dick, in their boots and heavy sweaters, would always get around to telling the story of how they'd met and broken up. Dick went off to graduate school at Stanford, and Susan went to New York, where she worked as a copywriter and auditioned for plays. Then Dick showed up again just as Susan was about to go out with some old friends. Dick suggested they get married instead. Not to wait, no reason to wait, they should get married right then. And so they did. Every year they celebrated Wedding Week, because for all their Yankee reserve, theirs was not a love that could be contained by a single day. It was the love, the house, the field, the dog, the dishwasher, the long wooden table in the kitchen, the bowl of apples, the piles and piles of books, the three girls mostly grown and gone, that made me think having children could be okay, as long as they were like the Todd children, by which I mean not around, as long as my life was like the Todds' life.

II.

The kid in the newspaper was named Stevie, and he was eight. I was thirty-nine and lived by myself in a house that I owned. For a short time our local newspaper featured an orphan every week. Later they would transition to adoptable pets, but for a while it was orphans, children you could foster and possibly adopt if everything worked out. The profiles were short, maybe two or three hundred words. This was what I knew: Stevie liked going to school. He made friends easily. He promised he would make his bed every morning. He hoped that if he were very good he could have his own dog, and if he were very, very good, his younger brother could be adopted with him. Stevie was Black. I knew nothing else. The picture of him was a little bigger than a postage stamp. He smiled. I studied his face at my breakfast table until something in me snapped. I paced around my house, carrying the folded newspaper. I had two bedrooms. I had a dog. I had so much more than plenty. In return he would make his bed, try his best in school. That was all he had to bargain with: himself. By the time Karl came for dinner after work I was nearly out of my mind.

"I want to adopt him," I said.

Karl read the profile. He looked at the picture. "You want to be his mother?"

"It's not about being his mother. I mean, sure, if I'm his mother that's fine, but it's like seeing a kid waving from the window of a burning house, saying he'll make his bed if someone will come and get him out. I can't leave him there."

"We can do this," Karl said.

We can do this. I started to calm myself because Karl was calm. He was good at making things happen. We could do this. I didn't have to want children in order to want Stevie.

In the morning I called the number in the newspaper. They took down my name and address. They told me they would send the preliminary paperwork. After the paperwork was reviewed, there would be a series of interviews and home visits.

"When do I meet Stevie?" I asked.

"Stevie?"

"The boy in the newspaper." I had already told her the reason I was calling.

"Oh, it's not like that," the woman said. "It's a very long process. We put you together with the child who will be your best match."

"So where's Stevie?"

She said she wasn't sure. She thought that maybe someone had adopted him.

It was a bait and switch, a well-written story: the bed, the dog, the brother. They knew how to bang on the floor to bring people like me out of the woodwork, people who said they would never come. I wrapped up the conversation. I didn't want a child, I wanted Stevie. It all came down to a single flooding moment of clarity: he wouldn't live with me, but I could now imagine that he was in a solid house with people who loved him. I put him in the safest chamber of my heart, he and his brother in twin beds, the dog asleep in Stevie's arms.

And there they stayed, going with me everywhere until finally I wrote a novel about them called *Run*. Not because I thought it would find them, but because they had become too much for me to carry. I had to write about them so that I could put them down.

12.

André Previn was a pianist, a composer, a conductor. He had four Academy Awards, ten Grammys, five wives, ten children. He was the musical director for several major symphony orchestras. He was the principal conductor for several major symphony orchestras. He wrote film scores, played jazz. He was ninety when he died, or something like that. No one was exactly sure what year he was born, only that his family got out of Berlin ahead of the Nazis.

Sometimes I think about people in terms of units of energy. André Previn must have come into this world with a thousand times more energy than I did, or else he must have marshaled his resources much more effectively. I have just enough energy to write, keep up with the house, be a decent friend, a decent daughter and sister and wife. Part of not wanting children has always been the certainty that I didn't have the energy for it, and so I had to make a choice, the choice between children and writing. The first time it occurred to me that I wouldn't have both, I was still years away from being biologically capable of reproduction. History offers some examples of people who've done a good job with children and writing, I know that, but I wasn't one of those people. I've always known my limitations. I lacked the units of energy, and the energy I had, I wanted to spend on my work. To have a child and neglect her in favor of a novel would be cruel, but to simply skip the child in favor of a novel was to avoid harm altogether.

My friend Elizabeth McCracken and I used to talk about this when we were writing our first books. She was twenty-three and I was twenty-six. She had chosen writing as well. "Unless," she said, "I fell in love with someone who absolutely wanted to have children and was willing to take half the responsibility. Then I'd think about it, assuming it was clear that he'd be a really great father."

We were sitting in the Governor Bradford, our favorite bar in Provincetown, in the dead of winter. We had the time to imagine and dissect every conceivable scenario for our future, but I couldn't quite envision what she was suggesting: a man who wanted children; a man who wanted to have those children with me; a man who wanted those children with me so much that he would claim half the work, half the love and responsibility, and I would be able to believe that he was telling me the truth, and that the truth wouldn't change a few months in. He would be a wonderful father. He would make sure I still had the time and space to be a writer.

I shook my head. I had never met such a man, nor did I believe in his existence.

"But if you did meet him?" Elizabeth asked. "Would you want to have children?"

I wasn't sure. I think I would have needed to have seen a prototype much earlier in my life so I would know how to recognize him. I certainly wasn't looking.

Years after that conversation, Elizabeth found him, or he found her, and together they had two spectacular children.

Together, together, together.

13.

"Even if you don't want a child," someone said to me once, "you should have one anyway, because later on you'll wish you had one, and then it will be too late."

14.

I don't remember any of my close friends ever asking me when I was going to have children. I suppose by definition of our being close they knew me. But their husbands asked me, or they told me: I needed children. It was important. I suspect it had less to do with my best interest and more to do with the fact that I made them nervous walking through the world unencumbered. I was setting a bad example.

People want you to want what they want. If you want the same things they want, then their want is validated. If you don't want the same things, your lack of wanting can, to certain people, come across as judgment. People are forever asking if I'd mind if they ordered a hamburger. "Not unless you force me to eat it," I say. This gets trickier when applied to alcohol. I stopped drinking a long time ago. People feel much more strongly about having a drink than they do about having a burger.

"So then just a glass of champagne."

"I don't drink."

"But you'll have champagne for the toast."

I shake my head.

Does my declining a glass of champagne mean that I judge your glass of champagne?

It does not.

Does my choice not to have children mean I judge your choices, your children? That I think my life is in some way superior?

It does not.

What it means is that I don't want children. Or a hamburger. Or a gin and tonic. That's all it means.

How I came not to care about other people's opinions is something of a mystery even to me. I was born with a compass. It was the luck of my draw. This compass has been incalculably beneficial for writing—for everything, really—and for that reason I take very good care of it. How do you take care of your internal compass? You don't listen to anyone who tells you to do something as consequential as having a child. Think about that one for a second.

15.

After eleven years of dating, Karl and I married. I was forty-one and he was fifty-seven. People said to me, "How wonderful! You can still have a child." These were the same people who had always asked when I was going to have a child, and the news of our late-life legitimacy gave them the excuse to remind us of what we otherwise might have forgotten: reproduction was still biologically possible, or possibly possible. I guess they thought we'd just been waiting for the paperwork to come through.

After Karl and I married and I'd moved into his house, after another year or two elapsed and the clock had run all the way down to midnight, even the most hopeful of bystanders were forced to concede. It was right around that time that I learned a lesson through my own thoughtlessness. Some neighbors who lived a few blocks away had just had their fourth daughter, and when I went to drop off a loaf of pumpkin bread, I met the mother-in-law in the driveway, a woman I knew and liked. "Do you think this is it?" I asked her. "Or do you think they'll have more?"

Inside that house, a woman with three tiny children and a baby in her arms had just come home from the hospital, and I had asked her mother-in-law if there were plans to have more children.

The mother-in-law did her best to hide her dismay at my inquiry, but it was hard. I knew, because I'd been trying to hide my dismay for years. "I wouldn't think of asking them something so personal," she said to me.

Yes, exactly. It was so personal. I might as well have asked, *What do you imagine the outcome of your son's sex life will be in the future?* I was appalled at myself for doing the very thing that had so annoyed me for my entire reproductive life, but the error came with a valuable revelation: I didn't care if they had more children. Of course I didn't care. I was standing in a driveway making the idlest conversation, just as plenty of the people who had asked me when I would get married and when I would have children were making idle conversation. It was nothing but noise, a question for the sake of speaking and not for the sake of inquiry.

Some of them cared, but not all of them. I should have realized that earlier.

16.

Throughout my life, the people who held the most urgent opinions on the subject of my childlessness were the members of my immediate family. My mother, my father, my stepfather, my grandmother, all showered me with positive reinforcement when, as a child my-self, I said I didn't want children. As I grew up and grew older, they never missed the opportunity to voice their approval. Even my sister, who loved her own children, would at times say to me wearily, "I admire your life choices." Whether this was because the people who knew me best thought I'd be a bad parent, or they wanted the resources I represented for themselves, or they wanted me to know they supported my decision, or they just didn't like children very much—the messiness, noise, trouble—I was never certain, though if I had to guess, the last option seemed the most likely.

17.

Karl's grandfather, Grover VanDevender, worked as a railway con-ductor on the Southerner. His run was the last leg of the trip—from Meridian, Mississippi, where they lived, to New Orleans. Grover and Karl liked to look at *National Geographic* together and talk about all the places in the world they wanted to go. When Grover died in 1968, he left Karl $2,000 in hopes that he would one day have the kind of great adventure they had dreamed of together. Karl put the money in the bank, and in 1980, when he was thirty-three, he took his five-year-old daughter Josephine trekking in the Himalayas for a month while his wife stayed home with their two-year-old son. For most of the trip, Josephine was carried by a Sherpa in a wicker basket and was fed a diet of chocolate bars and Coca-Cola, which another Sherpa carried in a different basket.

On the trip home, Karl lost Josephine in London Heathrow Air-port. He was standing in a ticket line and when he looked down, she was gone. She was missing for over an hour before being found by airport security, asleep in a chair, rolled into a little ball, the kind of ball one might have grown accustomed to after spending a month in a wicker basket.

This story is the centerpiece of the VanDevender family lore, and rightfully so. It's a weird story. Weird and somewhat admirable that Karl would trek to the Himalayas with a five-year-old in honor of his grandfather, weird and less admirable that he left his wife behind to take care of their toddler. But the weirdest and most telling aspect of the story was how the disappearance of Josephine at Heathrow was remembered: the way I always heard it, it was a story about Josephine being irresponsible. Josephine always wandering off. Josephine losing track of time and nearly making them miss their connecting flight home after a month in the Himalayas.

But Josephine was five. She had spent a month subsisting on Coke and chocolate. She had just flown to London from Nepal. The whole thing struck me one day when Josephine and I were together with her own son, who was five at the time.

"That's how old you were when you went to Nepal," I said.

"Yep," she said.

"When your father lost you in an airport."

She nodded. Josephine is, among many good things, a good mother and a forgiving daughter. "Crazy, right?"

It is possible to love someone with all your heart and still know your union would never have survived having children together. It was one of the many things that made Karl and me such a good match: I didn't want children and he already had them. I thought it when I caught him pouring half-and-half on the dog's kibble. It was best this way.

18.

Having a dog is not the same thing as having a child.

Writing a book is not the same thing as having a child.

Owning a bookstore is not the same thing as having a child.

Having wonderful stepchildren does not make me a mother.

I know these things to be true, no matter how many times people tell me otherwise.

I am not using the dog or the book or the bookstore or the stepchildren to fill a hole left by not having children, because there is no hole. I can love those people, that dog, those books, for exactly who and what they are.

19.

I was in New York on business and checked in with Marti, who was about to have a baby. She said she and her husband, Barry, were on their way to the hospital and I should come by and hang out. "We can walk the halls," Marti said cheerfully. Marti had a tendency to make difficult things look easy. She was thirty-one and this was her second child.

"Won't you be really busy?" I asked.

"Well, sure, but you're here," she said. "I want to see you."

So I went to the hospital, and her husband and I took turns looping the ward with Marti on our arm. At regular intervals she would stop, take a breath, look up at the ceiling and say, "Okay," then start to walk again. Back in the room, the nurse would check her dilation. Everything was going according to schedule. "Do you want to just stay?" she asked me.

"If you stayed, you could take the pictures," her husband said. They were trying to make me feel welcome, useful, even though it didn't seem like a party I should be crashing at the last minute. On the other hand, I couldn't imagine telling them I had plans. I must have had plans, but I don't remember what they were. I stuck around to see Katherine being born. It wasn't much of a wait. Marti was all business.

That was the one part of the decision not to have children that did in fact make me feel like I missed out. I am deeply moved by what a woman's body is capable of, but just because I could do something didn't mean that I should. Marti and Barry gave me a tremendous gift that day by letting me stay and watch their daughter come into the world. Katherine! From the first minute she was a force every bit as recognizable as her mother. That feeling of life coming into the room was unlike anything I'd ever experienced before, a flood of joy. I thought of it ten years later when I climbed into my grandmother's bed and held her while she died. The light pouring in and the light going out. I never would have known how close those two things were if it wasn't for Marti and Barry and Katherine.

20.

My friend Kate and I were talking about childhood, the way writers will. We are the same age. Our friendship had begun in the years when having children was no longer on the table.

"I could never do that to someone I loved," I said.

"Do what?"

"Childhood."

"Oh, that," she said, nodding. "I get that." Kate didn't have children either.

But the theory doesn't hold up, because my sister's childhood was much worse than mine, and all she ever wanted was to have children. Children gave her the chance to give someone else the kind of childhood she'd wanted, and, in doing so, to find a repository for her enormous love. I, on the other hand, just wanted to get the hell out of there.

The uncertainty, the complete lack of autonomy or control, leaving places you never wanted to leave to go to places you never wanted to go, the fear, the bullying, the helplessness, the awkwardness, the disappointment and shame, the betrayal by your own body. To have a child required the willful forgetting of what childhood was actually like; it required you to turn away from the very real chance that you would do to the person you loved most in the world the exact same thing that was done to you. No. No, thank you.

21.

For one year of my childhood, we lived in a sprawling condominium complex where I would ride my bike up and down the cul-de-sacs and drives. One day a car pulled up and the woman inside asked if I babysat. "Sure," I said. It wasn't true, but I liked the thought of having a job, making money. She wrote down my phone number and told me where to show up at 6:30 on Saturday night. Then she drove away.

This was the mid-1970s, the low-water mark of parental oversight. The parents—I can remember nothing about them—said the baby was asleep and they would be home by midnight. Off they went, I didn't know where. No phone number was scrawled on a notepad in the kitchen. I was twelve years old, not that anyone had asked. I was not one of those misleading twelve-year-olds who could have passed for fifteen. I was a twelve-year-old who could have passed for nine. When the baby started to cry, I crept up the stairs to his room. I had never held a baby before, never picked one up. I got him out of the crib. We were both crying. I called my mother, who came over and stayed with the two of us until the parents returned. She tended to the baby, who, as it turned out, needed a great deal of tending.

I was an uncomfortable child, a small adult biding my time. Despite my visible awkwardness with other people's children, I went on to become an extremely popular neighborhood babysitter when we moved again. By nature I am appalled by mess, and people with children lived messy lives. I would put away the books and toys, wash the dishes in the sink, wipe down the counters, run the vacuum. The children in my care were more or less left to their own devices, but they never got hurt and they didn't complain, and the parents came home to a house that bore no resemblance to the house they had left. Looking back, I wonder if they didn't go out to dinner just so I would clean their house for a dollar an hour.

22.

We all think that things are different now, that men and women are different, and the roles we play are different, that society has evolved, that we are safer, wiser, kinder. We look back at the generation before us and the generation before that and wonder, *How did they live?* It's how the next generation will look back at us, shaking their heads at the horror of our ways. Things do change, but in increments too small for us to perceive.

It doesn't matter how old you are. This applies.

23.

I met the illustrator Robin Preiss Glasser at the bookstore while she was on tour for the final installment of the Fancy Nancy series. We hit it off, and so Robin, force of nature, force of life, suggested we do a picture book together. While I didn't know a thing about children's literature, Robin was willing to teach me. I was thrilled, not only at her friendship but at the chance to collaborate, to try something new. We made a book together we were both proud of.

But with the book came the book tour. I hadn't been thinking about that part. In my mind I'd only gotten as far as the inherent pleasure of making lambs talk. Now I was supposed to travel the country pitching our book to people who didn't come up to my hip. I was uneasy, but decided to rely on the same strategy that had served me thus far: I would follow Robin's lead. She lived to stand in front of a roomful of children, to make them laugh and teach them something, to stir them up and then settle them down again. (She does this by clapping her hands three times. She tells every group before her talk begins—she will clap three times and they will settle themselves, effectively hypnotizing them into complete submission.) In bookstores, in school gymnasiums, in community centers, we went to meet them, vast seas of squirming bodies decked out in sequins or dirty T-shirts. Armed only with a lamb puppet and a chicken puppet, I tried my best to mimic her charm, but mostly what I did was stand back and watch the children watch her: starstruck and in love.

As they lined up with their stacks of tattered Fancy Nancy books and their pristine copy of our book, *Lambslide*, Robin asked them if they liked to get dressed up, and if they liked ice cream. She pulled them into her lap when they came around the table for a picture. She pulled up their shirts and nibbled their stomachs.

"Are you allowed to do that?" I asked. I wasn't kidding. Was she allowed to touch other people's children?

"Try and stop me," she said, kissing them again.

When a child came to the table crying or about to cry, she would ask if they wanted a butterfly on their hand. Through bleary sobs they would give the slightest hint of a nod, and Robin would take hold of that hand and marvel at it. Then, using a fat permanent marker, she would add a butterfly to the skin, explaining how to do it as she went along, just in case the child had the opportunity to ink up someone else later on. Then the child would stop crying. They'd stare at the butterfly, incredibly pleased, and often climb into Robin's lap for a quick cuddle before moving along. I didn't see this happen once or twice. I saw it day after day, city after city, with approximately every tenth child in every signing line. And every time it happened, the light that is Robin Preiss Glasser glowed brighter.

Had I met Robin early in my life, might that have made the difference? If someone had looked at me like that when I was a child, might I have had children?

No, but it would have come closer to changing my mind than the hypothetical man who might have taken half the responsibility for our hypothetical offspring. Each time we took the stage (or, in many cases, the floor) Robin was astonished by every child restlessly bobbing before us, and when we were done she threw open her arms to welcome them in with no consideration for fear. Every single one of them thrilled her: their beauty, their possibility, their life. *Look at you!* she is saying. *My god, look at you!*

It's the same way she looks at me—me with the books and no children—like not having children was some spectacular idea that I alone came up with. That is, after all, Robin's superpower: to love the person in front of her as she is, to see all the glorious light inside them and reflect it back, everywhere.

· A Paper Ticket Is Good for One Year ·

When I was twenty-nine and living in Montana with my boyfriend, I took a year-long fellowship at Radcliffe College and moved by myself to Massachusetts at the end of the summer. At the time I thought it was too great an opportunity to pass up, but by the middle of October I could see what the decision was going to cost me. When I called our apartment in Missoula late at night, no one answered, and when I did manage to reach my boyfriend, he was distracted, evasive.

Brokenheartedness was not upon me yet, but I could see it clearly up ahead—the bright lights of a car heading in my direction. I considered going back to Montana to stake my claim, but if the damage to our relationship was already done, and I suspected it was, then leaving Radcliffe just meant I would be out both a boyfriend and a fellowship.

In Cambridge, the days grew shorter and colder. I trudged back to my tiny apartment from the library, past the Brattle Theatre, past

Sage's Market, past the American Express travel agency. Something about the travel agency stopped me. I looked at the posters hanging in the window: the Eiffel Tower, the white-sand beaches of Tahiti. Maybe my assessment of the situation had been too limited. Maybe I didn't need to be in Montana or Cambridge. I put my hand on the door and went inside.

I'm sorry travel agencies don't exist anymore, at least not as the plentiful dream shops they used to be, those wide windows advertising the beauty of the world, the men and women behind the counter always there to help you go.

When I went to Europe in college, it was Vienna that stuck with me, the cafés that lined the Ringstrasse, the catacombs beneath St. Stephen's Cathedral, the glorious Hofburg Palace. I always believed that someday I'd go back. And so I left the travel agency that night with a plane ticket in my coat pocket and a week's confirmed stay in a pension. I would go in December for my thirtieth birthday. The travel agent was impressed by my spontaneity, as was I. I didn't have a lot of money in those days, but I had enough for a single impetuous decision. Walking back to my apartment, I found I had a different view of myself entirely: I was independent, adventuresome. I wasn't sitting around waiting to see what someone else decided about my future. I was the master of my fate. I was the captain of my soul.

"Vienna?" my boyfriend said to me over the phone. "By yourself?"

I pictured a distant future in which people sat around a table at a dinner party, reminiscing in turn about what they had done on their thirtieth birthdays. I would tell them I went to Vienna. By myself.

I got a booklet of traveler's checks and $200 in Austrian schillings. I got a new passport. At the end of November I told my friends in Cambridge goodbye, and they wished me an early happy birthday.

I packed my bag and put it by the door. My plan was to call for a taxi to take me to the airport at five o'clock. I sat down on the edge of my bed and waited. It was four, and then it was four-thirty, and then it was five. I kept telling myself to pick up the phone and call the taxi. I told myself that I could walk to Harvard Square and find one. It was five fifteen. I had planned to get to the airport early. There was still plenty of time to make the flight. I sat and looked at the clock. It was a quarter to six.

Was it bravery I lacked? Was I afraid of missing the boyfriend I'd be losing soon enough? Was I sick? Scared? Was I having a premonition about a plane crash that I didn't understand? I had no idea. All I knew was that I wasn't standing up. I wasn't picking up my bag. I wasn't picking up the phone. It was as if something very heavy was sitting on my head, holding me in place. It was six o'clock. I lay back on my bed, still in my coat, and cried from the shame of it all. Four hours later I woke up with a fever and started vomiting. It went on like that for five days.

I was never so sick, or so relieved. Whatever it was that struck me down in my apartment would have struck me on the plane. And then what? I would be this spectacularly sick in the airport in Vienna. I would have made it to the pension somehow, boiling with fever, infectious, not speaking German.

I called a friend, who left ginger ale and soda crackers outside my door. I slept through my thirtieth birthday and the day after that. My boyfriend called to check on me. I got better. After Christmas he confessed that he'd fallen in love with one of his students.

We had lived in a furnished apartment in Missoula and didn't own much. He mailed me what was mine in a few large boxes. Everything hurt and nothing killed me. I took my paper ticket back to

American Express. The prepaid room in the pension was a complete loss, but the travel agent told me I had one year in which to use the ticket to Vienna.

The following autumn I was living in Nashville. All year long I heard the plane ticket ticking towards its expiration in my desk drawer. I still planned to go and go alone but, having failed at my departure once, I was having a harder time making a commitment. In the meantime, I had been on three dates with a nice man named Karl. His wife had left him and he was very much adrift, having to rethink what he knew about his life. On our fourth date, I looked at him across the table in the restaurant. He wasn't a stranger, he worked with my mother, and yet he wasn't someone I actually knew. But what did life ever come to without a few risks? I asked him if he wanted to go to Vienna.

Yes. He said yes, and then he said it again without giving it another thought: Yes. It reminded me of the night I walked into the travel agency. I told him that, because of my ticket, we would have to go soon. He told me that soon was not a problem.

I hadn't meant this as a dating strategy, but it functioned as one just the same, so I pass this along as advice: if you meet someone you like and you have the means to do so, ask that person to go with you to Vienna.

As it turned out, we were in Vienna for Karl's birthday, which was a couple of weeks before mine. We ate pastries filled with marzipan and walked along the Danube holding hands. In the catacombs we struck up a conversation with a young woman wearing a backpack. She was traveling alone. She was, I think, from Alabama. When we walked away, Karl said she looked tired and broke and that we should invite her to dinner, and so we went back and found her and brought her with us to a wonderful restaurant called Drei Hussars. We drank little glasses of freezing, syrupy vodka with peach pulp in it. I wondered if some benevolent stranger might have invited me to dinner had I made it to Vienna a year before, and then I remembered no, I would never have been able to leave my room.

Karl and I had made plans to spend half of our trip in Prague, but on our way to the train station he saw a very old set of silverware in a shop window. After some discussion with the proprietor, he bought the forks and spoons and knives and had them shipped to Tennessee. The transaction took longer than we expected, and because of this we missed our train, the last train to Prague until the next day. We stood in the vast station with our suitcases, looking up at the departures board.

"Budapest," he said, scanning over our options. "I've never been to Budapest."

I allowed that I had never been to Budapest either, and so we took that train instead. It mattered less where we were going and more who we were with. In fact, that continues to be the case. Karl bought me a thin gold ring in Budapest to commemorate the day, and eleven years later I married him. We had been in such a rush and then we were in no rush at all, proving that we were impetuous and prudent in the extreme. Proving that we were in love, and that the trip was worth waiting for.

· The Moment Nothing Changed ·

The days are shorter now, it stays dark longer. I tell myself this is why my husband and dog and I have slept until six thirty this morning. We never sleep until six thirty. An entirely different set of neighborhood dogs are out when Sparky and I go for our walk. At five thirty, our usual time, it's just Chloe the German shepherd and a handful of runners: Byron the cardiologist, who lives a few blocks away and works at the same hospital as my husband, Henry from across the street, our neighbor Bob. But at six thirty Scout the English setter is out, Violet the Havanese, Moose and Shaka the chocolate Labs, and Molly. I don't know what Molly is. All of the runners have run home. It's a dog party. We discuss Isabella's new harness, which is a smart houndstooth. Isabella is the prettiest little Cavalier King Charles spaniel that has ever been put on this earth. She is the kind of dog I'd want to carry in my purse at Bergdorf's were I the sort of person who went to Bergdorf's with a spaniel in my purse.

When we come home, I fill the blender with spinach, a banana, an avocado, two dates, some lemon juice, water and ice, and my husband and I drink the results for breakfast. From time to time I believe I've found The Answer to Life, and right now I think it's spinach.

Sparky and I go to Parnassus. There are as many dogs in the bookstore as there are dogs on my street. Opie, a large hound, belongs to Andy the store manager. Belle comes to work with Cat. Bear, who is ancient and has to wear a belt with a Kotex in it because otherwise he pees on the books, belongs to Sissy. Mary Todd Lincoln, a fancy dappled dachshund, lives in a cross-body sling on Niki's chest. The dogs mostly stay in the back, where it's easier to beg for treats. The dog treats are kept in the staff bathroom, and whenever Sissy goes into the bathroom the dogs stand outside the door in a pack and wait for her. Sissy slides dog biscuits under the door. We yell at her to stop because Opie is better at the game than the rest of them and winds up getting all the biscuits. Opie's vet has made it clear he's supposed to be cutting back.

I'm at a big table in the back office signing copies of my new book for the store. I have sixteen hundred to sign and I feel like I'm losing my mind. Mary Laura pulls up Old Spice commercials on her computer, and Cat and Niki and I watch them over and over again until we know all the words and can act them out ourselves. *Look at me*, we say to one another, *now look at your man*.

The next morning I'm up at the regular time. I wave to Chloe the German shepherd from the other side of the street. Sparky, who weighs about fifteen pounds, is intimidated by Chloe despite her persistent friendliness. The runners run by.

I have a meeting at the bookstore with people who are flying in to discuss a future bookstore project. I'm wearing a dress. It's early and the store isn't open yet. I gave these people my cell-phone number so they could call me when they arrived and I could unlock the door for them. I turn my cell phone on about ten times a year, and only for occasions such as this. When it rings it's Byron the cardiologist. "Byron?" I say. I can't understand why he would be calling on my cell phone when I never carry it and no one has the number anyway. He says his name again, and tells me to come over to the hospital, even though he's pretty certain my husband is not having a heart attack.

MY HUSBAND IS not having a heart attack. By the time I arrive (minutes later) this fact has been established. The tests have all turned out perfectly. Karl sleeps off the Versed while I sit beside his bed in the tiny cardiac observation room. While watching him I think about a flight we were on years before. We were leaving Russia, and while we were going through all the various lines in the airport in Moscow, we noticed that nearly everyone had a baby. There was no overlooking it. We struck up a conversation with an American couple ahead of us in line. They were going home to Atlanta with a beautiful little girl they'd just adopted. We congratulated them and said that we were on that flight to Atlanta as well. They were radiant in their happiness, this couple and their Russian baby.

The closer we got to our gate, the more babies we saw: tiny infants, just-walking toddlers. When the announcement came that it was time to board our flight, everyone who had a child gathered up their strollers and diaper bags and got into line. One direct flight from Moscow to Atlanta, and everyone who had come to Russia from the States to adopt a baby was on it. We were a little nervous at first, more than a hundred babies on a twelve-hour flight, but as it turned out they were all happy—happy parents, happy babies. None of them were anywhere near being tired of each other. The couple we'd met in line sat right across the aisle from us, their sweet girl in their arms. How random it all was, who got which baby, where they would all go later on connecting flights.

Once we were airborne, the parents began to walk up and down the aisles, talking to one another, bouncing their infants in their arms. There was almost no crying until several hours into the flight when the woman across the aisle from us came back to her seat. She was crying. Her husband was asleep.

Karl asked her what was wrong. She waved him off, but he persisted. Karl persists.

"A woman in the back told me something was wrong with her." She was looking at her baby. "Can you see it? The woman said she wasn't holding her head up enough. She said I should take her to see a neurologist as soon as we get home."

"Give me that baby," Karl said. He told her he was a doctor, that he had delivered hundreds of babies. He held out his hands and she passed the infant over.

Karl studied the baby carefully. He looked in her eyes, sat her upright, let the baby grab his finger. He did whatever he could think of to appear as medical as possible. "I've looked at all these babies," he said to the woman. "This is the best baby on the plane."

She leaned over, touched her daughter's head. "Do you think so?"

"I'll give you twenty thousand for this baby."

The woman and I both looked at him. "What?"

"I'd love to have this baby," he said. "We can wait in Atlanta. My accountant will wire the money."

"I don't want to sell her," the woman said. She had the look on her face that anyone would have if the stranger holding your baby had just offered to buy her.

"This is the best baby I've ever seen," Karl said. "If you don't feel sure about her, you could get another one."

I thought the woman would call for the flight attendant, but instead I watched her grief break apart. Grief dissipating, evaporating, vanishing. "No," she said. "No, I don't want to sell her."

Karl handed the baby back with some regret, then gave the woman his card. "In case you change your mind."

She thanked him and thanked him. He had offered to buy her child and, in doing so, had restored her to joy, which served to underscore what I am constantly learning: Karl has an understanding of humanity that eludes me.

"Was the baby really okay?" I whispered to him later.

He didn't look up from his book. "There's nothing wrong with that baby," he said.

The woman had just needed someone to remind her how valuable her daughter was, how lucky they were.

I remember again how valuable he is, how lucky we are. Karl isn't having a heart attack. Byron didn't know what might have caused the pain. Indigestion? Stress? It didn't matter. Karl is beside me. The meeting I'm missing doesn't matter, and Sparky is fine with his dog friends at the bookstore. For as many times as the horrible thing happens, a thousand times in every day the horrible thing passes us by. A meteor could be skating past Earth's atmosphere this very minute. We'll never know how close we came to annihilation, but today I saw it—everything I had and stood to lose and did not lose. Thanks to this fleeting clarity, the glow from the fluorescent tubes on the ceiling of this small cardiac recovery room lights up the entire world.

· The Nightstand ·

Every year when friends ask me what I'm going to do on my birthday, I tell them I'm going to answer the phone. The phone rings all day on my birthday—good wishes, good cheer—problems I'm lucky to have. This year, Sparky decided to celebrate by running out the front door while I was getting the mail. He came back minutes later with something sticky on his shoulder and reeking of death. I lathered him up in the tub while the phone rang. It was ringing again when I finished drying him off. I ran back into the bedroom and grabbed the handset without looking at caller ID. A young man's voice asked to speak to Ann Elizabeth Patchett.

"This is she," I said, thinking it could be someone trying to deliver flowers. It was my birthday, after all. Fifty-seven.

"My mother found a letter in her nightstand from the Veterans of Foreign Wars," he began. "The Voice of Democracy Program? It was an award." This piece of news was followed by silence, as if he were waiting for me to jump in.

"Okay," I said finally. No one sending flowers would use my middle name.

"The letter was about an award."

"I'm not sure why you're calling," I said.

"I've been trying to find Ann Elizabeth Patchett."

"You found her." I sat down on the bed in the early dark of winter, wondering if this was the beginning of a complicated phone scam.

"Did you win an award from the Veterans of Foreign Wars in 1980?"

It wasn't the sort of thing that would have come immediately to mind in 2020, but yes, in fact, I had, when I was a junior in high school. I didn't understand what that had to do with his mother's bedroom furniture.

"She bought the nightstand at an estate sale. I took out the drawers to clean it. I found the papers, some poetry. There's a picture of a cheer squad."

My papers were in her nightstand. That would be a picture of Tavia, not me. I'd tried out for the cheerleading team and didn't make it. I won the essay competition. "I'm still not sure what you're trying to tell me."

"I've been looking for you so I could give these papers back. The letter from the VFW, that's important. Winning that award is a very big deal."

I wondered if such awards still existed. "How did you get my phone number?"

"Whitepages.com," he said.

My phone number was unlisted. Or it was supposed to be.

"You must really want these," he said. "I mean, I know it must be exciting for you."

"You're nice to go to all the trouble but no, I don't want them back. You can throw them away." Had I found them in my own nightstand, that's what I would have done.

"I can't throw this away! It's a big deal." In the background I could hear a baby fussing, and then a young woman's voice calling out from someplace nearby, "You won!"

Was I on speakerphone? "I wrote an essay in high school. I think I won a hundred dollars. That's it." I was a person who entered contests, working off the theory that you have to play to win.

"From the Veterans of Foreign Wars!" he said. "It changed your life."

"I promise you, it didn't."

"Maybe you don't remember."

"This is a strange question, but I have to ask. Do you know who I am?"

"No ma'am," the voice said.

"I'm a writer." Sparky was running around the bedroom. A bath always seemed to turn the key of his small dog engine. "I'm a pretty successful novelist."

"You're Ann *Patchett*?" He let out a small cry, and then the woman who was in the room with him did the same thing. They whooped as if they'd won something big. "Oh my god, oh my god, I didn't think you were going to be *her*. I'm totally fan-girling right now," he said.

It was starting to feel like a scam again. "It would make complete sense if you'd never heard of me, but it makes no sense that you didn't think Ann Elizabeth Patchett wasn't going to turn out to be Ann Patchett." A middle name is a very thin disguise.

"There are lots of Ann Elizabeth Patchetts," he said defensively.

"There aren't."

He ignored my point. "You have to have these papers. This was the start of your whole career."

We went around on this point again. He wanted me to know he wasn't the kind of person who would sell what was in his possession on eBay.

"No one exists who would buy those things on eBay," I said. "And if they do, I don't want to think about it." I told him he could either mail me the papers or he could throw them away.

"I'll mail them to you," he said, disappointed. He had made the movie of this phone call in his head, and in that movie I am speechless, bowled over by the wonder of being reunited with the paperwork of my youth. He kept giving me additional opportunities to live up to his expectations.

"Who are you?" I asked. "Where are you?"

He told me his name was Damien. He was calling from Wartrace, Tennessee. I gave him my home address. Should I have given him my address? Then, because I was feeling bad about my stunning lack of gratitude, I told him it was my birthday. We'd been on the phone long enough for me to know how much he'd like that.

"Your birthday!" he said, and the woman in the room with him cried "Happy birthday!" while the baby kept up its patter. It was the gift he'd been hoping for, proof of kismet. "I can't believe I called you today, on your *birthday*. This is the most incredible thing ever."

FOR WHATEVER REASON, the VFW essay was clear in my mind: When pledging allegiance to the flag at the beginning of each school day, we must discipline ourselves to consider the privileges and free-doms afforded to us by the veterans of foreign wars. We must never run through the declaration of citizenship by rote, as if brushing our teeth.

I feel certain it was that teeth-brushing comparison that secured my win. I'd written the essay without a flicker of patriotism, and all the craven calculation of a fifteen-year-old girl wanting to lay claim to a hundred bucks. I take no pride in this. Not only did I not want to see the letter again, I didn't particularly want to think about it.

I was, however, plenty curious as to how the letter had wound up in Damien's mother's nightstand in Wartrace, a dot of a town an hour and a half from Nashville. Here's my theory: I was a kid who stuffed whatever papers and trinkets I had into the five shallow drawers of the small chest beside my bed. Those drawers remained so perpet-ually overfull that I had to yank to get one open. It stands to reason that a letter informing me of my win, along with a handful of poems and my best friend's picture, could have slid out the back of one drawer and fallen behind the others.

My mother and stepfather moved while I was away at college, at which point I lost my designated bedroom. My grandmother moved into the new house with them, and my nightstands took up their posts on either side of her bed. When I went to graduate school and had to furnish my first apartment, I wasn't about to take the night-stands away from my grandmother. Instead, I went down to the cavernous basement (a veritable furniture showroom) and took my grandmother's old nightstands, the ones she'd grown tired of after so many years. These nightstands—which I remembered so clearly from childhood—were old-fashioned, tall and narrow with a small drawer on top and two roomier drawers underneath. They had come into our family by way of my grandfather's first wife, Frances, who died of a brain tumor in the early 1930s.

My grandmother and my nightstands lived together in my mother's house for the next seventeen years. From there, they moved to assisted living, and finally to that facility's memory-care unit. I was in that unit, lying in my grandmother's bed with her when she died. She owned so few things at the end of her life, and when she was gone, my mother and sister and I each took what we wanted. None of us wanted the nightstands, and so we left them: a letter announcing my win for a high school essay competition, some poetry, and Tavia's cheerleading picture still wedged behind the drawers where they had fallen all those years before. I was forty-one when my grandmother died. I cannot tell you where those tables spent the next sixteen years, or if they remained a set. It hadn't occurred to me to ask Damien if his mother had bought one nightstand or two.

What unsettled me about the story was not the singular strangeness of it, but that it kept happening. Several months before, the Librarian of Congress had contacted me, wanting my papers. I told her I didn't have papers. I wrote my novels on a computer and didn't print out my drafts. More to the point, I didn't write in drafts. I worked on one chapter, one page, one paragraph, a single sentence, over and over again until it was right, then I moved ahead. I made no record of any of that. I had nothing to collect.

"Look again," the Librarian of Congress said to me.

But I didn't want to look again. I had boxes of correspondence and dull journals that made note of what I was reading on a given day and how much I'd written and whether dinner turned out well. There were some old stories in the back of a file drawer that I didn't want to read. I wasn't interested in revisiting all the things I'd gotten wrong, and was even less interested in having a stranger see it. Dead or alive, I wanted to be judged by my best work, the finished product. The librarian, whose collections had no doubt been built on tenacity, encouraged me to put off making a decision, even though I had told her my decision. She said she would circle back again.

Of course I had papers, just not the kind of papers anyone would want. Months before, while cleaning out a closet of her own, my mother had presented me with a heavy box full of short stories and letters I'd written in college and graduate school and all the way through to the publication of my first novel. When I told her I didn't want it, she ignored me. She told me to put the box in my car.

"If you're going to throw those things away, then give them back," she said the minute I picked the box up. I told her once I took it out of her house she was forfeiting any say in the matter.

I would have thrown the box away were it not for the fact I took a quick look inside and saw a photograph of my grandmother right on top—eight by ten inches, in color; my cousin Chad had taken it—such a beautiful, happy picture of her that none of us remembered. My smiling grandmother made it clear that I would, at some point, have to pick through the contents before sailing it into a dumpster so as not to lose anything this important.

Still, I was more than a little annoyed that I would have to deal with things I'd never made the choice to save. Coincidentally, a few weeks later, my sister came across a similar, though smaller, stash of Ann-memorabilia. My sister is someone who saves things. She'd held on to poems I'd written, stories, letters, notes on cocktail napkins. It wasn't as if I'd said to my mother and sister, "There's been interest in my papers, what do you have lying around?" The chickens were coming home to roost all by themselves. I put my mother's box and sister's box with the giant box my stepmother had mailed me when my father died. My father was a true archivist. He'd saved everything he could find about me. Five years later, my father's box was still sitting there, unopened. Now the boxes could keep their own society.

"I'M GOING TO drive to Nashville," Damien said when he called again the next morning. "These papers are too important to put in the mail. What time can you meet me at the bookstore?" Damien knew I owned a bookstore.

"Don't do this," I said.

"I want to see the joy on your face when I present you with your papers."

"Damien, please, there isn't going to be any joy on my face. This isn't worth your time. Just put them in the mail."

"How's one thirty?"

I was part of a story that was writing itself. All I was being asked to do was show up. "Sure," I said, defeated. "Sure, one thirty."

My deep aversion to my early work—my desire to be spared any piece of my juvenilia—comes from the belief that it wasn't good. I wondered how my teachers had given me so much encouragement, and decided they'd pushed me along not because I was talented but because I was the hardest worker. They understood I had no backup plan. I needed to be a writer because I didn't know how to be anything else. Human beings cobble together their own mythologies over time: *I was unloved, I was too loved, I was popular, a loner, misunderstood, persecuted, stupid, a winner.* We use the past to explain ourselves. As many times as I told myself that I was going to open those boxes one day, sort through and see what was in there, I never got any closer to actually doing it. It was Pandora's lesson: don't lift the lid.

WERE IT NOT for the toddler they brought with them, I would have sworn Damien and his wife were still in high school. He had a short brush of black hair and black stud earrings. Her hair was a shade of blond that was very nearly white, thick and pulled into a ponytail. The son, cheery and pale, favored his mother. Damien gave me the papers, gently unfolding each of the poems, saving the VFW letter for last. In return I gave their child some books, as well as a book for his mother that I inscribed in honor of our mutual nightstand.

"It was a scholarship," he told me, although the letter from the Veterans of Foreign Wars made no such reference. "Maybe that's why you got to go to college."

I got to go to college because I went to a private Catholic high school. I got to go to college because my teachers encouraged me and helped me past my shortcomings, because my parents had the money to send me, because I grew up in a rarefied world where the gift of education was a given. In addition to winning an essay contest, I had won something so enormous and pervasive it could not be named. My guess was that Damien had never seen so much luck. He had driven to Nashville to give me a laurel I dropped, because who drops laurels? Who wouldn't want such a treasure returned? I remembered to thank him profusely before they headed back to Wartrace.

January 8, 1980

Dear Ann,
I wish to take this opportunity to congratulate you on being chosen
First Place Winner of the Voice of Democracy Program sponsored
by the VFW Post 1291. I further congratulate you for being chosen
Second Place Winner at the District Six Level.

I WONDERED WHO had won First Place at the District Six Level, and how life had turned out for him or her.

The letter went on to inform me that the two awards would be presented at two separate dinners, and that my parents and teacher should plan on attending both events. Had that happened? The letter was so brittle and brown it looked like it had been fished out of the back of Abraham Lincoln's nightstand.

"It's foxed," my friend Jennie told me when I showed it to her. Jennie is a novelist who had spent much of her life working in advertising in New York. "Foxed" was a classy way of describing age-related deterioration of paper. Forty years in the back of a nightstand was long enough to become foxed. The three poems and the notes I'd made for a forensics tournament speech were foxed unto disintegration. The photograph of the seven-member cheer squad was badly crumpled and torn, but Tavia, kneeling high up on the shoulders of Lisa Lawson, was unscathed.

I looked through what Damien had given me and found that it affected me not at all. The poetry was awful but not in any special way, just the average awful poetry of fifteen. I had recently slept at my neighbors' house to be with their children while they attended a funeral out of town. The twelve-year-old daughter told me the plot of a story she'd been working on for school. "It's about these people who kidnap children," she said while looking through the refrigerator for whipped cream. "Every week they kill one of the children, so the ones who're left decide to escape. But then the kidnappers find them and kill them, too. I don't know though, I might not finish it. I have another idea about a girl whose brother suicides."

Sweet girl. I would have wrapped her in my arms had she not been foraging. "I'd be so worried about you," I said, "were it not for the fact I remember writing those same stories when I was your age."

She turned from the open refrigerator to beam at me.

WHAT DAMIEN HAD given me, along with my award letter and terrible poetry, was insight. What was I so afraid of? If this was my early work, then I could open those boxes. All I'd needed was a warm-up, a test case.

The box my mother had given me was a heavy-sided rose-covered affair with metal handles, faux-foxed to look like the stuff of memories. And how. The thick stack of stories in the bottom were buffeted by a deep, dark woods of personal correspondence, letters I'd received in the summer of 1989 while I was away at two different artists' colonies, the letters I'd written home, as well as all the letters that came after I'd left those colonies. The box contained a day-by-day documentation of the summer I slipped out of my brief first marriage at the age of twenty-five, quit my teaching job, and moved into my mother's guest room. It was not a time I wanted an accurate record of. How had so many letters from one time come to be in one box?

I'd moved home right after I left those artists' colonies, my suitcase bursting with a summer's worth of mail. I dumped my prodigious correspondence into the nightstand in my mother's guest room—a nightstand that, coincidentally, was the same style as the one I'd had in high school, the same one my grandmother had downstairs. A fleet of identical nightstands had been purchased at some point in our family history. They were everywhere. When I moved home in 1989, my stepfather, Mike, had just moved out for the final time, and for a while my mother, grandmother and I lived together, the three of us. True to form, when more mail came, I jammed that mail into the nightstand as well. When I moved to Cape Cod many months later, I left all those letters behind, and when my mother moved again, she scooped everything out and dropped it into the box of the stories she'd been keeping for me.

Read more than thirty years later, the mail of 1989 amounted to a series of incorrect predictions coming from every possible direction: *I want you to come to Greece; I will love you forever; I will finish this novel; It looks like I'm going to get the job; Soon you'll come home.* None of those things happened. We thought we were making plans when in fact we were only guessing, and it was a crazy reckless guessing at that, like throwing tarot cards at a dartboard while blindfolded. At every turn we believed we were onto something big, the absolute truth of our lives. We were wrong about nearly all of it.

"You asked if I spent much time wondering about how my life will work out," my friend Jack wrote in July of that year. He was finishing his doctorate in evolutionary biology at Stanford.

Only six or seven hours a day . . . things like water policy, waste disposal and road repair interest me a lot. I don't really know what the best way to go would be, getting back into journalism, going to law school or getting into politics but I think that I really should do something. Of course I still spend a lot of time fantasizing about trekking to the South Pole alone. I think that this is the major conundrum for me, whether to devote myself to the public good or personal growth. I'm not sure why they seem so separate but they do.

ONLY MY FRIEND Lucy had it right. She wrote to me from Scotland that summer.

Two weeks ago I saw the new Indiana Jones movie. It's amazing how easy it is to die in the movies: BLAM!, and that's it. In Shakespeare you even get to announce it: "I am slain"—"Mother, he has killed me" (Romeo and Juliet and Macbeth, respectively). It would be interesting to see something like The Oxford Book of Death, *which would give a complete listing of Deaths in Literature, with subheadings for mythic, heroic, bathetic, futile etc., etc. Literature makes too much of death (or perhaps not enough, I'm not sure). I've been thinking lately of Christ dying on the cross, and it's occurred to me how important it is that he cries out and is lonely and thirsty on the cross: <u>no</u> death is glorious or triumphant, and in this story of everlasting life, the obscenity of death is kept intact. I suspect this is to remind us of the holiness of the ephemeral: we're always so busy looking towards (for) the eternal.*

She would manage to stay alive for another thirteen years. Going through those envelopes was unbearable at first—a too-hot bath—but in not much time I adjusted, then relaxed, and then wanted to get out. There were many pictures of the kitten my mother got that summer, as well as a picture of the man my mother was in love with, sitting on a beach in Israel. What was he doing in my box along with the letters from my sister and grandmother? Who knew. The box is never the dominion of just one person. Even if it was labeled as my box, we all intersected there. I picked up a short story I had written, but I couldn't make myself read it. I went down to the basement with a knife to open up the box of things my father had kept. It had, after all, been waiting a very long time.

Whereas my mother's box was a jumble of stories and letters, a time-capsule free-for-all, my father's box was a meticulously curated collection of three-ring binders full of plastic sleeves, each sleeve containing publicity materials, reviews, highlighted best-seller lists, magazine articles I'd published, stories I'd published, pictures of me at readings, pictures of us together at readings. My mother kept the drafts, the handwriting, the scrawl, while on the other side of the country, my father saved very little of what I had written and a great deal of what had been written about me. Together (separately) those two collections added up to something quite complete. Sitting on the floor of the basement closet, I leafed through not my writing but my career—my first review in the *New York Times*, the program from England's Orange Prize ceremony. I opened the third binder and out fell the mug shots of the Manson Family—Charlie and Tex (who is also Charles) and Clem (who is Grant) and Linda and Leslie and Sadie Mae (who is Susan), all of them in triplicate, one shot staring straight ahead, one shot in profile. One set of the pictures had my father's neat handwriting on the back:

Charles Milles Manson
M/C 11–11–34 5–6 130 BRN BRN
FBI # 643 369A
LA# 312 168-M

Dad, what the hell? Why all those murderers stuck in the binder? Why are they, of all people, not confined to a plastic sleeve? My father had been the person to connect the Tate and LaBianca murders. He had been one of the first people to question Manson, and he had been in the group that went to Death Valley to find him and the Family at the Barker Ranch and bring them back to Los Angeles. I remember asking my father about it when I was in high school. I said there must have been something powerful about Manson, something bewitching, to have gotten so many people to follow him like that.

"Those people would have followed parked cars," my father said without drama or hesitation. It was just a fact.

Looking at their faces now, I could see it. These were blank-eyed kids, remorseless and half laughing, having been dragged in to be charged for slaughter. That trip to Death Valley came just a couple of weeks after my mother moved my sister and me to Nashville. I shuffled the pictures back into a neat deck and brought them upstairs to my office. They didn't belong in the binder or in the box, but then again, they didn't belong anywhere.

Oh, Damien, see where you've brought me?

"I have those, too," my sister said later when I showed her the mug shots. "Mine don't have Dad's writing on the back, though. You got the better set."

"I got the better set of Manson Family mug shots? My god, do you want mine?"

She did not.

I've always had the impulse to protect myself, but somewhere along the way I got confused about what I needed protection from. Funny enough, the short stories didn't turn out to be the problem. The reason not to go in the boxes were the letters from my first husband, and the letters from my darling dead friend, and the Manson Family in the binder of press clippings for *The Magician's Assistant*. Those are things that stop the day. I'd been afraid the stories of my youth would be as bad as my youthful poetry. I'd been afraid I'd somehow been given a life I hadn't deserved, but that's ridiculous. We don't deserve anything—not the suffering and not the golden light. It just comes.

THE PREPONDERANCE OF the stories saved came from my sophomore year of college—the fall of 1982 through the spring of 1983—when I was eighteen and then nineteen. It was the year I studied with Allan Gurganus in the first fiction class I ever took. I say these were the majority of stories that were saved, but it would be more accurate to say they were the majority of the stories I wrote. Much of the work I turned in for the rest of college, and all the way through graduate school, were rewrites of stories I'd written for Allan. I'd intended to be a poet but, as the pages from Damien's mother's nightstand proved, I was bad at it. ("Then, in the distance breaks my wave. / The poet cannot run from life, / For they are life. / We must stand the experience.") After my freshman year of college it was clear that to be a writer, I'd need to pivot.

The thing about short stories is that they are themselves little boxes of the past, even if you'd never meant for them to be. With few exceptions, I had no memory of having written them. How could I so clearly remember the VFW essay and have practically no memory of the short stories? The answer is volume. I wrote dozens of stories. Sitting on the couch in my office, I found myself reading them with a curiosity as to how they would end. I wrote a lot that was overtly southern that year, leaning heavily into my love of Eudora Welty and Carson McCullers. That had less to do with who I wanted to be as a writer than with my own attempt to seem the smallest bit exotic in the extremely exotic world of Sarah Lawrence College and Westchester County. Lou Reed's then-wife, Sylvia, was in Allan's class that year, beautifully decked out in leather everything. It was a school of actresses and models and boarding school girls who went to Switzerland to ski on winter break. I tried to distinguish myself by playing the only card I had, which was that I alone in this talented group hailed from Tennessee.

Below is a page from a story I wrote called "Badge." Please note, I have transcribed the original exactly, resisting the powerful temptation to edit, or at least to supply the bucketful of commas that are missing. (What did I have against commas when I was young?)

He doesn't look like any of us even though we are first blood cousins. Edith came home crying one day last year from art class because someone said we were all pasty-faces. I think that pretty much fits. I tried to tell her that red hair is good luck, fellows going off to the service always want to pat our heads and stuff. Everyone wants to play it down, we all get pale blue sweaters for Christmas and lots of stocking caps. I for one have always wanted a red dress, flame red, like the neon sign in Henson's Luncheonette or a poinsettia leaf or a bottled cherry; a dress with long sleeves and a big full skirt that I would wear every Sunday until it was threadbare. Aunt Grace has kin from Italy or New York or somewhere and that's where Badge got his hair, it's jet black when it's wet and almost that dark when it's dry. While the rest of us cook like french fries in the sun and have to lie still all night smeared up with Noxzema, Badge just gets this nice color, like the inside of a Heath bar.

His real name is Henry, a fact known only to his truest friends. When he joined the cub scouts after they first moved to Memphis he did very well and by the time he was a year into the boy scouts he had earned every possible badge a person could earn, including cooking and kindness to animals. The other kids weren't even jealous since he always acted very natural with them. Everyone has always called him Badge since then, he doesn't talk about it but once when I asked him to show them to me he did. He keeps them in the zipper compartment of his suitcase. He took out this green felt sack that had a long green felt sash inside, the kind Miss Americas wear with the name of their state, only wider. Covering the front and the back were these little patches about the size of coke tops when they've been run over, all attached in neat little rows (Aunt Grace sews very well) I asked him to put it on but he said he didn't want to, so he put it on me. It came way down past my knees, we stood for a good ten minutes in front of the full length mirror in the hall closet just looking. I was a Christmas tree, covered with lights and glass balls and peppermints, really, it was a beautiful thing.

• • •

AS MUCH AS I played up my southernness (by way of Southern California), plenty of stories in the box were not remotely southern. I had written from the point of view of women and men, boys and girls, white people, Black people, Asian people. I had written stories in a floating omniscient voice, something I found impossible to pull off when I tried it again years later, forgetting completely that I already knew how to do it. Seeing those stories now was like finding out that I used to speak French and play the piano—I wouldn't have believed it and yet look, there I am. I marveled at the scope and bravery I found. I marveled at my willingness to fail. But mostly, I marveled at Allan Gurganus and his clean, distinctive penmanship in the margins of my work. He didn't bother with my missing punctuation or phonetic spelling. Instead, he nudged and praised and critiqued and urged me on:

> *A,*
>
> *It's much better. The shape is more apparent & the voice has somehow purified itself. The bros. don't get underfoot now & the cousin (the Boy Scout stuff is lovely) feels more erotically <u>there</u>.*
>
> *My one quibble: I think you need to definitely place the narrator on that porch & connect the speculative scene more fully to her. Otherwise, one palpably misses her & waits for her return.*
>
> *Consider the last page switch to present tense.*
>
> *You have made a good thing better. Inside of a Heath bar, Lord just let me <u>live</u> there.*
>
> *Allan*

• • •

IT'S DIFFICULT TO explain how much it meant that Allan Gurganus palpably missed my narrator and instructed me to place her on the porch so he would know where she was; that he ignored my more trivial errors in order to concentrate on making me stronger—not only to make the story stronger, to make *me* stronger. This was the second draft of "Badge" that I'd found in the box. There were first and third drafts as well. Allan did not roll his eyes or turn away when I tried again. Instead, he pointed me in the direction I needed to go, which is to say here, towards this present life. On the back of a story called "Catching Cold" he wrote:

> A,
> *The speed of this works for it. It has an immediacy related to fevers.*
> *I feel for her and poor Sam—so eager to help. Her claustrophobia is*
> *well-done—simply done. I <u>see</u> the old couple & Walter.*
> *Her final recovery & resolve seems laden w. interesting & perverse*
> *reasons all her own.*
> *A resurrection.*
> *(Atlantic—C. Michael Curtis*
> *Nyker—Charles McGrath*
> *Paris Review—Mona Simpson)*
> Allan

WHAT DID I do with such information? Nothing, I'm sure. I wasn't writing to be published, I was writing for Allan. I wanted so much to be like him. I wanted so much for him to love me. When he was

no longer my teacher, I saw a marked decline in both the quality
and quantity of my output. The evidence of this was made clear by
what isn't in the box. Without the easy pressure of his hand on my
back, I lost my way, went into a kind of hibernation. In the years
that followed, I learned less about how to write and more about
how to internalize what he'd already taught me. I was a garter snake
digesting a gazelle. It took time.

"Allan, Allan," I wrote to him in an e-mail a few days ago, "how
did you manage? How were you able to give so much? It's mystifying."

Forever attentive, he wrote me back in minutes. "You mention our
working together at Sarah Lawrence. The pleasure was on my side.
You were all for learning everything you could as soon as possible.
And each lesson STAYED learned. That lent a natural momentum
to how much could be accomplished in quantum leaps. Gosh, I love
teaching and still have dreams of getting panicky phone calls from
Stanford and Iowa. 'Your class is here and waiting.' 'Sorry, hold them
there. I'll catch the next plane.' "

Our work together. That was precisely how he made me feel. No
one was ever as lucky as me, except, of course, for all his other students. We are legion.

When I told Allan I might be changing my mind about giving
my papers to the library instead of the fireplace, he said he, too, had
considered pulling a Willa Cather and incinerating everything, but
decided to send his papers to Duke instead. Always the overachiever
(and archivist), he had mailed in fifty-two boxes to date, fifty-two
and counting. I think were I to scrape together every last thing I had,
including this essay, I might come up with three boxes.

Of course, without my mother and father and sister, I'd have a
shoe box. Though I'd held onto a few of the stories I'd written in

college, my mother seemingly had them all. That was because every single week I mailed her my homework.

"Writing goes well," read the note I attached, "but at the rate of one story a week, I am terrified of having a one-week block or God forbid, the flu. Ah well, we can't deal in negatives. Aside from more work than I can possibly survive, I am one happy clam. I seem to have very up days right after my story is turned in and very nervous days right before it's due. Subsequently it feels like my weekends begin on Tuesday and the work starts on Friday."

And then: "Well, it's three weeks in coming but here is the 'Badge' revision. There were a lot of questions about how Belle would know what had happened at the fair, so I'm letting her imagine it. I think it is stronger now. Let me know.

"P.S. Many thanks for the October funds."

And then: "I am starting to feel a bit guilty about monopolizing so much of your time. I just want you to get a sense of the *quantity* I am turning out these days."

And then: "I thought about saving a bunch in postage and waiting until you got here to give this one over, but perhaps the continuity is nice.

"P.S. bring envelopes!!"

Week after week I wrote stories, got them back, and mailed them home. Week after week, my mother read them and then put them in a box to save. She believed in my stories and so she saved them. She loved me and so she saved them. She knew me well enough not to let me make a decision about what would happen to them until I'd passed the midpoint of my fifties. She answered all my letters when I was in college. I always had envelopes in my mailbox at school, though sometimes they were notes from a boy named Larry whose work-study job it was to sort the mail at the campus post office. Larry wrote to me on the days I didn't get letters.

I wish I'd saved those notes from my mother, the notes from Larry.

I CAN'T IMAGINE what kind of work it would take to actually put the past in order, to make sense of what was there while resisting the urge to expunge the worst of it and correct the rest—not just my atrocious spelling, but my exhausting efforts to affect a tone that I thought of as witty and urbane. My fiction wasn't autobiographical, but the voice in those stories was much closer to who I was than the girl I tried to be in those letters. "I've been thinking a lot about great literature," I wrote to my mother. "It seems to me that the majority was banged out on a manual. What else could Hemingway have used . . . a 75-pound IBM Selectra? Hah! The current in Paris is hardly the current in Barcelona. As we can tell, *A Farewell to Arms* would not have materialized to be the book we know and love.

"Love? No, not yet, not any. Not a glimmer of hope on the horizon. Just me and my Hermes. Mon aimé."

Good lord.

I keep pens in the drawer of my nightstand now, scratch pads, a tiny book light. I've found that when some thought wakes me, writing it down is my best hope of going back to sleep. Three o'clock in the morning isn't the time to think about a letter that needs to be written, or that the dog is out of biscuits, or that once again I dreamed I missed my flight. Sometimes (rarely) what wakes me is important, a scene from a novel I've yet to write, and this is a piece of luck so sacred that I will always be ready to meet it.

What if the notes I made in the middle of the night were to fall behind the drawer of the nightstand? It could happen. When I woke up in the morning I'd never think to look for them. Half the time I have no memory of waking up.

And what if, years from now, the circumstances of my life were to change, and I were separated from this nightstand? They're beautiful; Karl bought the pair long before we married. Someone would want them. What if the person who bought them at an estate sale found the dreams and the grocery list, the few sentences that pointed towards a novel, and then went to all the trouble to track me down? Would I tell them to throw the notes away? Would I say that a dream and a grocery list and a possible idea from so many years ago meant nothing to me now, only because I was afraid to look?

No.

I would tell that person how I used to do that all the time, write down ideas in the middle of the night. I would say, *You're reminding me of just how much of myself I put into my nightstand. You're reminding me how lucky I was to have the nightstand there.*

The drawer where everything from the past was crammed turned out to contain equal measures of darkness and light, or maybe more light because Tavia was there in her cheerleading uniform, along with the veterans who'd fought for our country in foreign wars. I wonder how I had ever slept beside such luminous furniture. Were something like this to ever happen again, I would approach the past with considerably more tenderness. I would marvel at my youthful fifty-seven-year-old handwriting, the paper foxed at the edges. I would say, Damien, thank you. Thank you, Lucy and Jack, for writing me those letters. Thank you, Allan, for holding the lantern high. Thank you to my father and sister and grandmother for saving parts of the story, and thank you to my mother for saving all of it. Or for saving me, depending on how you read this.

A Talk to the Association of Graduate School Deans in the Humanities

As a rule, I avoid speaking to professional organizations, because really, what can I tell you about your work that you don't already know? I get a lot of requests to speak at medical conventions, but I won't do those anymore. You can't tell a doctor anything, and they text while you're talking. Still, there was something enticing about speaking to a roomful of graduate school deans in the humanities. Any group of people who've spent as much collective time in the classroom as you have are bound to be a good audience. Definitely no texting. And while I'm sure I can't tell you anything about your job that you don't already know, I can tell you some things about my job you can probably relate to.

A few years ago, I published a novel called *Commonwealth* that was fairly autobiographical. Many people were horrified by the lack of adult supervision the children in that book grew up with. "It was the seventies," I would tell them. "We were feral. All children were feral in the seventies." Well, in my experience, graduate school was feral in the eighties.

I went to Sarah Lawrence College in 1981 and had as good an undergraduate experience as any writer could dream up. I studied with Allan Gurganus and Grace Paley and Russell Banks, and each of them taught me things about how to write and read and, most importantly, how to be a decent person, that I am still leaning on to this day.

I was a very promising kid. I published my first story in the *Paris Review* when I was a senior. When I left college, I got it in my head that I needed to go to work and not back to school. I wanted to write stories about how people lived, and I felt it was important to go out and meet those people.

I made a clear decision not to go to graduate school. I moved back to Nashville, back to my mother's house, and got a job as a cook in a restaurant. I wanted to make a living with my back and save my brain for writing, which is a beautiful idea, except for the fact that I was tired all the time. Post-college lesson number one: manual labor is hard and should not be romanticized. One day I burned myself while cleaning the grill at the end of my shift. I was already covered in bruises and cuts. The woman who owned the restaurant told me I needed to go to graduate school for my safety. And so I did. It can take very little to be pointed in the right direction—or the wrong direction for that matter—when you're twenty-one.

I got into the Iowa Writers' Workshop. I didn't get in anyplace else I applied, nor was I wait-listed anyplace else I applied.

This was 1985, and the Iowa Writers' Workshop had three levels

of financial aid for first-year students: the best gig was teaching literature to undergraduates three days a week. It was the most money
for the least amount of work, and you got in-state tuition. The second-
best gig was teaching rhetoric and composition four days a week.
You were paid less money for more students and more work, but you
still got in-state tuition. The third level of financial aid was office
work, where you worked five days a week and were paid next to
nothing and didn't get in-state tuition. Another group of students
got no financial aid at all. This system did not foster friendly feelings
among classmates.

My dearest friend and constant companion was my roommate,
the poet Lucy Grealy. We had both been assigned literature fellowships, though neither of us had ever thought about teaching. We
hadn't thought about much of anything. We were just happy to have
gotten a good financial aid package.

We showed up at the end of summer for our training program. We
were told to pick two novels, one contemporary and one classic, not
from a list but out of the air. I chose *One Flew Over the Cuckoo's Nest*
and *Madame Bovary*. One Shakespeare play (I chose *Othello*), one
contemporary play (*A Raisin in the Sun*). A standard Norton anthology was used to put together a section on the short story and a section
on poetry once it was time to teach the short story and poetry. We
filled out our order forms for the bookstore. We were given the room
numbers of where we would be teaching and the name of our supervisor. Our training was then complete. I never met my supervisor.

Lucy and I went to find our classrooms in the English and Philosophy building, which everyone called Eggs and Peanut Butter. I
remember it was very hot. We sat on the desk and swung our legs
back and forth. I had picked out novels and plays and stories I liked,

but Lucy's list represented her aspirations. The books she ordered for her class were books she wanted to read. Most weeks she managed to stay one chapter ahead of her students.

We were teaching literature to kids who were nineteen or twenty. When we collected our student evaluations, we read them and threw them in the trash. When my supervisor sent me a note telling me the day she was coming to observe my class, I sent a note back saying I was going to give a quiz that day so there would be nothing to see. I didn't know how to teach and I didn't want someone watching me do it. Fortunately, I never heard from her again.

I can only liken this experience to getting pregnant at twenty-one and having the baby on my own. The idea being that I was biologically capable of procreation, and that I could be a mother because I'd had a mother and seen other people's mothers and so I should know how things worked.

I was teaching literature not because I had the training, skill, or desire to do so, but because the short stories in my application for graduate school, the same stories that were turned down by three other programs, had been deemed better than someone else's. Don't get me wrong, I was grateful. Even though I was making the most money possible, it still wasn't quite enough to sustain my extremely minimal existence. To avoid taking out loans, I got a job babysitting for the two-year-old daughter of Jorie Graham and Jim Galvin, married poets who taught at Iowa. The poets and fiction writers had different schedules, so a fiction writer was needed to look after the child of poets. I was no more qualified to take care of a two-year-old than I was to teach literature.

Who taught your classes, who was in your classes, and your financial aid package were the reliable predictors of how your time at the Iowa Writers' Workshop would go. Unfortunately, we had no control over any of those things. Jack Leggett, the director of the program, said on our first day when all the workshop students were together, "Take a good look around. You will become lifelong friends with some of the people in this room. You will have sex with some of them. You may well marry someone in this room, and then you will probably divorce them." Jack had been at Iowa a long time and he knew what he was talking about. All of those predictions came true.

The financial aid for our second year was handed out in the spring of our first year. Students submitted stories and poems and the faculty judged them. It was like something out of *Gladiator*. The winners were called TWFs, pronounced "twiffs"—Teaching-Writing Fellows. In our second year, Lucy and I were both TWFs. TWFs taught an undergraduate workshop one day a week and made nearly twice as much money as the people teaching four days a week, not because we were better teachers—nobody had any idea what kind of teachers we were—but because we were deemed to be better writers. Our time was considered more valuable. Again, I will say it was not a system that engendered good feelings among classmates.

In the same way that I had drawn a spectacular series of good hands at Sarah Lawrence, I drew consistently bad ones at Iowa. Two semesters I studied with visiting faculty who had no interest in teaching, and two semesters I studied with long-tenured faculty who had no interest in teaching. All four of those people are dead now and I will not speak ill of the dead, but oh, I could. The problems in those classes were not trivial. For example, one semester the very old and extremely unwell visiting professor regularly conducted his workshop in French. I don't speak French. There you have my graduate school experience.

I believe the problems I'm talking about here were probably solved decades ago, and that this or any other MFA program should not be judged by my experience. I am bringing back a report from the Dark Ages. In those days, the workshop still fostered the Cult of Insanity which has played such a big part in the mythology of being a writer and artist—that misery, mental illness, drug addiction, and alcoholism were proof of your sensitivity and talent. Or to put it another way, the worse you were, the better you were. We still believed in Papa in those days, in the righteous dominance of masculinity. We believed the hallmark of literary greatness was going to war, racking up a long string of wives, and then blowing your head off in Idaho.

How, you might ask, does a graduate program foster such ideas? Like this: I was at a party one night at the house of a famous visiting professor who was not my teacher. He came up to me late in the evening and began to drunkenly harangue me in a loud voice, telling me he had never believed in natural talent, that *he* believed in hard work and perseverance, but clearly *I* had natural talent, which ruined things for everyone else. "I can only hope you die young and alone in a closet," he said to me. I was twenty-two.

What I learned in those two years of graduate school came not from being taught, but from teaching. This new skill was something I took seriously. Teaching made me a better reader and a better thinker. I became more conscientious about how I expressed myself, which in turn made me a better writer. Still, I would like to apologize to every student I had during those two years. I'm sorry that their Introduction to Literature class happened to be the place I was learning to teach. I'm sorry that they took out loans, or that their parents forked out money, to pay for those classes, but thanks to them, I got better at it.

Graduate school also made me tough. It helped me develop a canny sense of whom to listen to and whom to ignore. Like boot camp, Iowa wrung every ounce of sentimentality out of me. I had been a tender thing when I arrived, and by the end I cared about nothing but writing better stories. Those workshops taught me to seek smart people who could help me make my work better. Nothing is more valuable than a good editor and a sharp critic, and I learned how to be that for other people as well. After two years in workshops, I would say it's almost impossible to hurt my feelings, and that has served me well through eviscerating reviews and all manner of internet weirdness.

In the winter of my second year, at the very end of 1986, I attended my first Modern Language Association conference. I had three published stories and from that landed twenty-one interviews, most all of them for tenure-track jobs. Of all the astonishing tales I bring from the Old World, this may be the most shocking fact of all, since no one would be interviewed for those jobs today without at least one book, probably two.

I don't know this, but I'm guessing MLA interviews haven't changed much in the years since I last went. The conference took place in a giant hotel. The interviewee would call from the lobby and say "I'm your eleven o'clock," and then go up to the room and knock on the door. It was impossible not to feel like a hooker, especially since the search committee members sat on one bed while I sat on the other. I remember arriving to one interview soaking wet from a sudden downpour on my way to the hotel, and when I started to take my raincoat off, the chairman said, "Have we told you about the wet T-shirt portion of the interview?" I pulled my coat back on and sat down on the bed, making a giant wet spot.

I got an on-campus interview at the University of Missouri. Those were wonderful people. They could not have been nicer or more welcoming. The poet Sherod Santos hosted a dinner party for me at his house, and before I ate with the search committee he called me into the kitchen. At the stove he told me, sotto voce, that they were going to offer me the job, and that I should not under any circumstances accept it. He said it would ruin me. He said I had a real chance to make it as a writer and a tenure-track job would kill that.

But of course I was going to take the job. I didn't *have* a job. I wanted health insurance and a TIAA-CREF account like everyone else. Before I left, everyone kissed me and said they couldn't wait to see me in the fall. They didn't offer me the job.

The past can look shocking, even when seen from not so terribly far away: the savagery of financial aid, the fact that there wasn't a single student of color in any of my four workshops and I didn't think to notice, that teachers slept with students, that students slept with visiting writers, that everyone was drunk, that favoritism was the order of the day, and the thing that troubled me most of all, both then and now, a tenured member of the workshop faculty who encouraged her students to shoplift. She told us that when we went to readings at Prairie Lights, the wonderful local bookstore, we should lean against the shelves while the author was reading, then slip the book we wanted in our pocket. We were poor artists, she told us. We deserved those books. Dear God! What was going on?

But then I imagine what an older faculty member might have said in 1985 if he—and it would have been a he—were asked to describe his graduate student experience thirty years before. What will your own students say thirty years from now? Because in this present moment we always feel that we have fully arrived. We believe we are

fair and sensitive, helpful, kind, no longer predatory or racist. But
the future will call us out just the same. As the old saying goes, every generation believes they invented sex and war. I will add to that
list: graduate school. And honestly, at the time it was kind of fun.

Here's a happier story: when I was at Iowa, I was flying home to
Nashville for Christmas. I was changing planes in Chicago and got
lost in O'Hare. Remember when it was still possible to get lost in an
airport? I was lugging a heavy bag full of steel plates I was engraving
for a printmaking class, because—I failed to mention this earlier—I
was actually taking classes in the MFA programs for both creative
writing and printmaking for my first year in Iowa. I was that kid. I
got in completely over my head and eventually dropped out of the
printmaking program, but on this particular Christmas vacation my
steel plates and I were heading home, where I planned to do some
drypoint in my spare time.

I was walking back and forth in the terminal looking for arrows
that pointed to gates when a young man in a pink Oxford shirt and
khakis who looked like John Denver asked me if I was lost. I was
lost, and I was also flattered because he was cute. He took my ticket
and said I was indeed a long way from where I needed to be and that
he would walk me there. He took my heavy bag from me. I asked
him if he worked in the airport and he said sort of. He was a Hare
Krishna. I was briefly terrified, thinking I was going to be snatched
up and forced into a cult, but he had both my ticket and my plates
so I followed him. Of course when we got to the gate my plane was
delayed, and so he sat down with me. I decided I could either fight
it or go with it.

I asked him about his life and we talked for more than an hour
while we waited. He said, "Imagine loving God so much you'd be

willing to stand in an airport day after day trying to tell people what it was like—to love God, to feel so loved by Him. What if this joy you felt, this love, was so great that you wanted to share it with everyone, but they all rushed right by you, looking in the other direction?"

All these years later, it's still the best description of how I feel about books. I would stand in an airport to tell people about how much I love books, reading them, writing them, making sure other people felt comfortable reading and writing them.

I've had a few teaching jobs in my life, mostly visiting writer positions, but for the most part I followed Sherod Santos's advice and stayed outside. I spent years writing for *Seventeen* and *Bridal Guide*. I've been a waitress, a cook, a travel writer, a writer for the *New York Times*. I published my first novel at twenty-seven and pieced together a slim financial existence until I wrote my fourth novel, *Bel Canto*. After that I bought a house, protected my privacy, and worked.

An MFA is a funny degree. Unless you're completely delusional, and many artists are, you don't think it's going to land you a job in your field, and yet MFA programs are thriving. I think, more than anything, it's the idea of finding like-minded people, people who care about words, color, light, meter, chapter breaks, and ideas more than they care about food and shelter. As much as I look back on my time in Iowa as complete and utter madness, I did love being in the company of people I understood.

I love the fact that Lucy and I memorized so many poems, that we tried to memorize the first chapter of *One Hundred Years of Solitude*, and that we danced in the kitchen every night after dinner. I love that the students went to bars after class to talk about Alice

Munro and Raymond Carver, that we couldn't stop talking about Denis Johnson's stories in *Jesus' Son*. I felt that my entire life had been changed by Donald Hall's *The Ideal Bakery*. I saw Stephen Jay Gould give a talk about evolution. I saw Tobias Wolff read "Back in the World." I saw Czesław Miłosz read his poems in quiet, formal English, then turn around and thunder them out in Polish. I saw Louise Erdrich not long after she published *Love Medicine*. She was a vision of all that was good in the world.

Lucy and I went to readings two or three nights a week, and on the other nights we watched foreign films at the campus theater. I remember going to see Cocteau's *Orpheus*, and how thrilled we were when a fight broke out in the Poet's Café, a fight over the importance of poetry! We would fight for poetry! Lucy and I walked home from the theater that night, arguing over which of us was more in love with Heurtebise. We were two girls in love with a dead French actor who was playing a dead French chauffeur. When you're a writer, it's worth two years of your life to feel like you've found your people.

That's what owning a bookstore has been like for me: it's reminded me of what I loved about graduate school. It's made me realize that I could use the tools I'd been given in ways I never knew they could work. I've made a soft place for an ever-expanding group of friends and strangers to come and exclaim and argue over books. Some of us have lives that revolve around the humanities the way planets circle the sun. It's not who we're trying to be, it's who we are. In the last month I've seen the Korean film *Parasite*, the four-hour Philip Glass opera *Akhnaten*. I staged a table reading of *Our Town* with neighbors in our living room, and am reading *How to Catch a Mole*. I'm pretty much the poster child for how to incorporate the humanities into your life. It is my greatest love, my deepest joy, and all I want to do is share it, to use books and writers to bridge the lonely technological divide we find ourselves stuck in. And I'll tell you, as satisfying as it is to see the store packed to the rafters for Colson Whitehead, it was even more amazing to see it jammed with the people who'd come to meet Pat Summit, the legendary coach of the Lady Vols who was dying of Alzheimer's, or Antoni from *Queer Eye*, who had a new cookbook out. They brought an audience of people who might not have been in a bookstore in a long time, and they eyed the place with wonder.

When I went to graduate school, hoping to be a writer, I had no idea that owning a bookstore was one of my career options. But I believe I've done more good on behalf of culture by opening Parnassus than I have writing novels. I've made a place in my community where everyone is welcome. We have story time and poetry readings and demonstrations from cookbooks. I've interviewed more authors than you could even imagine. Many of them sleep at my house. I promote the books I love tirelessly, because a book can so easily get lost in the mad shuffle of the world and it needs someone with a loud voice to hold it up and praise it. I am that person.

As every reader knows, the social contract between you and a book you love is not complete until you can hand that book to someone else and say, *Here, you're going to love this*. I always thought that sharing the books I loved with my students, requiring them to read those books, was the biggest perk of being a teacher. But at the bookstore, people who actually want my recommendations walk through the door all day long. The students were captives, the customers are volunteers. It's a dream to hand a stranger a copy of a Jane Gardam novel, or to connect just the right person with Halldór Laxness's *Independent People*.

And it isn't just about books. Yo-Yo Ma came in one day and played a Bach suite for the twenty people who happened to be in the store. Emanuel Ax once played a Brahms intermezzo on our upright piano until I thought it would leap straight off the floor. High school kids come in and play that same piano. We have puppet shows and jazz workshops. Artists exhibit their paintings. My ideas about what constitutes beauty and culture and art are continually expanding. Book clubs meet regularly to discuss and praise and disagree. People sit and read with a dog in their laps, all sorts of people, all political stripes, coming together to talk and listen and read.

When people used to come up to me in the grocery store to tell me how they felt about my books, it made me uncomfortable, but since we opened Parnassus they want to talk to me about the bookstore, they want to thank me. They tell me what they're reading and ask me what I'm reading. They introduce me to their children. "I know you," a girl said to me once. "You're the person who owns all the libraries."

"Not exactly," I said, "but you're close."

Here's something they didn't teach me in graduate school: if you want to save reading, teach children to read. Engage children in reading. "You have to raise your own customers," a bookseller friend told me before we opened, and he was right. We have a magnificent children's section. We have a story-time reader who can play the ukulele. Our children's book buyer and our children's booksellers have an ability to match books and children with such pinpoint accuracy, they should be studied by educators worldwide.

One night in the grocery store a couple of rock star hipsters asked me if I was the bookstore lady. I told them I was. They said their daughter, to whom they had read since birth, was not herself a comfortable reader. They'd bought her *The Secret Garden*, they'd bought her *Anne of Green Gables*, they'd gotten nowhere. "What can we do?" they asked me in the cheese section, and to my own astonishment, I knew the answer because I had seen it played out time and again. I told them to bring her into the store, give her a copy of *Captain Underpants*, and let her sit on one of the filthy dog beds with a shop dog in her lap and read the book to the dog.

They brought their daughter to the store the next night, and she read to a very old dog who worked in our store. I cannot overstate how much this thrilled me.

I'm sorry I made my students back in Iowa read *Madame Bovary*. I love *Madame Bovary*, but these were not literature majors. They were kids who may have had one shot in college to feel thrilled and engaged by reading, and I'm fairly certain I blew it for them. At the time, I thought that *Madame Bovary* was the essence of a liberal arts education, but the essence of a liberal arts education is the ability to be flexible and curious, to be able to teach *Othello* and then write for *Bridal Guide*, to publish several novels and open a bookstore, to promote the work of living writers, to evolve. I once believed that nothing could surpass winning a big literary award, but I was mistaken. The thing that's been so much better has been to create jobs in my community, to be part of the Parnassus Foundation, which buys books for children who can't afford books so that they can know the thrill of owning the book they love, to find as many ways as possible for literature to make a difference in the lives of as many people as possible.

I have become a spokesperson not just for Parnassus but for reading, and for independent bookstores everywhere. Amazon has opened a brick-and-mortar store in the mall across the street from us. People want to know how well we are doing. I'll tell you how well we're doing: they've come to kill us. But we'll survive. Nashville has been incredibly kind. They value all things independent, and as a Nashvillian, so do I.

Not everyone is going to open a bookstore, I understand that, but it's one of the choices. That's what I hope students in MFA programs now can understand—the future is not one thing. So many possibilities can arise as a result of intelligence, education, curiosity, and hard work. No one ever told me that, and I'm sorry it took this long for me to figure it out.

Did I need an MFA to write a novel? No, I did not. Did I need an MFA to open a bookstore? No again. But I was a solitary kid, and I imagined a solitary life for myself. My MFA showed me the importance of community. We are social creatures. Even the introverted readers, the silent writers, want a place where they feel welcomed and understood. I had wanted that once, and now I can give it to others. That's how I've wound up putting my degree to work. That's how I discovered that my truest destiny was a thing I never saw coming.

· Cover Stories ·

When I sold my first novel, *The Patron Saint of Liars*, I was twenty-seven years old. I knew as much about book jackets as I did cars, which is to say certain models appealed to me but I had no real understanding of how they worked. My publisher hired Thomas Woodruff, who had painted the cover illustration for Anne Tyler's extremely successful novel *Breathing Lessons*, in hopes that if he painted the cover illustration for my book, the legions of Anne Tyler readers would absorb the subliminal message of similarity and become Ann Patchett readers. I suppose they were on to something, because almost thirty years later people still tell me my novels remind them of Tyler's. For *The Patron Saint of Liars*, Woodruff sent in a painting of a field at sunset with a house in the distance and a night sky full of stars. In the foreground was a votive candle, a small flame twinkling in a glass cup. It was a beautiful painting.

But instead of saying thank you, I said I didn't like the candle. The symbolism seemed contrived—light a candle against the darkness—and too overtly Catholic, though the novel was nothing if not overtly Catholic. The art director went back to the artist to explain that the young novelist did not like the candle, and so the artist snuffed out the candle and replaced it with a dandelion whose seeds were blowing loose and floating up into the stars. When I saw the second incarnation, I realized the candle had been a good idea.

This took place before the digital age. The dandelion was not photoshopped in; it was painted over the place where the candle had been. This time I kept my mouth shut. The book was published in 1992, the year that brought us Donna Tartt's *The Secret History*, Cormac McCarthy's *All the Pretty Horses*, and Dorothy Allison's *Bastard Out of Carolina*, three books with startlingly beautiful covers that used photography and crisp graphic design to grab the readers' attention. The fact that all three novels were brilliant only served to reinforce the point: original illustration was out, photography was in.

"Never judge a book by its cover" is a good way of saying that people shouldn't be evaluated on the basis of looks alone, but the adage doesn't apply to actual books. Where books are concerned, covers are what we have to go on. We might be familiar with the author's name or like the title, but absent that information, it's the jacket design—the size and shape of the font, the color, the image or absence of image—that makes us stop at the new releases table of our local independent bookstore and pick up one novel instead of another. Book covers should entice readers the way roses entice bees—like their survival depends on it.

My second novel had a bad title and a worse jacket. Like every other novel that came out in 1994, *Taft* (I told you it was a bad title) had a photograph on the cover, having been influenced by *The Secret History*, *All the Pretty Horses*, and *Bastard Out of Carolina*. But my cover photo was muddled and confusing—a bar full of long-legged barstools that looked like spider's legs, and, in the distance, a young white woman, even though the book was about a Black man. I hated everything about it. After a great deal of back-and-forth with my publisher, I pointed out that I had the right to refuse the cover written into my contract. When I reminded them that I could turn it down, they reminded *me* that they could print two thousand copies of the book and fail to distribute them. I was learning things about publishing all the time.

I switched publishers for my third novel, *The Magician's Assistant*, and I loved the cover they came up with: a photograph of a 1960s model turned 90 degrees so that she appeared to be floating in midair on her back. I also loved the cover for the paperback—a giant white rabbit sitting in an armchair. Generally speaking, if a book is a big seller in hardback, the cover doesn't change when it goes into paperback, and if a book hasn't been such a hit, they'll try something new. I liked the publisher of my third book, but by the time I'd written my fourth book, everyone I knew who had worked there had either left or been fired. I left, too.

When it was time to publish my fourth novel, something remarkable happened. My new editor sent me a whole stack of preliminary cover ideas called mock-ups, each one glued onto heavy black cardboard.

Bel Canto
A NOVEL BY
Ann Patchett

they read in bright red, in navy blue, in the shape of an open mouth, on a line of music, on piano keys, in camouflage. I propped my choices up on windowsills and asked friends to vote. The truth was I liked them all. The strong colors and simple graphics made my novel look like a work of serious literature. Any of them could have been the cover of a John Updike novel. (Updike, who designed many of his own covers, was my personal gold standard for good taste in those days.) This new publisher did an equally good job when they changed the cover completely for the paperback. The paperback sold well, and the book won prizes and was taken seriously. The covers had promised the reader it was that kind of book.

Bel Canto was published in more than thirty countries, and none of those publishers asked me for my opinion on the cover art. Over time, boxes of books from China and Romania and Argentina started showing up at my house. The Swedish cover had a picture of a mansion flanked by palm trees, its windows lit with what appeared to be burning crucifixes. The Dutch cover showed a woman in a ball gown holding a violin, even though no one in the book plays the violin. The Slovenian cover featured an incredibly cheerful-looking blonde in a plunging red dress who may have been on her way to the disco. The Russian cover looked like a James Bond novel—a man in a tux with a gun, a sports car, and a large-breasted woman in towering heels. In many countries' editions the emphasis was on a woman's luxuriant hair, I don't know why. Other foreign editions featured musical notes or guerrilla fighters or, in a few cases, both. Sometimes I could convince myself that the publishers must know their audience in ways I could not, other times that charity was too much of a stretch. Foreign covers, I decided, were like translations: their quality was outside my control.

When I did speak up about a foreign cover I didn't like, things didn't improve. I got to see an early mock-up of the UK paperback of my fifth book, *Truth & Beauty,* which featured a photograph of two girls sunbathing on a beach towel. One was pretty and wearing sunglasses while the other had an open book covering her face. Since this was a memoir about my friend Lucy, who'd had cancer of the jaw as a child and suffered serious disfigurement because of it, I didn't like it at all. We weren't those girls, and covering up one face was coy. I objected strongly. When the final copy of the book arrived, I saw the publisher had solved the problem by simply cropping out their heads. Now the jacket featured two headless torsos lying on a towel, their necks stopping just at the jacket's upper edge.

My problems with my covers hit an all-time high, or low, with *Run,* my fifth novel. While I'd been sent eight possible covers for *Bel Canto,* for *Run* I got ten, then twenty, then thirty. No one, including me, had any idea what should be on the cover. One contender was a photograph of a snowy path in New York City's Central Park (the book is set in Boston) with a trash can right in the middle of the composition.

"Why are you sending me a cover with a trash can on it?" I asked my new editor.

She told me it wasn't a trash can, and then, after looking at the design again, said oh, yes, in fact, it was a trash can. She hadn't noticed. One of the choices that I absolutely loved included a photograph of two goldfish swimming in a plastic bag. Since the book is about two brothers, one of whom is an ichthyologist, I thought it was perfect. I bought my editor an expensive handbag, put that mock-up inside and mailed it back to her. Finally! We had a winner.

"You can't have that one," she said, thanking me for the handbag. "Everyone here hates it."

"Then why did you send it to me?"

"Because you need to know we're trying."

The hard-won final image was a shimmering blue snowstorm. I liked it very much, but I also understood that a tremendous amount of time, energy, and goodwill had been expended in the process. That was when I realized that book covers were like birthday presents: How could someone give me what I wanted if I didn't know what I wanted?

That turned out to be the epiphany that changed everything, and by "everything" I mean more than just my relationship to cover art.

I was halfway through writing my next novel when my husband came home one night and put a record on the turntable. (I love my husband, who still has records and a turntable.) He was listening to *An Historic Return: Horowitz at Carnegie Hall*, and when I saw the album cover on the coffee table—the cream background, the intricate filigree around the edges that called to mind an ornate tangle of leaves—I thought, *that's* what this book should look like. Somehow it was the embodiment of everything I was trying to write. A year later, when I turned in the finished manuscript of *State of Wonder*, I sent along a color photocopy of that album cover. It didn't need to be this exact thing, I said, but this was the place to start. I wound up with a beautiful jacket.

THROUGHOUT MY LIFE, Allan Gurganus has proven himself to be a continuing oracle of good advice. When I sold my first novel, he sent me a bouquet of tiny white roses, along with a note that said it was up to me to steer my ship. "It's your name on the book," he said. "You're responsible." I think about that when a typo gets by me or some fact in the published book turns out to be wrong: it's on me.

Allan told me I should never hesitate to rewrite jacket copy or ask to see ad layouts, and that while every piece of the process—contracts, editing, publicity, marketing—might be another person's job, it was my life. I would be judged in the world by my books, every part of them, and I had to attend to their details.

After we opened Parnassus Books, I started noticing not only dust jacket designs but the paper stock the jackets were printed on, what was most likely to crinkle at the edges after coming out of a box, and what inks were easily scuffed. I unboxed a lot of other people's books. The covers of literary fiction were almost always printed on matte paper, while the covers of commercial fiction were glossy. These were the trends in book-cover design: five years ago this wasn't the case, and at some point the fashion would shift again. I knew which typefaces demanded to be read, and what got lost in a busy image. I saw a cover recently whose title and author's name were bold when held in one direction, then vanished (by design) when the book was slightly tilted. It was a catchy illusion but a really bad idea if you approached the book from the wrong side.

I've also learned that cover art gets recycled. One day a famous author who was visiting the store pulled another author's book down to show me. "This was the first cover they offered me," she said, pointing to the utterly generic graphic of leaves and vines. "I told them I didn't like it and six months later they gave it to her."

I didn't know the second author personally, but I'm betting she had no idea it was possible to ask for something better, or at least for something else.

There is no universal list of elements that comprise a good book jacket, but we all know one when we see it. The covers for my next two books, *This Is the Story of a Happy Marriage* and *Commonwealth*,

came together perfectly. I turned in my ideas with my finished manuscript, and the art director and the editor and the sales force and I
all listened to one another. I showed the sample covers to my friends
at Parnassus and asked for their opinions. By this point in my career
I understood I was going to have to look at these covers for a long,
long time, which gave a whole other level of incentive for getting
things right.

Sometimes knowing what you don't want is an important step in
figuring out what you do want. When I finished *The Dutch House*, I
knew I didn't want a house or any part of a house on the cover, not a
door or window. The house had to exist in the reader's imagination.
That ultimately led me to be certain that I wanted Maeve on the
cover. For a long time I had planned on calling the book "Maeve,"
and without that title, the cover would have to make my intention
clear: it was her story. I thought back to Thomas Woodruff and his
beautiful painting on *The Patron Saint of Liars*. I wanted something
like that. All I needed was to find a painting that would stand in
for the portrait of Maeve that was in the novel. I began to scour the
internet for portraits of black-haired girls, and while I found many
that were beautiful, the ones that were sufficiently classical were
of girls in pinafores or bonnets. The face would be right but the era
was wrong. Nothing I found came close to the portrait of the girl
in my head. I knew a painter in Nashville named Noah Saterstrom
whose work I loved. Couldn't I ask Noah to paint Maeve's portrait?

My editor and the art director liked the idea, but first they wanted
to put together a list of artists, get some preliminary sketches, and
decide who would be best for the job. I got off the phone and thought
about this for a minute. I didn't need to ask anyone's permission to
commission a painting. If things worked out well, then we'd have

our cover, and if they didn't, then I would have bought a painting from someone whose work I loved. What could be the harm in that? I asked Noah if he could paint a portrait of an imaginary ten-year-old girl with black hair and a red coat. The painting would have been done in 1950, but should be in the style of portraits of the 1920s. Oh, and the painter would have been Scottish, if that was helpful. I sent him the two paragraphs from the book in which the painting was described. I told him I wanted Maeve's gaze to be direct. One thing that drives me crazy about portrayals of women on book jackets is that their faces are almost universally turned away, or covered by a hat, or obscured by a tree branch, or, as in the case of the UK cover of *Truth & Beauty*, simply lopped off. Maeve would look at the world straight on. She would expect the world to look straight at her.

"Sure," Noah said. "I'm on it."

The thing to know about Noah Saterstrom is that he has three young children and a big career. He doesn't have time to mess around. Four days later he called to say the painting was finished. When I saw it, I was looking at my heroine. I was standing in the Dutch House and looking at the portrait of Maeve.

I've had some very good covers in my life, but this was a great one, and while I've worked with many other people to get things right, I've never had a true collaborator. Noah's painting is actually part of the book, and it makes the book better. At a certain point the reader comes across the mention of the painting and realizes that the painting she's reading about is the painting on the cover. The moment comes with a small jolt of electricity.

Noah's painting is hanging in my house now. "Where did you *get* that?" people ask. They're stunned by it—Maeve's red coat, her piercing stare, the wild swallows darting behind her. I wondered if

I would get tired of looking at something that had become my book jacket. The answer is no, and I never will. The painting informs my life.

And Noah informs my life. Through this unexpected circumstance, we've become good friends. He comes over once a month or so for breakfast and I make him poached eggs and we talk about art. The cover plays a part in the book, the artist plays a part in my life. Both of those things have turned out to be a joy. Book, art, friend: I learned the lesson and carried the lesson forward.

Which brings me to the book you're holding now. My friend Sooki Raphael was home in California when she sent me a picture of a painting she'd just finished, a woodpecker bracketed by a stack of books on one side and a tree on the other. Everything inside me leapt up. It was the image I wanted on the cover of what was then a half-written book. Sometimes the world hands you exactly what you need when you need it. Sometimes your friend paints exactly the right bird. I asked Sooki if I could buy the painting and she said no. She sent it to me as a gift instead. Not long after, I got an e-mail from my editor saying he'd had a dream that I was writing the sequel to *State of Wonder* and that he'd brought me back a giant, brightly colored parrot from the Amazon. "What do you make of that, Dr. Freud?" he asked.

I told him he was close. "It's a sequel to *This Is the Story of a Happy Marriage*, and it's a pileated woodpecker." I e-mailed him a photo of the painting. He was in.

Months later, when I took the painting of the woodpecker to be professionally scanned for the cover, I brought along a painting that Sooki had made of Sparky. She was thinking of having cards printed; this way she'd have a high-resolution digital file. When I sent the woodpecker painting to my editor and the art department, the painting of Sparky was in the same file. The art director mocked up a set of jackets with Sparky and another set with the woodpecker. They were completely different and both completely perfect, and none of us was able to decide between the two. And when I say we weren't able to decide, everyone who saw them changed their minds, first one, then the other, then back again, which made me think the book should have two covers. Not two separate jackets—that's a gimmick that confuses people to no end—but one jacket that essentially had two fronts. Some people would put it on their nightstand with Sparky face up while other people would choose the woodpecker, or they could get halfway through the book and change their minds, because the cover didn't have to be one thing or seen one way, just as the book didn't have to be one thing or be read one way.

My editor and the head of the art department agreed. I could not only have the cover I wanted, I could essentially have two covers I wanted.

It made me wonder if my visual discernment had improved as I'd aged, or if I had a better track record. Maybe I finally knew how to ask for what I wanted. I was following Allan's advice and taking responsibility for what had my name on it. I would send my books into the world wearing the best suit of clothes I could find, because they were my books, and I knew that that was how they'd be judged.

· Reading Kate DiCamillo ·

Kate DiCamillo came to Nashville while on tour for her novel *Louisiana's Way Home*. It's the middle book of a trilogy that started with *Raymie Nightingale* and ended with *Beverly, Right Here*. Kate and I had crossed paths a few times over the years and had a kind of "Hey, hi, how are you?" relationship, which is to say we had met but didn't know each other. She was doing her event for *Louisiana* at the Oak Hill School and I picked up lunch for her and her publicist and drove it out. I did it because our events manager at Parnassus Books asked me to. She told me Kate was a fan of mine. Niki rarely tells me what to do, but when she does I listen because she's always right.

Kate and her publicist and I sat on tiny chairs at a tiny table in the school library and ate our salads. They made a big fuss over how nice I was to bring them lunch. The whole thing lasted less than thirty minutes. Then Kate gave a talk in an auditorium packed with kids and their parents. I hadn't meant to stay but I did. She talked about her mother's vacuum cleaner and how it had inspired a novel about a squirrel who types poetry. I was, along with every ten-year-old in the room, transfixed.

And that would have been the end of the story, were it not for the fact that the next day I got an e-mail from the writer Nell Freudenberger. Nell asked me if I knew Kate DiCamillo.

"Funny you should ask," I said. "We had lunch yesterday."

Nell went on to tell me that she had just finished reading *The Miraculous Journey of Edward Tulane* to her son, and that it had cracked them open and made them better people. "You have to tell her that for me," Nell said. "Will you do that?"

I didn't have Kate DiCamillo's e-mail address, but I was pretty sure I could find her. Except that I didn't want to find her. I knew she was a fan of my work, but I hadn't read anything she'd written because in my adult life I'd never made a habit of reading children's literature. Even after having lunch with her and hearing her speak, it hadn't occurred to me to read one of her books. I'd been operating under the assumption that children's literature was a matter for children, but what if I changed my mind? If owning a bookstore had taught me anything, it was to broaden my interests and forget my assumptions about what I liked and didn't like. Instead of going to look for the author, I decided to find the book.

The Miraculous Journey of Edward Tulane is the story of a three-foot-tall china rabbit of great privilege who has an extensive wardrobe and is owned by a doting child. The laws of the novel's universe adhere to the laws that children believe: The rabbit is a toy who cannot speak or move but has the interior life of any human. He knows love and fear, comfort and suffering. He can communicate with other inanimate objects but not with people. Edward Tulane is an imperious, nonverbal, immobile china rabbit who is laid low by fate. When his world falls apart it goes fast. He's passed along from one truly harrowing situation to the next, utterly defenseless and struggling to keep some sense of himself intact. It's not unlike the story of childhood itself: no matter how well or poorly you start out in life, someone can drag you off to a place where you aren't safe. You'll have no say in the matter, and after you've bravely assimilated to your new circumstances, someone else can come along and take you to a place of new and even greater peril.

"Once there was a princess who was very beautiful," Edward's owner, a little girl named Abilene, is told before bed. "She shone as bright as the stars on a moonless night. But what difference did it make that she was beautiful? None. No difference."

Because nothing makes any difference. Life is coming for you.

The rabbit learns humility and compassion in the course of his trials, but at such a high cost that I wished for him no more hard lessons. I wished for the imperious rabbit what I would wish for anyone: a little love, a little bit of safety and consistency. It turned out to be an enormous ask.

What kind of a writer puts an inanimate object at the center of a novel? Who would set herself up for such a task? And yet I'd been made to care about a china rabbit in such a way that I couldn't sleep. Nell Freudenberger was right: *The Miraculous Journey of Edward Tulane* is a perfect novel. It made no difference what age it was written for. I felt like I had found a magic portal, and all I'd had to do to pass through was believe that I wasn't too big to fit.

I went back to the store and got more Kate DiCamillo novels— *Raymie Nightingale* and *Because of Winn-Dixie* and *Flora & Ulysses*.

Not only were they beautifully written with gorgeous narrative arcs, there was something emotionally satisfying about being able to read a book in one sitting. The plots twisted in ways I didn't see coming, and did not shy away from despair (obviously) or joy or strangeness (see: squirrel who can type). They were, each one, sui generis, each one extraordinary.

And so I decided to read all of Kate DiCamillo's books, because I loved them, because I felt bad about having ignored them, because I was mystified by the scope and energy of her imagination. The novels fall into two camps—tragic childhood and magical animals—though there's plenty of overlap, inasmuch as the realistic tales of children slogging their way through the complex and painful landscape of adults almost always contain at least a moment of solace from an animal, and the stories of magic animals (or their china incarnations) never lose sight of the suffering children.

Along with the novels, I read the chapter books for early readers, a series called Tales from Deckawoo Drive that features an assortment of lost souls, including two elderly sisters, Eugenia and Baby Lincoln, one a bully and the other bullied. When the bullied sister strikes out to find independence, the result is *Where Are You Going, Baby Lincoln?* I wouldn't have thought it was possible to write a book for young children about an old woman getting on a train because she wants to experience a moment of autonomy. She wants to take a Necessary Journey. I hadn't understood that this particular emptiness and longing was a part of life children would be able to understand.

But a story is all in the telling, and these stories are expertly told.

I didn't read the books in any sort of order. I didn't finish the

Deckawoo Drives and then start on the Mercy Watsons (stories of an amiable house pig who likes hot buttered toast—those are written for even younger readers). I skipped around. I bought the backlist in its entirety and carted them home. Whenever I finished a stack, I passed them along to a young neighbor, who in turn drew me thank-you notes.

Somewhere in the DiCamillo immersion, I got very sick, that kind of winter sickness that lasts a month or more, the kind of sick that seemed bad because it happened before COVID. I took a particular comfort in the books when I was awake. Kate DiCamillo's work bursts with loyalty, the fierce loyalty of childhood that makes you stick a pin in your finger so that you can hold your blood tight to the blood of your friend as a symbol of your unbreakable bond. The suffering and cruelty the characters endure was a kind of clear, bright bell. How could she be telling these stories to children? Ah, yes, because children suffer. We had grown up and grown out of it, while they were still in the dark woods, listening for the voice of solidarity.

I went to those dark woods again. Sometimes I was moved and other times, honestly, I felt ill just having to remember.

I don't remember at what point I reached *The Magician's Elephant.* I want to say it was the end of my journey, the last DiCamillo left in the stack, but that's probably me turning this into a fairy tale, which is fine. In a very real sense, it is a fairy tale. *The Magician's Elephant* turned out to be my favorite of all of the books. It's the story of a girl in an orphanage, her loyal brother, and an elephant brought into a life of bondage by a magician who simply made a mistake. I was reading in bed and Karl had fallen asleep. I kept my light on. It was New Year's Eve.

Before he came to serve Madame LaVaughn, however, Hans Ickman had lived in a small town in the mountains, and he had there a family: brothers, a mother and a father, and a dog who was famous for being able to leap across the river that ran through the woods beyond town.

The river was too wide for Hans Ickman and his brothers to leap across. It was wide even for a grown man to leap. But the dog would take a running jump and sail effortlessly across the water. She was a white dog and small, and other than her ability to jump the river, she was in no way extraordinary.

Hans Ickman, as he aged, had forgotten about the dog entirely; her miraculous ability had receded to the back of his mind. But the night the elephant came crashing through the ceiling of the opera house, the manservant remembered again, for the first time in a long time, the little white dog.

Standing in the prison, listening to the endless and unvarying exchange between Madame LaVaughn and the magician, Hans Ickman thought about being a boy, waiting on the bank of the river with his brothers, and watching the dog run and then fling herself into the air. He remembered how, in mid-leap, she would always twist her body, a small unnecessary gesture, a fillip of joy, to show that this impossible thing was easy for her.

MY OWN DOG Rose had been just such a dog—small and white and talented. It was late and I was sick and now my mind was full of my beloved dog long passed. I'd never forgotten her, but still, I'd forgotten so many things. These books had given me the means to look backwards. I marveled at the resilience of children who were strong enough to read such sad and beautiful novels full of prisons and dungeons and hunger and sorrow and knives. I marveled at the resilience of children for their ability to survive their own childhoods with joy.

Any Kate DiCamillo novel I started I would finish that same night. They take only an hour or two to read. A hundred pages later, not too far from the end, I came to this:

> *The manservant looked into the boy's eyes and saw himself, young again and still capable of believing in miracles, standing on the bank of the river with his brothers, the white dog suspended in midair.*
>
> *"Please," said the boy.*
>
> *And suddenly it came to Hans Ickman, the name of the little white dog. Rose. She was called Rose. And remembering it was like fitting a piece of a puzzle into place.*

ROSE. A LITTLE white dog named Rose.

I remembered what it had felt like as a child to read a book and be certain the author was speaking directly to me. The work of Kate DiCamillo had opened something in me, an ability to see and feel things that were very far from me now. It was midnight when I read the last page and turned out the light. Still awake, I asked my little dog Rose to come back, and she did, running. She had been waiting for me to call. She was perfect in her joy and I held her and kissed her. I called for my father then, just to see, and he came to me too, and took me in his arms, me and my little dog. My father was nothing but love, a love so certain and pure there was no space to doubt it. I called for my grandmother, my dearest Lucy, my stepfather, and each one came and folded me in her arms, in his arms. There never had been a moment like this in my life, so much love, and all of it free from doubt or exhaustion or misunderstanding. This love had always been there, it would always be there, no matter how I rewrote it or forgot it. I stood inside my gratitude and cried until finally I fell sleep.

That's what I got from these books, the ability to walk through the door where everything I thought had been lost was in fact waiting for me. All of it. The trick was being brave enough to look. The books had given me that bravery, which is another way of saying the ability to believe.

· Sisters ·

I was probably ten the first time a cashier in the grocery store asked my mother and me if we were sisters. At the time I thought that the cashier meant we resembled one another, and to some extent that was true. I was a blonde and fair like my mother, with small shoulders, but my eyes were green and hers were blue. My sister had brown hair and skin that tanned to gold just by walking out the door. People were much less likely to ask my mother and my sister if they were sisters, though surely that had to do with the fact that my sister was three and a half years older than I was and made it her personal mission to never be with us in the grocery store. (No one ever asked my sister and me if we were sisters, probably because we *were* sisters, and even though we didn't much resemble one another when we were growing up, the electrical current that ran between us was self-evident.) The question posed by the cashier was a compliment for me—your mother is beautiful—but mostly it was meant as a compliment for her: You look so young! How could you be the mother of this big girl?

My mother was twenty-six when I was born, and her twenties was the decade in which she took up indefinite residence. Her youthfulness was such that she was carded in bars late into her forties. Everyone got older but her. When I was in high school, I wore one of her nightgowns to the prom. She was out of town and I didn't know it was a nightgown. As far as I was concerned it was just another great dress hanging in her closet. (Note: my mother hung up her nightgowns.) Later, when I told my mother about the dress, and she told me what I'd done, my friends and I all laughed about it. Her nightgown was better looking than their prom dresses. My friends were all in love with my mother, with her zip-up boots and E-type Jaguar and her thick yellow ponytail. My mother would write notes for anyone who had spent the night at our house and was late for school the next morning. "She's more like a sister," my friends would say, not meaning that we looked like one another.

By the time I was in college, whatever resemblance we had shared before was harder to see—not exactly gone and no longer obvious. My hair had faded to a color I liked to call "dead mouse" and I'd put on weight, two things that hadn't happened to my mother. I was a little taller than she was. I no longer fit into her clothes. I came home from school and the bank teller stared at us earnestly, as if she were coming upon someone she couldn't quite place. "Are you two sisters?" she asked. And that was exactly what she meant: Are the two of you the offspring of one set of parents?

My mother, who looked like a cross between a Hitchcock heroine and one of John Derek's wives, had drawn a winning ticket from the genetic lottery. Had she followed my example and done nothing more than wash her face and walk out the door in the morning, she would still have been the most beautiful woman you would see on any given day, but my mother left nothing to chance. She skipped desserts and dinner rolls, was fully committed to moisturizer and sunscreen. She had a collection of silk tap pants and camisoles, teddies, chemises in every color, and when she changed her clothes, she started at the beginning and changed her lingerie as well, the things no one would see, because the lingerie was all part of it. The best hours of my childhood were spent sitting on the edge of the bathtub watching her put on her makeup and roll her hair. The bag boys in the grocery store argued over who would push her cart out to her car, and once or twice the winner tried to kiss her. She had to have checks printed without her phone number because the man in the liquor store would call and ask her on dates. Was gorgeousness such a rarity in those days? In restaurants someone would inevitably come to the table to tell us, just in case we didn't know, that my mother was a vision—truly, they had never seen anyone like her. My mother would thank the person while the rest of us kept eating.

I grew up, grew older. I didn't color my hair or buy mascara. I aspired to a look that was clean, well-kempt, invisible, and in this I was successful. I had seen the benefits and costs of beauty and decided to pass. A lucky call on my part, since even though I was nice enough looking, I possessed neither the raw material nor the volition to try to improve what I had to work with. I like to think my mother's beauty saved me time, by which I mean years and years of my life. Despite all indications to the contrary, most women harbor some secret hope that they might be beautiful, that the right dress or lipstick or diet could turn the tide in their favor. As someone who had lived so close to exceptional beauty, I harbored no such illusions.

People love to believe that beautiful women are narcissists, and that they'll be punished for what they've unfairly received. While she was certainly punished for her beauty by jealous husbands and envious friends (and by her older sister, who liked to announce to anyone who would listen that my mother got the looks but she—the sister—had gotten all the brains), my mother was never a narcissist. She worked as a nurse for most of her life. She possessed an uncanny knack for comforting people, for knowing the right thing to say, and knowing when to say nothing at all. Men liked her best, but so did dogs and children. She was funny and kind and, no matter what her sister would tell you, smart. She was also beautiful.

As I moved through my thirties and forties, my sisterhood with my mother became a given. The questions were no longer questions, they were statements of fact. When someone said, "Sisters, right?" I said, "You got it." In fact, I was starting to be the older sister. I could imagine a time when I would be the mother.

If my mother was the one who answered the question, she always told the truth. She was the progenitor after all—she was proud of me. Once, when I was in my forties, we stopped by my publishing house in New York to drop off some papers. The security guard at the desk took our IDs. "You two sisters?" he asked suspiciously.

"She's my daughter," my mother said.

The man handed us back our driver's licenses and looked at me. "What are you doing wrong?"

I laughed. "You're supposed to ask her what she's doing right."

"I know what I said." His tone was flat, accusatory. "I said what are you doing wrong?"

Every now and then I did it right, and that's when trained professionals were paid to do it for me. When I was on television or had my picture taken for a magazine, other people dressed me in clothes that weren't mine and then someone else straightened, curled and sprayed my hair while a third person painted an entirely new face on top of my face. Then even I must admit I looked something like my mother. Sometimes I went to see my mother after being photographed as an author and we went out to lunch before I could get hold of a washcloth and scrub my face. The twenty-six years my mother had on me could almost balance out the inequality, assuming we were both wearing a layer of makeup. The waitress put her hand to her heart. "Seriously?" she said. "Are you two twins?"

"Sisters," I said.

We came close to evening out one other time, and that was when my mother was sick. It happened before she turned eighty. She had such a terrible pain beneath her lower ribs that I drove her to the hospital in a rainstorm, in the middle of the night—no time for makeup, no time to pack. The doctor in the emergency room sent her straight to the intensive care unit, where we stayed for a week. She slept in a bed inside a glass room and I slept in a chair beside her. She was diagnosed with a walled-off infection in her upper duodenum. She sweated through her nightgown and sheets, and shook so hard I would climb into her bed and hold her. Doctors and nurses and phlebotomists and the housekeeping staff moved through her fishbowl room every fifteen minutes to check on one thing or another, and there they observed the two pale women in a single bed who didn't eat or sleep or wash but who lay together, arms around waists like a mother and daughter, in bed beneath the buzzing fluorescent lights. It would be safe to say we had never looked worse.

"You look so much alike," the nurse would say quietly, not wanting to disturb us more than we were already disturbed.

"Like sisters?" I asked.

She shook her head. "No," she said. "Like the same person."

· These Precious Days ·

I can tell you when it all started because I remember the moment exactly. It was late and I'd just finished the novel I'd been reading. A few more pages would send me off to sleep, so I went in search of a short story. They aren't hard to come by around here: my office is made up of piles of books, mostly advance-reader copies that have been sent to me in hopes I'll write a quote for the jacket. They arrive daily in padded mailers—novels, memoirs, essays, histories— things I never requested and in most cases will never get to. On this summer night in 2017, I picked up a collection called *Uncommon Type* by Tom Hanks. It had been languishing in a pile by the dresser for a while and I'd left it there, based on an unarticulated prejudice that actors should stick to acting. Now for no particular reason I changed my mind. Why shouldn't Tom Hanks write short stories? Why shouldn't I read one? Off we went to bed, the book and I, and in doing so put the chain of events into motion. The

230

story had begun without my realizing it. The first door opened and I walked through.

But any story that starts will also end. This is the way novelists think—beginning, middle, and end.

In case you haven't read it, *Uncommon Type* is a very good book. It would have to be for this story to continue. Had it been a bad book, or just a good-enough book, I would have put it down, but page after page, it surprised me. Two days later I sent an endorsement to the editor. I've written plenty of jacket quotes in my day, mostly for first-time writers of fiction who I believed could benefit from the assistance. The thought of Tom Hanks benefiting from my assistance struck me as funny, and then I forgot about it.

Or I would have forgotten about it, except that I got a call from Tom Hanks's publicist a few weeks later, asking if I would fly to DC in October to interview the actor onstage as part of his book tour. As the co-owner of a bookstore I do this sort of thing, and while I mostly do it in Nashville where I live, there have certainly been times when the request was interesting enough that I've gotten on a plane. I could have said I was busy writing a novel, which would have been both ridiculous and true. Tom Hanks needs a favor? Happy to help.

"Do you even realize your life isn't normal?" Niki said to me when I announced the news of my trip. Niki has opinions about my life. "You understand that other people don't live this way?"

HOW OTHER PEOPLE live is pretty much all I think about. Curiosity is the rock upon which fiction is built. But for all the times people have wanted to tell me their story because they think it would make a wonderful novel, it pretty much never works out. People are not characters, no matter how often we tell them they are; conversations are not dialogue; and the actions of our days don't add up to a plot. In life, time runs along in its sameness, but in fiction time is condensed—one action springboards into another, greater action. Cause and effect are so much clearer in novels than in life. You might not see how everything threads together as you read along, but when you look back from the end of the story, the map becomes clear. Maybe Niki was right about my life being different, but maybe that's because I tend to think of things in terms of story: I pick up a book and read it late into the night, and because I like the book, I'm asked to interview the author who is also an actor.

I went to DC by myself. I was going only for the night. I walked from my hotel to the theater and showed my identification to a guard, who led me to the crowded green room. I met the hosts of the event and a few people who worked for them. I was introduced to Tom Hanks's editor, Tom Hanks's agent, his publicist, his assistant, Tom Hanks himself. He was tall and slim, happily at ease, answering questions, signing books. Everyone was laughing at his jokes because his jokes were funny. In the small room the people around him arranged themselves into different configurations so that the assistant could take their pictures, each one handing over his or her cell phone. Audience questions arrived on index cards, were read aloud and sorted through. The ones Tom Hanks approved of were handed to me. I would ask them at the end of the event, depending on how much time was left. The green-room crowd was then escorted to their seats in the theater and we were ushered to the dark place behind the curtain to wait, Tom Hanks, his assistant, and I. The assistant was a tiny woman wearing a fitted evening coat with saucer-sized peonies embroidered onto black velvet. "Such a beautiful coat," I said to her. We'd been introduced when I first arrived, but I didn't remember her name.

The experience of waiting backstage in the dark just before an event is always the same. I can never quite hear what the person making the introduction is saying out on the stage, and for a minute I wouldn't be able to tell you the name of the theater or even the city I was in. There's usually a guy working the light board and the mics who'll talk to me for a minute, though that night the guy talking to me was Tom Hanks. He wanted to know if I liked owning a bookstore. He was thinking about opening one himself. Could we talk about it sometime? Of course we could. We were about to go on.

"I don't have any questions," I whispered in the darkness. "I find these things go better if you just wing it." Then the two of us stepped out into the blinding light.

The first thing he said to the audience once the roaring thunder of approval eased was, "She doesn't have any *questions*." He pointed to me.

WHEN THE EVENT was over and more pictures had been taken and everyone had said how much they'd enjoyed absolutely everything, Tom Hanks and his assistant and I found ourselves alone again, the three of us at the end of a long concrete passageway by the stage door, saying good night and goodbye. A car was coming to pick them up.

"Come on, Sooki," he said, his voice gone grand. "Let's go back to the hotel. I need to find a Belvedere martini."

I hoped he would ask me to join them. I'd spent two hours on a stage talking to Tom Hanks, and now I wanted to talk to Sooki.

Sooki of the magnificent coat. She said almost nothing and yet my eye kept going to her, the way one's eye goes to the flash of iridescence on a hummingbird's throat. I thought of how extraordinarily famous a person would have to be to have someone like that working as their assistant.

Neither of them asked me out for drinks.

AGAIN, IT WOULD appear that story had reached its conclusion, but a few months passed and I got an e-mail from Tom Hanks early one morning. He was in Nashville. Could I meet him at the bookstore in half an hour? I couldn't. My friend Sister Nena had just called. She'd fallen down some stairs outside of church the night before and twisted her foot and now that foot was swollen and sore. She needed me to take her to the hospital for an X-ray.

I e-mailed him back. "I've got to take care of my nun."

"*Your* nun?" he wrote (as opposed to what most people would say: "Your *nun*?").

I told Sister Nena the whole story while we sat in the waiting room, her foot propped up on the edge of a wheelchair. She was disappointed. "I want to meet Tom Hanks," she said.

I called the bookstore to let them know Tom Hanks was on his way over. He thrilled them, buying stacks of books, signing books, taking pictures, going next door to the Donut Den for an apple fritter. I had missed my chance, but months later there he was again. His wife, Rita Wilson, is a singer who writes with people in Nashville. (In Nashville, songwriting is a group activity.) It turned out Tom and Rita came to town less than regularly but more than I would have guessed. On this visit we sat in the cramped office at Parnassus and talked about the bookstore he might want to open in Santa Monica while my dog slept in his lap. I was already years ahead of myself, thinking of all the good Tom Hanks could do for independent bookstores. Could any business wish for a better spokesperson?

Here's a Universal Truth: people are interested in helping Tom Hanks. Our hearts have been filled with the comfort his films have given us, and that, coupled with the fact that he's a nice man, made it easy to line up a group of booksellers who were ready to pitch in. But over time the idea drifted to the back burner. When we were in touch, it was less about bookstores and more about books. One more reason to like Tom Hanks: he's a reader. He recommends books and asks for recommendations. I had just finished my own novel, and on a lark of the highest order, I sent him an e-mail asking if he might record the audiobook. He responded:

[MAR.17.19] Hey! I'm in Albuquerque shooting a movie. I'd love to do your audiobook! But when? I have limited time as I work till mid May, then leave the US in June until I come back to start another movie in September. So what are the deadlines, days needed, etc? Books are fun!

I sat at my desk trying to make sense of this: time when there was no time, and talent all out of proportion to the task. It hadn't occurred to me that he might say yes. Had I thought it through in the first place, I never would have had the nerve to ask. A year and a half had passed since I had picked up his book in my office, and this was where it had taken me: Tom Hanks was willing to narrate *The Dutch House*.

I'd been in touch with Sooki once or twice when Tom was thinking of opening a bookstore in Santa Monica, and now I pinned my hopes on her as she dug into his schedule at Playtone, his production company. Wonderful Sooki! She made the time, stitching days together. As we worked our way through trying to get contracts signed and making arrangements with the audio producer, our e-mails became an affectionate exchange.

[APR.30.19] I imagine your kindness comes from you being kind. Just a guess.

[APR.30.19] My kindness comes from sincerely wanting this recording to happen. I am a huge fan of your work (and Tom's, of course) and it just thrills me that you are collaborating on this! So happy to be the connector of good things.

This sort of thing wasn't out of the ordinary for me, as I'm sure it wasn't for her. E-mail tilts towards the overly familiar. I tilt towards the overly familiar.

Sooki had two young grandchildren in San Diego and made plans to bring them to an event I was doing there for my new children's book, but they didn't show. I lost her for a while, and then she was back again. She apologized for her late response, saying that she'd had a medical procedure and hadn't been in the office.

I asked if she was okay. I had met Sooki, after all. We'd stood together in the dark of a Washington theater for a matter of minutes a year and a half before. I had admired her coat, those pink peonies as big as my hand.

[MAY.21.19] Thank you for your concern about my medical procedure. I am doing my best to keep it pushed off to the side, but

I was diagnosed with pancreatic cancer in November (caught it early) so I've been dealing with surgeries and chemo. I'm still here—at Playtone and in general.

She had been diagnosed with pancreatic cancer a year after we met. There was no reason she would have told me this. We didn't know each other, and for the most part our correspondence had come after this defining fact. Ours was an ephemeral connection common to the modern world. Except it was Sooki, and I liked her very much.

A week later, Tom Hanks began recording *The Dutch House* at a studio in Los Angeles. Sooki went with him every day. She sent updates—chapter eight now, chapter twelve. The director of the audiobook sent me an article about Sooki from a 1978 issue of *New York* magazine. Sooki had gone to work for the New York City Department of Health, Bureau of Animal Affairs, right out of college. She was the bat squad. She was Batgirl. The pictures of Sooki at twenty-two showed a beautiful dark-eyed girl, her gloved hands holding a bat and a net while standing on somebody's desk in little canvas tennis shoes. I was struck by an overwhelming sense of wishing I knew her, of not wanting to miss Sooki while she was here.

. . .

THIS IS WHAT it's like to write a novel: I come up with a shred of an idea. It can be a character, a place, a moral quandary. In the case of *The Dutch House*, I'd started to think about a poor woman who suddenly became rich, and because she was unable to deal with the change in her circumstances, she left her family and went to India to follow a guru.

Sister Nena shook her head. "Not a guru. She's Catholic. She doesn't have to go to India. She helps the poor like Dorothy Day."

We were sitting at the bar at California Pizza Kitchen at four o'clock in the afternoon. It was our place, what Sister Nena referred to as "vacation." She ordered the house merlot and I had a seltzer with cranberry juice. She wanted to know about the book I was going to write next, the book I had just barely started thinking about.

"This woman goes to India," I said.

"She could be a nun." Sister Nena picked up a piece of bread and swiped it through the olive oil in the saucer between us.

I shook my head. "She's married," I said. "She has children. She has to have children."

"It could happen. Plenty of nuns were married before."

"They were widows, not divorced."

"You never know." Then she looked at me, her face suddenly brightened by a plot twist. "She could work for Mother Teresa. If she really wanted to go to India and she wanted to serve the poor, that's what she would do."

I wasn't sure why I was negotiating my character's future with my friend, but there I was, listening. Did my character want to be a nun?

When I'm putting together a novel, I leave all the doors and windows open so the characters can come in and just as easily leave. I don't take notes. Once I start writing things down, I feel like I'm nailing the story in place. When I rely on my imperfect memory, the pieces are free to move. The main character I was certain of starts to drift, and someone I've barely noticed moves in to fill the space. The road forks and forks again. It becomes a path into the woods. It becomes the woods. I find a stream and follow it, the stream dries up, and I'm left to look for moss on the sides of trees. For a time, the mother in this novel went to India to work for Mother Teresa. I tried it out but it didn't work. What about the children who were left behind in that house she hated? What became of them? And what about the women who cleaned that house, who fixed those children their dinner? The ones who stayed turned out to be the ones I was interested in.

Putting together a novel is essentially putting together the lives of strangers I'm coming to know. In some ways it's not unlike putting together my own life. I think I know what I'm doing when in truth I have no idea. I just keep moving forward. By the time the book is written, there's little evidence of the initial spark or a long-ago conversation in California Pizza Kitchen. Still, I'm able, for a while at least, to pick up the thread and walk it back. Everything looks so logical going backwards—*Yes, of course, that's what we did*—but going forward it's something else entirely. Going forward, the lights may as well be off.

· · ·

SOOKI AND I kept up a sporadic e-mail exchange once the audiobook was done. I thought of her time as precious now. We wrote about painting because she painted. I sent her books on color theory. We wrote about artists we liked, about Pantone and the color wheel. *Dear* gave way to *Dearest*; *Love* became *Much love*. Then this:

[JUNE.21.19] As of last week, my 6-month chemo run is done, and I had a follow-up CT scan. My doctor paired up some words I never thought I would hear together: "pancreatic cancer" and "you're in remission!" It seems like an early declaration, but I'll take it! Here's to more time to explore color and enjoy all the people—like you—who make life colorful.

LATER IN THE summer she had radiation, just to be safe.

[AUG.5.19] Radiation has become a fascinating routine over the last 5 weeks. 22 sessions down and 6 to go. Only on weekdays and not on the Fourth of July, because apparently cancer knows to take weekends off and observe federal holidays.

I leave the house at 6:30am every weekday morning to make it down to the bottom basement—floor 2B—at UCLA's Westwood Medical Center by 7:30am. There is a bright therapist named Hassan at my assigned machine, always the same, with a sweet attitude. He has me repeat my name, birth date and area-of-radiation each time before I enter the room. I want to envision it as a healing room, but it reminds me of a meat locker: freezing cold—I'm guessing the temperature favors the delicate machinery—with a rack of blue torsos lined up on hooks. My blue torso, the mold made on the day I came in for my fitting and tattoos, is already on the radiation bed and I need to bare my abdomen and slide onto the table so they can line up the laser beams with all my tattoos and red-sharpie X's before they cover me with a warmed flannel sheet.

I was impressed that first day when the therapists swarmed

the table forming the mold around me and explaining about tattoos. I was told that although not everyone wanted to commit to having the tattoos, it was the most accurate way to align the radiation field that had been so meticulously laid out by a team of physicists working alongside my radiation oncologist. The only other option was to go with "stickers" which could shift or come off in the shower. Of course I opted for tattoos. Precision seemed like a good decision here. Three blue tattoos on the same plane as my prominent abdominal scar, it would hardly matter. So, I was surprised on my first scheduled day of radiation to have another technician pop in with a red sharpie to make three large X's near the tattoos as additional points of reference and stick clear round stickers over them.

Now I look like an improvised elementary school art project, and in addition to owning my permanent tattoos, I have to nurture my three little stickers and hand-drawn sharpie marks so they last 6 weeks. I feel like I could pop into Trader Joe's and have them replaced with those happy little stickers they hand out to well-behaved children—it undermines my confidence in the sophisticated nature of the whole process just a bit.

I sent more books: books I'd written, books I thought she'd like, Kate DiCamillo books to be read with her grandchildren. In return she sent me pictures she'd taken of Los Angeles: a woman in an orange sari sailing past a city bus on a bicycle. The world that Sooki inhabited was electrified by greens and blues, purple bougainvillea draping over hot-pink walls, colors too vivid to be explained. She would pour color into my in-box for a while and then be gone again. Winter came without a word. I worried, and thought it was not my place to ask. Did Tom even know Sooki and I had become friends? Would he think to tell me if something had happened? I wanted to say hello very quietly so as not to bother her. I didn't want to be one more person tugging at her coat, but I was.

[DEC.27.19] Sweetest Ann, I am traveling today—just for the day—up to Stanford for a second opinion, with the magician's elephant in my carry-on bag.

I didn't need to hear about the first opinion to know what that meant. I said good luck because what else was there to say? Could I say that I would like to come and see her? That I would like to meet her in the way I had wanted to meet my pen pals as a child? This was what I knew about Sooki: She lived in Los Angeles. She had a son and a daughter-in-law with two children who lived south of her and a daughter and son-in-law who had recently moved north. She painted. She once caught bats for the City of New York. She worked for Tom Hanks. She had cancer.

I saw Tom and Rita two more times in Nashville. The second time they came because Rita was singing at the Grand Ole Opry. Karl and I sat in a dressing room with them for an hour and a half between sets. Dionne Warwick came in with her son. We talked about singing and touring and about the Opry. I told them that when I was a child, my sister and I would come to the Ryman on Friday and Saturday nights with the man who was then the house doctor at the Opry. He would bring us with his own two small girls, and the four of us would sit in the coils of power cords backstage and fall asleep in dressing rooms, in this dressing room. Every childhood is strange in its own way.

[FEB.7.20] When last we typed you were on your way to Stanford for a second opinion. I think about you often and hope for the best. Much love. Ann

[FEB.8.20] I have wanted to write—every day—for forever. As I got ready to send the details of my second opinion, I was already looking to the third opinion and rethinking the story.

My cancer marker—CA 19-9—is nonspecific to pancreatic cancer (it can indicate other inflammation in the body) but, it's an indicator and is supposed to be at 35 U/L or less. It was normal in October, 3 months post-chemo and radiation—great news—but then started rising.

It has been an exercise in creative storytelling to try to think up more and more reasons why the number might rise while the scans (CT's! MRI's! PET scans) were showing no sign of disease. I looked up every anomaly online, settling on too much black tea, or maybe the wrong color shoes. As the number spiked this week at 1700 U/L, I ran out of excuses, and my PET/CT scan on Wednesday showed a return of the cancer to my liver.

I am now sitting at the airport waiting to catch a plane to my next opinion, at Sloan Kettering in NY. (It was not reassuring to know that one of the nurses at UCLA thought that "Sloan Kettering" was the name of the doctor I'd be seeing.) It looks like I'll have chemo and maybe a clinical trial ahead. I will keep you more closely posted as I move ahead (in the right color shoes).

The last few months, the oncologists were watching the numbers and Western medicine offered nothing to do but to wait and see where the cancer showed up. I was convinced it wouldn't show up and embarked on a full scale exploratory mission into holistic healing, prayer, juicing, yoga, meditation, sound waves and magnetic magic (this last one, highly recommended by a friend, but in a clinic run by a reality tv star). I gained back 20 pounds, and have been back hiking the trails and at work full time. I feel great.

But the doctors say, as they expected, the cancer is back, and they are ready to start up chemo again.

My reading on this flight is a book called "Radical Remission." I am hopeful and feeling radical.

I promise to be a more reliable friend and pen pal. I miss our e-mails.

Much love,

Sooki

That night as my husband and I walked our dog around the block in the cold dark, I told him about Sooki. This was what we did at the end of the day. "Tell me the news of the great world," Karl would say when he came home from work, and since many were the days I didn't leave the house, I relied on books and phone calls and e-mails to have something to contribute. As Sparky stopped and sniffed, I offered up Sooki's recurrence as a story to tell, not a problem to solve. Sooki had been treated at UCLA, Stanford, Duke, and Sloan Kettering. This wasn't about an inability to get good medical care; it was about not being able to find a clinical trial for recurrent pancreatic cancer that both matched her cancer and could take her into the study immediately. The months she'd lost not being in chemo while they struggled to locate the new tumor had put her perilously behind in her treatment.

"Tell me how you know her again?" he asked.

I told him she worked for Tom Hanks, that we'd struck up a little friendship over e-mail.

Karl said she should send him her records if she wanted to, and that he would talk to Johanna Bendell, an oncologist at the hospital where he worked. He said they were running more trials for pancreatic cancer than Sloan Kettering.

I had thought this was a story about Tom Hanks, the friendly actor-writer who had recorded my book, but I was mistaken. I kept up with a great number of people and I didn't remember to what extent I'd told Karl Sooki's story before, and if I had told him, I didn't know if he'd been listening, but now I had his full attention. To introduce Karl into this narrative as a general internist (he calls himself a "pediatrician for adults") would be reductive. Simply put, Karl makes rain. He solves the problems that other people have tried and failed to solve for years. Other doctors are quick to do him favors because he's done so many favors for them. He holds a kind of medical currency, saved then spent, and when needed, he can marshal all necessary parties into immediate action, bringing them together so fast that whatever needs to happen can happen yesterday.

I told him about Sooki that night, but it was equally possible that I wouldn't have. He didn't know her, and I didn't exactly know her either. I made it a point not to tell Karl sad medical stories at the end of his long day of sad medical stories. I might have chosen to let it go had there been something else to talk about, maybe his mother or my mother or the spigot that had frozen in the garage. I might have forgotten to mention Sooki altogether, because even though I followed her story with interest and concern, it was one of many stories. But I didn't forget. I told him.

When we got home from our walk, I e-mailed Sooki and said if she wanted Karl to check on the possibility of a trial in Nashville, she should send her files.

• • •

NOTHING IS MORE interesting than time: the days that are endless, the days that get away. Certain days of the distant past remain so vivid to me I could walk back into them and pick up the conversation in mid-sentence, while other days (weeks, months, people, places) I couldn't recall to save my life. One of the last things I understand when I'm putting a novel together is the structure of time. When does the story start and when does it end? Will time be linear or can it stutter and skip and circle back? At what point does our understanding of the action shift?

• • •

WE HAVE COME to the point in this story when time changes. It had been over two years since I met Sooki in a theater in Washington. We had never spoken on the phone. The number of e-mails we'd exchanged could be printed out and slid into a single manila envelope. But the clinical trial she needed was here in Nashville at the hospital where my husband worked. Karl's friend Dr. Bendell knew Sooki's oncologist at UCLA and her oncologist at Stanford and her surgeon at Duke. They reviewed her records together. I was copied on a barrage of e-mails I had no business reading, reports of molecular profiling, adenocarcinoma, tumor tissue for genetic analysis. I now knew that she'd had a Whipple procedure at Duke, and six months of Folfirinox followed by twenty-eight days of radiation over five and a half weeks at UCLA. UCLA had plans to start the same clinical trial that was up and running in Nashville, but not for another month or two, a unit of time that could not be lost to waiting. Plans were made for Sooki to come to Nashville. I told her I would pick her up at the airport. I told her, of course, that she would stay with us.

Let's go back to Karl for a minute.

This wasn't the first time I'd invited someone we didn't know to live with us. I once invited the daughter of a woman who ran the Pittsburgh Arts and Lectures series to live with us after she'd found a job in Nashville and couldn't find an apartment. Nell stayed for six months, and we loved her. Patrick, who lives in a tiny apartment in New York, spends a couple of weeks with us every year, writing in our basement—which, for the record, is nothing like a basement. He uses the library table to spread out his pages. Writers who come to read at the bookstore are often stashed in the guest room. Karl has never once complained. He claims our lives are better for all the people I bring into the house. He thanks me for it. Still, I wanted to double-check. Sooki was coming to be a patient, and more than a little of the work was going to fall to him. I e-mailed to ask how he would feel about me extending the invitation to stay.

[FEB.14.20] PS—Just to be clear, I ran all this by Karl first, who said, "I favor having her here." (Very Karl.)

[FEB.14.20] Oh, Ann. I don't even know how to respond to such generosity.

I would love to stay with you for my first night or two in Nashville—it would be wonderful to spend some time with you.

Once I'm there for chemo, I will find a place where I won't be worried about being a good houseguest. I just can't stand the thought of being so disruptive to your and Karl's (and Sparky's!) lives. I know that after my last round of chemo I would sometimes get up and eat in the middle of the night, or get up early and make noisy smoothies. I'm self-conscious about being in the way, especially if I'm not at my best through chemo. I just would worry too much about being a bad friend.

My husband, Ken, will come down for at least part of the time, once I've started chemo, and I may have other visitors, so I think I will explore some other options in the area, but I can't tell you how touched I am that you've extended the offer.

Sooki was married? I had pictured her going through this alone, a conclusion I reached based on a lack of information and a florid imagination. Had I known she had a husband, might I have assumed that she was taken care of and so not followed the story as closely? I tried to find a place for this new factor in the equation and all I could come up was the obvious—I didn't know her. I didn't know how old she was, I couldn't remember her face, but there have been few moments in my life when I have felt so certain: I was supposed to help. I was overcome by a sense of order in the world: if I hadn't chosen that book, if I hadn't gone to DC, if we hadn't stayed in just enough contact for her to tell me a year after the fact that she had had cancer, and if I hadn't mentioned it to Karl, she wouldn't have found her way to the only clinical trial in the country that both matched her cancer and could take her in immediately. I wrote again.

[FEB.15.20] I will try to keep this quick as I know you have many fish to fry.

I hear you, and I know that if I were in your shoes and you were asking me to stay with you it would seem impossible. But I think once you're here and see the set-up you'll understand. The bottom floor of the house is an apartment, separate entrance, no kitchen. We call it The VanDevender Home for Wayward Girls. There is another guest suite on the main floor and we live on the top floor. There are people here all the time. You will not be called upon to be a good guest.

I live 14 minutes from the airport and five minutes from the hospital. I will pick you up very late on Tuesday and take you to see Johanna on Wednesday. Kate DiCamillo is coming later on Wednesday. You will love her. We are Southern, and it is like this here, always. Some people stay for months. It's like a Nöel Coward play but not as witty.

I didn't know you had a husband!! What a good idea. Ken will like it here, too. Wait and see. And you will be surprised by how comforting it is to be very sick with an actual doctor upstairs. Karl is the king of the hospital. He'll make sure you get everything you need.

They can't do the Stanford biopsy here?

Much love.

We went back and forth. She agreed to come for a few nights, but after that she said she would rent a car and find a hotel. Ken would come later. I tried to imagine chemo while living in a hotel. Surely sadder things happened all the time, but none of them came to mind. Tavia was staying with us while this discussion was going on. "Don't worry about it," she said. "Once she gets here and sees the way things are, she'll be fine."

Because if I didn't know that Sooki had a husband, how much did she know about me, about us? Nothing. We would meet on the level playing field of affectionate strangers.

BEFORE COMING TO Nashville, Sooki had to go back to Stanford for another biopsy to track the genetic markers of her tumor. She arrived the following Sunday, February 23, just after Kate DiCamillo left. I had described my car, and she waved when I pulled up in front of the terminal. She looked like a tiny rock star in her shaggy pale-pink coat and sunglasses and high boots. She looked like Los Angeles in winter. We hugged, and I hefted her enormous suitcase into the hatchback.

What had been a theory—*Sooki should come to Nashville for her chemo*—was now a fact. There she was in the passenger seat, a shy person with a quiet voice. I asked her about her trip to Stanford, her flight to Nashville. She repeated her gratitude and I waved it away. We did our best to pretend that what we were doing was normal. I asked her if she had ever been to Nashville before, and she said yes, once, with Tom a long time ago. There had been a meeting of some sort. She'd been here for only a couple of hours.

I was leaving the next day for an event in New York. I would be gone for the night, and when I got back my friend Emma Straub was coming. Emma and I would be speaking at a librarians' convention downtown. I would leave again on Sunday for Virginia. I had warned Sooki about all of this before she arrived. Everything was planned so far in advance, and my spring was packed with speaking engagements. I would be in and out, other people would spend the night, which was fine, plenty of room for everyone. We would all proceed with our lives except that now we would be together.

I had invited someone I didn't know to live with us for an undetermined length of time, and I was leaving the day after she arrived, leaving it all to Karl. Even if it wasn't a perfect plan, it was better than doing nothing.

Karl was home from work when we arrived, and together we showed Sooki around—the sitting room downstairs, the library, her bedroom and bathroom. I had cut a small bouquet of the Lenten roses from the backyard and put them on the night table. I set out a bottle of water, a blue glass by the sink. I told her to take her time settling in. We would have dinner whenever she was ready. She gave us a giant furry blanket that I loved. She had brought a squeaky toy for Sparky.

"She seems very nice," Karl said once we were in the kitchen. As I was agreeing, she reappeared.

"I'm sorry to bother you," Sooki said, looking around. "But have you seen my phone? It looks like a little purse on a long strap?"

I asked her if she could have left it on the plane but no, of course not. I'd been in the cell phone waiting area and she'd called me from outside the airport. "Let's try the car."

The cell phone carrier also served as her wallet—her credit cards, cash, identification, insurance cards, everything important was together. We looked in the car. We looked downstairs and in the kitchen and the den. She had only been in the house for a few minutes; there hadn't been enough time to lose anything. She gave me the number and I called it from the house phone, hoping we'd hear it ring. A man answered. The phone had been turned in to airport security.

"I must have dropped it. It must have fallen off my shoulder when I got in the car." Sooki was a tiny thing, with thick brown hair and olive skin. She told me she had gained back the twenty pounds she'd lost after the last chemo but she couldn't have weighed a hundred pounds now. "If I can borrow your car, I'll drive back to the airport."

I shook my head. "Then you'd have to park. It would be a nightmare."

Karl said he would go.

"They aren't going to give you her wallet," I said. "Go together. Karl can pull up and you'll run in. You two go and I'll have dinner ready by the time you get back." It was the practical solution, and so they left. While they were gone I tried to imagine it: the cancer back, the wallet gone, strangers.

Or maybe it wasn't as bad as that. The phone hadn't been run over, nothing in the wallet was missing. Karl and Sooki came in the back door together in the middle of a conversation. They were talking like old friends. "Sooki's a pilot!" Karl said. He wanted to know why hadn't I told him this. How could I not have known? Karl had started flying in Mississippi when he was eight. He had a single-engine Cirrus that he kept at the small hobby airport not far from where we lived.

"My mother was a pilot," Sooki said, and there she was, suddenly at ease.

"Sooki got her pilot's license before she learned to drive," Karl told me.

"Whenever I came to an intersection I would look to the right, the left, then up and down."

I lit the candles on the table and served the cauliflower cake and tomato soup I'd made in the afternoon. The phone sat beside her on the table quietly—the prodigal returned—while we asked the kinds of questions people ask on first dates: Do you have siblings? What do your children do? Where were you born? All three of us had lost our fathers, all three of us were close to our mothers. Now that things were going right, I felt the jolt of how wrong they could have been. But this was right, and we would all be fine.

I FLEW TO New York early the next morning, took a car to New Jersey, signed several hundred books, attended a cocktail party where I raised money for the Booksellers Charitable Foundation, gave a talk in a crowded town hall, got to my hotel room in Manhattan at midnight, got up in the morning to tape a piece for the *Today* show, then was back on a plane. It was such a short trip it hardly counted as being gone.

The house smelled of chickpea stew and rice when I came in the door that night. Sooki was making dinner. She'd gone to the Indian restaurant and bought bread stuffed with apricots and dates. Everything was lit up bright, the table set. In the twenty-six years that Karl and I had been together, I'd never had the experience of coming home to dinner being made. It was a minor footnote considering everything I got from Karl, but still, the warmth of it, the love, to walk in the door after a long two days and see that someone had imagined that I might be hungry knocked me sideways. This was what marriage must look like from the other side.

Our lives ran the way they always did, but with the addition of a quiet person who did her best to take up little space and be as helpful as possible. We took turns cooking or we cooked together. Back before she came, when she was still insisting on finding a hotel, I asked her if we could talk for just a minute on the phone. I wanted to know what her worst fear about staying here was, and after a pause she told me she was a vegetarian. I laughed. I should have thought of that one myself. It's why I don't like to go to other people's houses for dinner: I never want to tell people I'm a vegetarian.

Karl found a giant bright blue tarp in the garage and Sooki spread it over the floor and table downstairs, setting herself up to paint. We kept a common grocery list on the kitchen counter. Writers still came and spent the night, bookstore events were still packed. Most mornings Sooki set out in the darkness to walk the two miles to a power yoga class that started at 6:30 in the morning, despite the presence of my car keys on the kitchen counter with explicit instructions to drive. She walked to the hospital for chemo and then walked home. Treatments were on Wednesdays—three Wednesdays on, one Wednesday off—with immunotherapy (which constituted the trial) added in every other week. They took ten vials of blood on one visit, twenty-eight vials the next. How did she have twenty-eight vials of blood in her? When her white count was too low to get treatment, she would run up and down the stairs at the hospital, down from the seventh floor to the first and back up again, over and over, and then get retested. Sooki had been a marathoner, though her best event was a 10K trail run. Those she won. Miraculously, after a spate of vigorous exercise there would be just enough white cells to slip her in under the wire.

She asked if that was cheating and was told not to worry about it. It meant she didn't have to sit out chemo for a week. She liked the team in Nashville. She loved Dr. Bendell. The treatments left her tired but she was managing. She was painting. She was doing every part of her job that could be done over e-mail or on the phone. This chemo wasn't the nightmare Folfirinox had been, the chemo that had treated her first round of cancer. The plan was that she could go home to Los Angeles on her week off, and once UCLA started the trial, she would go home permanently. We were loaded with plans in those days.

I was leaving for Virginia. At night in bed I asked Karl, how did he think this was going?

He put down his crossword puzzle. "It's an honor, really. I think about all the people who would want her to live with them. It's almost unbelievable that she's here with us."

It made me think of something our neighbor Jennie had said. Jennie and I walked our dogs together after dinner, and Sooki came with us most nights, unless she had a phone call to return, unless she wasn't feeling up to it. "Do you ever miss being alone in your house?" Jennie asked me once. "Just you and Karl?"

I thought about it for a minute, shook my head. "No, it's wonderful having her here."

"Well," Jennie said. "She does seem like a saint."

Sooki exuded such an air of self-sufficiency that I scarcely thought to worry about her. Maybe it had something to do with her job. She had worked for Tom for almost twenty years, and part of her responsibility was to go out on location before he arrived, find a place to stay in Morocco, get a driver, arrange for food, make a list of the local attractions if there was any free time, which usually there wasn't. Navigating her way around Nashville was small potatoes for someone who had put together a Thanksgiving dinner for a film crew in Berlin.

• • •

I WENT TO Virginia to see my friend Renée Fleming in concert. Afterwards we sat up at the hotel and talked about this new coronavirus, and whether the rest of her tour would be canceled. A couple of authors who were scheduled for events at the bookstore had already pulled out. At first we'd rolled our eyes, but now I was wondering if it would be melodramatic to cancel my book tour in Australia and New Zealand in April. I surely would go ahead with the dates I had scheduled in the States. "Don't go anywhere you wouldn't want to get stuck," a doctor friend had said to me. I didn't want to get stuck in Auckland, but if flights were canceled and I was stranded in Tulsa, Karl could always come and get me.

While I was sleeping in Virginia, a series of tornadoes cut through Nashville. Karl's cousin was visiting from New Mexico, sleeping in the other guest room. As the warning sirens kicked in at four in the morning, only Sooki was awake. "I didn't know what I was supposed to do," she told me later. "Should I have woken them up and made them come down to the basement? Were they awake and choosing not to come to the basement?" She wanted to know what constituted being a good houseguest during a tornado.

What if you came to Nashville to take part in a clinical trial for recurrent pancreatic cancer only to be killed by a tornado? Sooki told me about evacuating for fires in the canyon where she and her husband lived in Los Angeles. It was a year and a half earlier, the night before she was scheduled to fly to North Carolina to have her surgery. She and Ken put what mattered most in the car and drove away, waiting to see which way the wind would shift the wall of flame. They were lucky and the fire skated past. They were lucky to get up in the morning to fly across country so Sooki could have a pancreaticoduodenectomy, also known as a Whipple procedure. Her best friends lost everything in that fire. All that was left was the wall around what had been their garden. But they had survived. Sooki had her surgery at Duke and survived. Twenty-five people died in Nashville the night of those tornadoes.

I CAME BACK from Virginia and took Sooki to see the daffodils at the botanical gardens, but we were too early; the grass was still brown and only a handful of the thousands of bulbs had opened. I took her to the J. M. W. Turner exhibition at the art museum. We saw two movies with my sister. One morning Sooki had coffee with Sister Nena and me before she went to a yoga class across the street from the restaurant we went to for breakfast.

"Oh, she's darling," Sister Nena said. Sooki had left for yoga just as the waitress was bringing our eggs.

"She has pancreatic cancer," I said.

Sister Nena stopped for a minute to lock Sooki in her heart. I could see her doing it. "I'd be grateful if you'd pray for her," I said, because while I was uncertain about prayer in general, I believed in the power of Sister Nena's prayers unequivocally. I'd seen her work in action.

Sister Nena nodded. "We all will."

Good, I thought. Get as many nuns on this as possible.

EVERY DAY SOOKI came upstairs looking spectacular—embroidered jeans, velvet tops, a different coat, a perfect scarf. The same outfit never showed up twice. "How is it possible?" I said as I complimented her again and again. "You must have Mary Poppins's suitcase."

"The clothes are small," she said. "And I roll them all up. I'm a good packer." She told me she had packed for good cheer, having had the reasonable expectation that times would be hard and cheer a necessity.

I said, "I have access to every article of clothing I own and I couldn't pull myself together to look as good as you do going to chemo."

She told me she thought she'd put too much of her creative energy into her outfits over the years since she hadn't been painting, though she might have said it to make me feel better.

I flew back to New York for two more events, the first one in Connecticut. I went to Marti's house in Harlem and she drove me out. We had left early, taking into account the traffic that turned out to be eerily absent. We found a diner down the street from where I would be speaking. Our conversation was continually derailed by the television hanging over the counter. It seemed we had just driven through the US epicenter of the coronavirus.

"Looks like we're sitting on the edge of the apocalypse," Marti said, leaving her French fries on her plate. Marti and I had been in some scrapes before. We both agreed that if this was the brink of extinction, it was nice to be together.

WALKING BACKWARDS IS an excellent means of remembering how little you know. On the morning of September 11, 2001, I was sitting in a café in the West Village with my friends Lucy and Adrian when a woman ran in and said a plane had just hit the World Trade Center. A plane? we asked. Like a Cessna? She didn't know. She hadn't seen it happen. We went out to the street on that bright morning to see a fire high up in the distance. The waiter came out and told us to get back inside. We hadn't paid the check. I paid the check. Lucy said she didn't have time for this. She was teaching at Bennington in Vermont, and this was the first day of classes. She had to make her train. We said our goodbyes and Adrian and I walked downtown to see what had happened. We both wrote for the *New York Times*. Surely there would be a story for one of us. We had just passed Stuyvesant Park when the first tower fell. I would tell you we were idiots, but that's only true in retrospect. In fact we were so exactly in the middle of history that we had no way to understand what we were seeing.

· · ·

I HAD THOUGHT I was writing a novel about a woman who left her family to go and serve the poor in India. That didn't work. The mistakes I had made were so clear once I had finished. I was interested in her children.

· · ·

AT THE COUNTRY club in Connecticut, the organizers of the event began to apologize as soon as we were through the door. What with all the news of this virus they thought chances were good people weren't going to show up. But everyone showed up, all four hundred of them packed in side by side, every last chair in the ballr~
cupied.

"Welcome to the last book event on earth," I said

onstage. It turned out to be more or less the truth. By the time I was done signing books that night, the event I had scheduled in New York the next day had been canceled. I had breakfast with my editor and agent and publicist, and when we were finished, they each decided not to go back to the office after all. I caught an early flight home. It was done.

After dinner that night, Sooki and I sat on the couch and tried to watch a movie, but her phone on its leash began to ding and ding and ding, insisting on her attention. Tom and Rita were in Australia, where he was about to start shooting a movie about Elvis Presley. He was to play Elvis's manager, Colonel Tom Parker. All the messages were about Tom and Rita. They both had the coronavirus.

I leaned over to look at her phone. "They've been exposed to it?"

She shook her head, scrolling. "They have it," she said. "The press release is about to go out." I sat and watched her read, waiting for something more, something that explained it. Finally she went downstairs to her computer. She was Tom Hanks's assistant and there was work to do. I floated upstairs in a world that would not stop changing. I was going to tell Karl what was happening, but he was looking at his phone. He already knew.

WEDNESDAY'S CHEMO WOULD hit Sooki on Friday afternoon. I could track the way her voice got quieter, the way she was less likely to look me in the eye. "How's the painting coming?" I would ask.

"I fell asleep."

"Then you needed to sleep."

"I need to go home," she would say, as if home were one more ᵖlace she could walk to.

"You can't go home, and we don't want you to go home."

"You've been so nice, but you didn't sign on for this." She stood in the kitchen, holding her cup of ginger tea.

"I signed on for this."

She shook her head. "I can't tell you how appreciative I am. But I can't just live with you and Karl for the rest of my life."

The direct flights to Los Angeles had been suspended, and even if she'd wanted to fly to Dallas to wait and see if the connecting flight would be canceled (because that's what flights did now), her weekly blood draws underscored the fact that she scarcely had enough white cells to qualify for chemo, much less protect her from a pandemic while on a commercial flight. And anyway, UCLA had suspended its plans to start the clinical trial for recurrent pancreatic cancer. All across the country, clinical trials were being postponed or abandoned in an attempt to deal with the overflow of patients being treated for COVID. All resources were now directed to a disease that was not the disease Sooki had.

"You can't kill yourself because you're afraid of being an inconvenience."

"I need to go home," she said.

"Let's wait and talk about it on Sunday. You can't go home before Sunday."

She was serious, but she was also tired, so I could get her to agree. By the time Sunday came the urgency would have passed. In time, all I would have to say was, "It's Friday. You always feel this way on Friday."

"I do?"

"That's what I'm here for," I said. "I chart your emotional life."

An important piece of information hadn't been made clear to

Sooki when she came to Nashville, which was that—unlike the Folfirinox which had carved twenty pounds off her over twenty-four weeks—this course of chemotherapy had no end. She was to stay in the trial, three Wednesdays on, one Wednesday off, until the regime was no longer effective, or, to put it another way, until she died. Sooki, I had learned, was sixty-four.

Karl was seventy-two. The partners in his clinic asked him to stay home and practice telemedicine until there was a better sense of how the pandemic would be resolved. His risk was too high. He agreed, and then kept finding reasons to go to work anyway. Old habits. I reminded him that in choosing to work, he ran the risk of killing our houseguest. That was how I saw the coronavirus—as something that could kill Sooki. Finally, he stopped. I went to the grocery store and piled up the cart. I had come late to pandemic stockpiling, but fortunately the staples I relied on—chickpeas, coconut milk—were still plentiful.

IF I KNEW nothing about Sooki before she arrived, I knew little more three weeks later, when we were spending all of our days together. Or maybe I should say I was coming to know her without knowing very much about her. People are not comprised entirely of their facts, after all. Our interactions stayed in the present: Do you want to go for a walk? How's the painting going? While we pored over every detail of dinner (Sooki was a great cook), we didn't talk about her family. I knew she worried about her ninety-four-year-old mother in Rye Brook, New York, and read to her grandchildren in San Diego over Zoom. When I asked her how she was feeling, she might admit to being a little tired or having a bit of a stomachache, nothing more than that. Tom Hanks was so completely absent from our conversations that I once asked if he knew where she was. She looked startled.

"I mentioned it to him," she said.

Somehow I imagined that she had mentioned she was in a clinical trial in Nashville but not that she was living with us, which didn't feel like too much of an evasion seeing as how she managed to live with us in the quietest way imaginable. She was indefatigably pleasant and warm while maintaining her distance. Whether she was trying to hold on to her own sense of privacy or what she perceived to be our privacy, I didn't know. The truth was, we had no idea how long we were going to be together. Daughter, husband, sister, friend—none of the people scheduled to visit her could come now that the world was on lockdown. She had set up her life in the bottom floor of our house, a place we never went. She painted and slept and did her work, she had her Zoom meetings and her Zoom gatherings with friends. Many nights after dinner, I would ask Karl where Sooki was and then we would start looking around for her. "She was right here," Karl said. It was more like a magic trick than someone turning in for the evening. She was there and then she was gone and we wouldn't see her again until the next morning.

"I don't want you to feel like you have to stay downstairs," I said.

"Oh," Sooki said, "I don't."

"We're just reading. You could sit with us and read if you wanted, answer e-mails. We could all be boring together."

But she rarely stayed. On the few mornings she didn't come up at her usual time, I imagined her sick, needing something, not telling me because she didn't want to bother me. That had been one of her greatest fears about coming to stay with us in the first place, that she would be unable to take care of herself, that she would be a burden, that she would embarrass herself.

I didn't worry about her embarrassing herself. I worried about her dying. I finally asked her to write down the phone numbers of her husband and son and daughter, telling her if she got sick, if she were in the hospital unexpectedly, I'd need to know how to get hold of them. The truth was, I had no idea how Sooki was doing, and I had no confidence that she would tell me.

"I wonder," I said to her one night while we walked Sparky around the block, "do you think you're a good assistant because you're a private person, or did you become a private person because you've been an assistant for a long time?"

"I think this is just the way I am," she said.

"You know that you don't talk about yourself, right?" We were living together. We were in the middle of a pandemic. I didn't see how it could hurt to ask. "I'm just wondering if you got in the habit of not talking about yourself because of the work you do." I told her about a friend of mine who worked as an assistant for a hedge-fund manager in New York, and how she parked every piece of herself at the door when she went to work in the morning.

Sooki thought about it, or she thought about having to tell me. "I hadn't meant this to be my career. I worked at the Bronx Zoo during school and then I did the whole bat thing. I made a documentary about my father. He had a program where he taught kids with Down's and autism how to ride bikes."

As it turned out, Sooki had done a lot of things. She'd worked on a documentary about George Romero called *Document of the Dead* (she was a zombie in *Dawn of the Dead*). She'd been a location scout, made wedding cakes, had a children's clothing company, taught ceramics. For a while she filled in for a friend and was the assistant to a director, and then another friend introduced her to Tom, who was looking for someone. Her kids were in school by then. She thought it would be fun for a while. But it turned out to be a good job, and Tom was a nice guy, and the travel was interesting. "Still," she said, "I can't help feeling like I should have done more with my life."

"Call me crazy, but that seems like a lot." We were well into March by then. The spring was cold and wet and endlessly beautiful because of it. The cherry blossoms hung on forever. Sooki hadn't answered the question, but that was the day I felt like we started talking.

What Sooki thought she should have done with her life was paint. She had wanted to study painting in college, but it all came too easily—the color, the form, the technique—she didn't have to work for any of it. College was meant to be rigorous, and so she signed up for animal behavior instead. "I studied what did not come naturally," she told me. She became interested in urban animals. She wrote her thesis on bats and rabies. "My official badge-carrying title at the New York City Department of Health's Bureau of Animal Affairs was 'Public Health Sanitarian.' The badge would have allowed me to inspect and close down pet stores if I wasn't too busy catching bats." Painting fell into the category of what she would get back to in time, but there wasn't time—there was work, marriage, and children. And then pancreatic cancer.

Renée Fleming spent two years in Germany studying voice while she was in her twenties. She told me that over the course of her life, each time she went back to Germany she found her fluency had mysteriously improved, as if the language had continued to work its way into her brain regardless of whether she was speaking it. This was the closest I could come to understanding what happened to Sooki. After her first round of cancer, while she recovered from the Whipple and endured the Folfirinox, she started to paint like someone who had never stopped. Her true work, which had lingered for so many years in her imagination, emerged fully formed, because even if she hadn't been painting, she saw the world as a painter, not in terms of language and story but of color and shape. She painted as fast as she could get her canvases primed, berating herself for falling asleep in the afternoons. "My whole life I've wanted this time. I can't sleep through it."

The paintings came from a landscape of dreams, pattern on pattern, impossible colors leaning into one another. She painted her granddaughter striding through a field of her own imagination, she painted herself wearing a mask, she painted me walking down our street with such vividness I realized I had never seen the street before. I would bring her stacks of art books from the closed bookstore and she all but ate them. Sooki didn't talk about her husband or her children or her friends or her employer, she talked about color. We talked about art. She brought her paintings upstairs to show us: a person who was too shy to say good night most nights was happy for us to see her work. The canvases displayed no hesitation, no timidity. She had transferred her life into brushwork, all those colors overlapping, compositions precariously and perfectly balanced. The paintings were bold, confident, at ease. When she gave us the painting she'd made of Sparky on the back of the couch, I felt like Matisse had painted our dog.

• • •

MOST OF THE writers and artists I know were made for sheltering in place. The world asks us to engage, and for the most part we can, but given the choice, we'd rather stay home. I know how to structure my time. I can write an entire novel without showing a page of it to anyone. I can motivate myself without a deadline or contract. I was happy, even thrilled, to stop traveling. I had spent my professional life looking at my calendar, counting how many days I had left at home. Now every engagement I had scheduled in 2020 was canceled. With each day, I felt some piece of long-held scaffolding fall away. I no longer needed the protection. I was an introvert again. Sooki had come to our house thinking she'd be staying with someone who was gone half the time and busy the other half the time. And there I was, going nowhere. It was just the three of us now, Sooki and Karl and me.

Sooki and I stood together in the kitchen, one of us washing the vegetables, the other one chopping, making it up as we went along. I wrote and she painted and then we made dinner. But our truest means of communication arrived in the form of old yoga DVDs. She couldn't walk to a class in the dark of morning—everything was closed—and so I asked her if she wanted to exercise with me. I did kundalini yoga in the morning, a type of practice that was built around a great deal of rapid breathing, and then I went on to other things.

But once we had finished that first short practice, she turned to me, blooming. "This is what I need," she said, excited. "This is what's been missing."

• • •

THIS STORY—WHICH BEGINS and begins—starts again here. Of course we would exercise together, it was good for both of us. Kundalini is nothing if not an exercise in breath, and as it turned out, breath was what Sooki was craving. More breath. Almost from the moment we finished that first practice, she identified it as part of her recovery, the thing she needed to stay alive.

I had never found a way of asking what having cancer had been like for her, or what it meant to so vigorously refuse your fate. With every passing day, I seemed less able to say, *Do you want to talk about this? Am I the person you're talking to, or are you talking to someone else downstairs late at night?* I was starting to understand what she needed might have been color rather than conversation, breath rather than words.

My continuous and varied relationship to exercise was an inheritance from my father. He was not one to miss a workout, and neither was I. I'd practiced kundalini devotedly for years and then drifted, picking up other things, and while I'd stuck with the short class, I had amassed no end of DVDs. Now Sooki and I sorted through the cache like they were old baseball cards. We did a different hourlong class every morning, identifying our favorites and then ordering more. All that breathing and twisting and flexing fed her, and the calm voice of the instructor seemed to be speaking directly to her. "This one is good for your liver." "This will help all your internal organs." "You are beautiful. You are powerful. You decide." We laughed at the simple optimism but we also caught ourselves listening.

Every morning before breakfast we waved our hands in the air. We danced. We did up dog and down dog in endless repetition. And then one night, for reasons I cannot imagine, we decided to do it all again before we went to sleep. And that was that. Yoga and meditation for an hour in the morning was augmented with yoga and meditation for an hour at night. Surely we would take off the Wednesday mornings, when she had to be at the hospital at seven. Never. She was going to be stuck in a chair all day, which was why it was necessary to do it again at night when she got home. We laughed at ourselves, at the practice, at the voice that told us we were flowers, we were leopards, but we didn't stop. I thought some nights my back would snap. I wanted to go to bed and read. But my sixty-four-year-old houseguest with recurrent pancreatic cancer asked for absolutely nothing but this. How was I going to say I was tired when she was never tired? She lit up with all that breath.

Or maybe it was the company. We had finally found a completely comfortable way of being together. I saw my mother and sister. I went to sleep with my husband. Most days I went to work at Parnassus for several hours, filling boxes with books. The bookstore was closed to the public, but we were still shipping. Yoga was Sooki's necessary social hour, and what I got in return was time with Sooki. So many other people would have done anything to be with her—her mother and husband, her daughter and son and grandchildren, her sisters and all of her friends. How thrilled they would have been to have even a few of the hours she wasted with us. *These precious days I'll spend with you*, I sang in my head.

Pay attention, I told myself. Pay attention every minute.

Even as Sooki's white count continued to hover in the neighborhood of nonexistent, her CA 19-9 cancer marker number (that unreliable indicator we relied on) was dropping. "Maybe it's the trial," she said, "but I think it could just as easily be the food and the yoga."

I told her it was all an elaborate hoax. "You think you're getting chemo three Wednesdays a month but really it's a test to measure the effectiveness of kundalini yoga and kohlrabi." I had signed up for a farm-share box, and every week we were overwhelmed with pounds of mysterious vegetables.

I knew a part of her believed that maybe what Nashville had to offer in terms of fighting cancer was happening in our house, that she was improving because she was with us.

THE DAY I picked Sooki up from the airport in February she had told me she would need to buy dry ice for Wednesday. She was supposed to wear a complicated Velcro gel pack (unfortunately called a penguin cap) on her head on the days she had chemo. The four frozen caps were to be stored in a cooler filled with fifty pounds of dry ice. She was supposed to lug this cooler with her to the hospital every week. They clearly didn't understand she meant to walk, though knowing Sooki, she probably could have carried it. The caps had to be switched out every twenty-five minutes during treatment to ensure that her scalp more or less stayed frozen. "It's supposed to keep your hair from falling out," she said. "Or it's supposed to slow it down." She hadn't lost her hair on Folfirinox, though she'd lost her sense of taste and smell, the feeling in her feet and hands, and twenty pounds. Folfirinox had also given her a profound aversion to cold.

"And you're going to freeze your head for eight hours every week?" At this point we'd been together for a matter of minutes. I had no business offering unsolicited opinions on a subject I knew nothing about to a person who had just gotten in my car, but the thought of a frozen gel cap on my own head struck me as boundless misery. Would it even work? I asked her. If she missed a session, would her hair fall out anyway?

Sitting in her shaggy pink rock-star coat, Sooki told me how much she'd come to hate the cold. I said I thought it would be easier to be bald. The caps were in the Mary Poppins suitcase, along with her paints and easel, the large blanket she had brought us as a gift, her extensive wardrobe.

A month later I still hadn't seen all the clothes she brought with her, and I never saw the cold caps.

"Just think," I would say to her on Wednesdays. "If it wasn't for me, you'd be walking around with a penguin on your head now."

Then one day she told me she was starting to shed. The next day she brought up the vacuum cleaner to vacuum off her yoga mat. The day after that she came upstairs wearing a sock hat.

"I'm going to have to have my hair cut," she said. "Something happened to it while I was in the shower."

"I can cut it."

She shook her head. "It's too weird."

"There's no weirdness left between us," I said. "And anyway, it's my fault. I was the one who talked you out of the fifty pounds of dry ice."

She took off her cap to show me the damage.

It was as if 98 percent of her hair had fallen out, but somehow in the process of falling, it had felted. The chemical tide that rose in Sooki's blood not only caused her hair to fall out, it caused that hair to mat into a solid surface. Small, flat islands of boiled-wool hair were resolutely attached to her scalp by the 2 percent of hair which had not fallen out. It was a science experiment that could never be replicated.

"See?" she said.

I picked up one of the bigger islands and moved it gently back and forth. It was anchored by a quarter inch of hair at most but it was indeed anchored. Sooki got a stool and a towel and went to sit on the back deck. I went upstairs to get the scissors out of my sewing basket.

"You have a pretty head," I told her when the job was done. "I guess you never know if you're the person who's going to look good bald until you're bald."

She went inside to see for herself. She wasn't about to tell me she looked good, but it was clear what I was talking about. There was a delicacy about her that was well suited to baldness.

"I need to go home," she said, looking at the pictures of herself she asked me to take with her cell phone. Then she went downstairs and went back to sleep.

Later in the day we sat side by side on our yoga mats, Sooki's head wrapped artfully in a scarf. With our hands on our shoulders we turned left and right, left and right, endlessly.

"It's so important to twist this way," the gentle voice-over of the yoga teacher reminded us. "You're detoxifying all your inner organs."

That was what we had to hold on to, and so we held on.

WHEN I LOOK back on those first few months of the pandemic, all I will remember is recurrent pancreatic cancer. Recurrent pancreatic cancer kept me focused on this present moment. I wasn't suffering the crashing waves of anxiety that battered down so many people I knew—though two hours of daily yoga and meditation surely contributed to keeping panic at bay. While other people were left to worry about a virus that might or might not have been coming for them, I worried about Sooki. I had a concrete reason to be careful about the germs I was bringing into the house. It wasn't just that I could kill someone, it was that I could kill her.

I was also greatly occupied by the bookstore. Unlike so many other small businesses, we had the means to pivot. We still had customers, even though they couldn't come in the store, and they were fantastically loyal. I was packing boxes, writing cards, and making cheerful videos in which I extolled the virtues of the books I loved. I would save what I could save, and along with my business partner Karen Hayes and the handful of fiercely loyal staff (including my sister Heather) who never backed down, I was determined to save Parnassus. Sooki was desperate to be helpful. Some mornings we went to the store at first light, when no one was around, to tape up boxes and stick on labels together. She was thrilled to get the chance to work. She kept saying she wanted to be the one to help me for a change. But all Sooki did was help me. She was the magnet in the compass. The very fact of her existence in our house kept me on track.

"What Sooki is," Tom wrote to me in an e-mail later, "is all that is good in the world."

We lived in that good world made up of yoga and chemo, the bookstore, cooking, painting, talking over dinner. We filled up the birdfeeders twice a day, scrubbed out the birdbath every morning, tracked the relationship of a pair of lizards who lived in the planter on the deck. Sooki told me they were skinks. Stranded at home, Karl studied to get his instrument rating as a pilot. He watched classes on his computer and worked calculus problems at the dining room table. He talked to his patients on the phone. He would tell me how lucky we were, the three of us together. And we were. We knew it.

ON THE FIRST Sunday in May, in the late afternoon, a storm kicked up, not expected but not a surprise either. Karl was sitting on the front porch and he called for me to come out. "Look at this."

I came and watched from the open door. The sky had turned a ferocious gray, the rain sheeting sideways. The wind was coming down the street like a train.

Karl spent a huge amount of time studying weather as part of his instrument rating. "I've never seen a storm come up so fast." He leaned forward over the porch stairs.

"Come inside," I said.

He wasn't listening. He was watching the weather.

A tremendous explosion rocked the house, something far beyond thunder. A transformer must have blown up somewhere close by. Up and down the street the lights clicked off; our house went dark. All the neighborhood dogs began to howl and bark. On the porch, Sparky joined in.

"We need to go downstairs," I said.

"In a minute."

"Hey guys?" Sooki called.

"God damn it, get inside," I said to my husband. Twenty-five people killed in the last round of tornadoes in Nashville two months before.

Sooki came outside and was caught by the spectacle of the storm. It would take nothing for her to blow away. I could already see her tumbling down the street. "Do you want to come downstairs?" she asked.

I tugged at Karl and we all went downstairs with the dog. By the time we sat down it was over. It had been no more than seven minutes start to finish. The rain went on for another half an hour, and when it gave up I put Sparky on his leash and the three of us went outside to wander and gape with our neighbors. About a quarter of the trees were down. Giant hackberries had fallen into maples and split them in half. A forest sprung up in the middle of the street. Telephone poles were down, and electrical wires snaked across the asphalt. They were dead, the wires, weren't they? Gingerly we picked our way forward. Catalpa flowers littered the sidewalk, though I hadn't realized the catalpa trees were blooming. I scooped up a handful for no reason and carried them with me. It was a straight-line wind, a freak occurrence that raged up out of nowhere. The trees were down but not the houses, and the trees, from what I could see, hadn't fallen on the houses. They'd fallen on the mailboxes. They'd knocked each other down like dominoes. Karl looked up the name for it on his phone. *Derecho.* Spanish for straight, direct.

"First the tornadoes," Sooki said, taking picture after picture, the giant root systems pulling up slabs of earth taller than Karl, the bright spring grass meeting the sidewalk at a right angle.

"Then the pandemic," I said.

"The freak wind," Karl said.

"And pancreatic cancer," Sooki said.

"Let's not forget the cancer," I said, and we laughed.

That night we lit candles. We lit the gas stove with matches and made dinner. We played Scrabble and did our yoga from memory after Karl went to bed. We breathed deeply and flexed our spines.

"Well," Sooki said when we were finished. We just kept sitting in the stillness, the kind of dark that electricity wants us to forget had ever existed. It was the last hour in a long day.

"Let's go outside," I whispered.

Sooki got her flashlight and blew out the candle. Sooki had been working for the bat squad in New York when a bicentennial parade went down the street in front of the Bureau of Animal Affairs. People were dancing, laughing, and so she went outside. She met a group of sailors who had sailed around the world. One of them was shirtless and had a colorful parrot on his shoulder. Sooki had had a toucan in college. Surely she was leaving out some piece of the story, because the next thing I knew she'd sailed off with them. She was twenty-one. She went to work as part of the ship's crew. They sailed to St. Barts in a beautiful old wooden boat named Christmas. She had once shown me a picture of herself standing in the surf wearing a bikini, a sarong tied around her narrow hips.

I woke up the dog and the three of us left in the darkness. We weren't the only ones who felt restless. People were sitting in their cars, in their driveways, charging up their phones from their car batteries. People were out with their dogs. They were on their porches, laughing. I didn't understand what it was, but something was in the air. Everyone was wide awake, waiting up to see if the world was going to end.

Sooki and I shined our flashlights against the smooth bark of the trees that lay across the streets. We shined them into the beds of purple iris that stood tall and straight, untouched. We climbed over branches, met an impasse, turned to walk another way. The water in the creek a block away skimmed the bottom of the footbridge. We talked and then we didn't. It was enough just to be together in all that darkness.

The power stayed off for four days, those rarest of days in Nashville when it was neither too hot nor too cold. I cleaned out the freezer and the refrigerator and at every moment thought, We are so lucky.

• • •

BEFORE I CAN start writing a novel, I have to know how it ends. I have to know where I'm going, otherwise I spend my days walking in circles. Not everyone is like this. I've heard writers say that they write to discover how the story ends, and if they knew the ending in advance there wouldn't be any point in writing. For them the mystery is solved by the act, and I understand that; it's just not the way I work. I knew I would write about Sooki eventually, I had told her so, but I had no idea what I'd say. I didn't know how the story would end.

"She'll die," Karl said. "People die of this."

But wasn't there also a scenario in which she didn't die? The chemo, the clinical trial of immunotherapy, the yoga and the vegetables, the prayers of nuns and all the time to paint—what if it added up to something? What if a strange alchemy existed in the proportions, something that could never be exactly measured, and as a result she lived, only to die later from the thing no one saw coming: a pandemic, tornadoes, a straight-line wind.

THERE IS A magnificent quiet that comes from giving up the regular order of your life. Sooki came to Nashville and stayed in one place, no more movie stars, no more trips to Morocco and Tan-Tan.

Tan-Tan had no electricity at night. She and Tom would walk in the desert in the early mornings and she would feed him lines from a script while he memorized his part, the cobras slipping across the dust just in front of them. Death was there on those long sunny days. Death was the river that ran underground, always. It was just that we had piled up so much junk to keep from hearing it.

SOMETIMES SOOKI WOULD leave money on the kitchen counter, "For groceries," she would say, "for gas, for the books."

I would shake my head. "Don't do this."

That was when her eyes would well up. Sooki, bareheaded, her silver earrings dangling down her neck. "I have to feel like I'm contributing. I can't always be the one who's taking everything."

But of course I was the one who took everything. Why couldn't she see that? The price of living with a writer was that eventually she would write about you. I was taking in every precious day. What Sooki gave me was a sense of order, a sense of God, the God of Sister Nena, the God of my childhood, a belief that I had gone into my study one night and picked up the right book from the hundred books that were there because I was meant to. The CA 19-9 had gone from 2100 to 470. The tumor in her liver was shrinking. A hundred thousand people in this country had already died of the coronavirus. We were still at the beginning then. Thanks to Sooki, I became aware of the quiet in my house, in my own mind. I could hear the river running underground, and I wasn't afraid.

Sooki worried about her mother, who had been admitted to the hospital for a urinary tract infection. Sooki left messages for the doctors and put her phone at the end of her yoga mat, waiting for the call back while we practiced. When they called, she asked them all the right questions. She was an expert in dealing with the medical system, after all. It made her crazy not to be there to help.

"I can fly you up," Karl offered, once her mother was safely home. "We can go up and back the same day."

Sooki had twice flown down to Mississippi with us to visit Karl's ninety-eight-year-old mother. She liked to fly: the idea of the considerably longer trip to New York was good news. Sooki's mother lived two miles from the Westchester airport. From her patio, she could watch the planes take off and land. Once a pilot, always a pilot. Sooki's two sisters, one in Connecticut and one in Massachusetts, could come to meet them, a family reunion at the airport. Everyone could bring his or her own sandwich and stay safely apart.

"It's too much," Sooki said.

Karl disagreed. "It's not too much. I'm supposed to be flying."

The trip came together fast. They would leave in four days. Karl worked out the plans. He would bring a copilot to split up the hours. They would stop each way to refuel in West Virginia. Her sisters were in, her mother was thrilled.

The problem wasn't how the trip would be organized, but what it meant—pandemic, cancer, ninety-four. Implicit in the idea of everyone getting together was the reality that this could be the last time it would happen. How do you fly from Nashville to New York in a single-engine plane for a two-hour visit? How do you get back on the plane to come home?

Sooki hadn't lost weight but she was losing her ability to project her voice. It had been happening for a while. Sometimes I had to get right in front of her to hear what she was saying. "It's so amazingly generous of Karl," she whispered uncertainly. She kept to herself, sleeping and painting, trying to wrestle it out. "Of course I want to go. It's just . . ."

I waited but nothing came. Nothing had to.

The next morning we went to the bookstore early and picked out presents for everyone in her family. We went to the bakery across from the bookstore and bought spinach-feta bread and cinnamon-raisin bread. We went home and baked a spectacular cake that was especially well suited to travel. "It's like you're going home to the Ukraine for the first time in ten years," I said as we loaded up coolers and bags. I had gotten up in the dark to make stacks of sandwiches. Whether all of this together was what helped, or whether she had made up her mind to see only the good, I couldn't say. Probably it was some combination of the two. By the time Karl and Sooki left for the airport she was happy.

They told me the story later: how after they landed, when they were all standing together on the lawn outside the small airport, a police officer came and told them they had to disperse. Westchester was still a hot spot of the pandemic and there could be no congregating, even outside. Karl, being Karl, took the officer around the corner to explain the situation.

"We have some picnic tables outside the police station," the officer said. "No one will bother you." The police station happened to be next door to the airport, so everyone picked up their coolers and walked over. All day long Sooki sent me pictures with her family and the subject heading *Where is our other sister?* She meant me.

When Sooki and Karl got home that night, they were elated. Karl had loved Sooki's family and they all loved Karl. He and the other pilot talked flying with Sooki's mother. "She told me that she had to put Sooki on a leash when she was little because she ran so much. No one could keep up with her. Every time her mother turned around, Sooki was gone."

Sooki, the middle daughter. "What about your sisters?" I asked.

"No leashes on them," she said.

In bed that night, Karl told me about how happy they all were, how kind. He said that Sooki was good when they left. She had made up her mind that it was going to be okay.

I turned out the light and kept thinking about the leash, the marathons, the trail running, the yoga, the walking in the desert, the painting and painting and painting. The energy it took to stay alive, the impossibility of quitting. I didn't know what I would have done in her place, but I imagined that upon getting the news of recurrent pancreatic cancer I would go to see my lawyer and settle up my tab with the house. Maybe I would find the fight in me, but I was never much of a fighter. Sooki wore a leash as a child, the energy in her tiny frame too much for her mother to control. Many were the mornings the yoga felt endless to me, and so I would give her a wave as I left the mat and headed off to my desk. To the best of my knowledge she never quit.

MORE NEWS ABOUT planes: friends of mine in Nashville who have a house in California and a jet that takes them there, the nicest possible friends, who knew what was going on with Sooki, offered her a ride home. They were flying out at the end of May. It was her only chance of getting back safely anytime soon. The same trial she was a part of in Nashville had finally commenced at UCLA, twenty minutes from her house. Her California and Tennessee oncologists had conferred so that she could transfer from one hospital to the other without missing a treatment. Everything was lined up—except Sooki didn't want to go.

My goal was to maintain neutrality. I told her as much. She shouldn't stay for us or leave for us. She was welcome. No one had ever been so welcome. "You can live here for the rest of your life," I said, and I meant it. These days were concentrated like no time I had ever known. She had moved in before the pandemic. We had been together for the duration of this new world. But of course the thing to do would be to go, wouldn't it? She must miss all those people she so rarely spoke of.

"I'm afraid if I leave I'll never see you again," she said in a voice I could barely hear.

It was possible, and I had no intention of thinking about it. "I wonder if it isn't easier here because you don't have to comfort us, you don't have to make us feel better about the fact that you're sick. You can just concentrate on yourself."

She shook her head. "It isn't that."

It's funny, but all this time I was sure it was exactly that. I'd come up with the answer months ago. Our house was a holding pattern, a neutral space without expectation where all that mattered was her recovery.

We were standing in the kitchen in the late afternoon, the time before dinner and between two yoga practices. "I like myself here," she said softly.

I had to listen to what she was telling me. I had to turn myself away from the movie of what I thought was happening, the movie I had made myself, so that I could see her.

It was so hard for her to talk. I stood close, willing myself not to fill in her sentences. She told me that at home she had become impatient and angry. She had wanted her life to be different, and now it was. She had wanted to be a better person, and here she believed she was better. She liked herself again. She wasn't just her illness. She was an artist. I saw her as an artist. "The fact that the two of you want me here, that you love me, that you believe in me, it makes me believe in myself. I don't want to give that up."

"You'll never have to give up the friendship or the love," I said. "And if you decide you want to stay, well, you don't have to give that up either."

Sooki the Tireless, Sooki the Indefatigable, looked like she was about to split apart. She said she didn't know what she was going to do. "I can't just stay here forever."

But she could. I had no idea whether it was a good idea, but she could.

That night I tried to explain it to Karl. "This whole time I've gotten it wrong. I thought I was helping and now I wonder if I've made it worse."

"How could you have made it worse?"

"By showing her what her life might have looked like and then sending her home." By seeing what I wanted to see instead of what was actually in front of me. Mine was the sin of misunderstanding, of thinking that a clinical trial was the point of the story.

The days went on and I could feel Sooki slipping, hounded by her own indecision. Here she was an artist who lived with a writer. Here she was the person she had meant to be. One night after we'd finished our yoga and meditation we were lying on our mats, staring up at the ceiling. Sparky had crawled onto my chest and gone to sleep. I asked her if she had any interest in trying psilocybin.

It's essential to the life of a novel to come upon the turn you never saw coming.

I knew people in college and graduate school who took mushrooms, and then about thirty years passed before I heard anything about them again. Now I knew several people who were using them as part of therapy. Plant medicine, they called it now. When you're young, you're getting high, and when you're old, you're using plant medicine, like herbal insect repellent. Still, wasn't it worth mentioning?

Sooki said she'd heard about it too, and knew other cancer patients who'd tried it, but she was hesitant, as any right-minded adult would be hesitant about adding the X factor of fungi into an already complicated chemical mix. We started looking up articles on the Johns Hopkins website. The reports on the studies were overwhelmingly positive:

> Psilocybin produces substantial and sustained decreases in depression and anxiety in patients with life-threatening cancer. . . . High-dose psilocybin produced large decreases in clinician- and self-rated measures of depressed mood and anxiety, along with increases in quality of life, life meaning, and optimism, and decreases in death anxiety.

"MAYBE," SHE SAID.

I don't drink. I'm a vegetarian. My only prescription was for vitamin D. If I'd had a coat of arms it would have read QUALITY OF LIFE, LIFE-MEANING, OPTIMISM. "Would you feel better about it if I did it with you?"

She looked at me. "Aren't we talking about doing this together?"

"Oh," I said. "We are. Of course we are."

This is how we arrive at the next chapter of the story.

THE TRICK WASN'T getting the mushrooms. I knew how to do that. The trick was coming up with the nerve to confess our plans to Karl. I presented him with the studies from Johns Hopkins. Seventy percent of participants rated it as among "the most personally meaningful and spiritually significant experiences of their lives." He rolled his eyes, but he read. Marriage meant that he would hear out what on the surface may have appeared to be a spectacularly stupid idea. Marriage also meant that I would listen if he tried to talk me out of it. I wasn't looking for permission, but it was a matter of mutual respect.

He finished reading several articles while I waited.

"Okay," he said.

"Really? You don't think this is crazy?"

"I didn't say that, but I know you're trying to help Sooki."

When we turned out the light that night, I felt myself buzzing with happiness: after nearly three months of lockdown, we were going to have an adventure. Travel while staying at home! I don't know why I didn't have the sense to worry, but I didn't. My friends who had tried it had all had positive experiences, new books extolled the value of seeing the beauty and connectivity of all life. It seemed possible that this experience, coming so far out of left field, might be just the thing Sooki needed.

It took a while to get the mushrooms. A friend who was well versed in the experience brought them over early in the morning on Memorial Day. I had interviews scheduled all day on Tuesday, Sooki had chemo on Wednesday, and my friends were leaving for California on Thursday. It was now or never.

My friend told us we should wear eye masks and cover ourselves with blankets. The Johns Hopkins team had put together a six-hour playlist of music that was meant to somehow guide you safely through the experience. Sooki had downloaded it on her computer. We were ready.

"It's important to think about your intentions before you start," my friend told us. We were sitting in the den at seven thirty in the morning. My intention was to help Sooki. What other reason would I have to be going on the cancer patient's journey?

"It's okay for us to be in the same room," Sooki said, a statement rather than a question.

My friend tilted her head. "I wouldn't. Things can get very confused. There aren't a lot of boundaries. Or I should say what you think of as boundaries tend to fall away. I wouldn't be on the same floor of the house."

She said we could expect to be in the thick of things for an hour and a half, maybe two hours, with some residual effects for another three or four hours after that. "And even when you're in the middle of it you can still get up and go to the bathroom. It's not like you're stuck in one place." I would have given her a hug but for the pandemic. I promised to call when it was over.

Then Sooki and I went to the kitchen, mixed our premeasured packets of mushroom powder in with yogurt, and poisoned ourselves. We headed upstairs to lie side by side on our yoga mats, deciding to disregard my friend's advice about staying on separate floors. We were in this together. That was the point of everything. Karl and the dog went out on the front porch to read the newspaper.

We put on the music, the eye masks, covered up. We waited. Then came the moment one feels on a roller coaster just as the bar locks into place and the car starts to pull up, the body pressing back into the seat, knees out ahead, and you think, Wait a minute, was this the best . . .

"Ann?"

I pulled up my eye mask. Karl was standing in the doorway. He told me he was going to take his grandsons to the river to go boating. It was Memorial Day, after all.

"You're not staying?"

He shook his head. I felt the car pulling up and up, just about to tip over the cresting track. Had we not talked about the part where he stuck around to oversee our health and safety? Maybe not. Remember in the future not to make assumptions. Click, click, click. I rose as I pressed against the floor.

"Is it working?" he asked.

"It's working," Sooki said.

And then, it seemed, he left.

The car was taking me into yellow, not a field of yellow but into the color itself. There are no words here, I thought. I had put a notebook and a pen beside me on the floor before we started. Forget that. The color was keeping time with the music, the color was breaking apart into tiles the size of Chiclets, the color of Chiclets, from which cathedrals rose in the sacred spirit of the Johns Hopkins playlist.

It occurs to me that I should put that playlist on again and listen as I'm writing this, but I will not. Vivaldi, Vivaldi, Vivaldi—that's how it starts.

THE COLOR WAS engulfing, stupefying, spinning, building, reconfiguring, splitting apart. I tried to enjoy it but it was difficult to breathe. The car I was locked into was now hurtling down through a million winking flagella, every one a different color. Who knew so much color even existed? It was my intention to vomit, but the idea of getting past Sooki was overwhelming. Sooki, in her eye mask, was lying so serenely beneath the furry blanket she had brought us from California that I wondered if she was dead. Still, it seemed possible I could get off the ride early by expelling the mushrooms. I desperately wanted to vomit, to turn back time. I crawled around her as carefully as I could and collapsed in the hallway.

Reading about other people's hallucinogenic experiences is like listening to other people's dreams at a dinner party. What's fascinating fails to translate. Suffice to say the car I was strapped into followed a tunnel down into dark and darker colors, narrower spaces. Where I was going was death. My death. Two words I kept trying to bring up as I convulsed on the bathroom floor.

"You okay?" Sooki asked. She was in the doorway, outlined in neon tubing.

"Sick," I said.

"Are you breathing? You have to remember."

Face down on a bath mat, I forced myself to take a breath.

"You should come back to the music," she said sympathetically.

I couldn't muster up whatever it would have taken to follow her, but I could hear the music fine from where I was, Górecki's Symphony No. 3, Arvo Pärt, pieces I had loved and would love no more. "We did this to ourselves," I said, or maybe I didn't say it. She was already gone. By the time the playlist had reached *Tristan und Isolde*, my skull was a horse's skull, dry and white and empty.

"I'M DYING," MY friend had said to me.

"I'll go with you," I said.

THIS WAS NOT a two-hour journey. This was eight hours of hard labor. I wanted Karl's comfort and was glad he wasn't there. I was sorry for what I'd done to him, by which I meant poisoning myself. We'd had a very good life. I felt like someone was slamming me against a wall, not in anger but as a job. My breath was roaring now, in and out, my lungs enormous bellows that would not tolerate my death. These months of exercise would save me. Save me. When I was very nearly at the end, I came to a beautiful lake, the kind you'd see on a Japanese postcard, or my imagined Japanese postcard, and lay down in the soft grass beside the still water, panting until it all started to slow down. That was my reward.

I had set my intention to help my friend, to hold her hand and go with her while she went to peer over the cliff, the cliff that, coincidentally, I fell off.

When it was over, I managed to make my way into the shower, perhaps the biggest single accomplishment of my life. Sooki went downstairs to her room. Karl came home and we sat on the couch and watched a storm tearing up the backyard. I thought he was angry and at the same time I knew my judgment to be flawed. I was angry at myself. I thought he *should* be angry at me. I pushed my face into his shoulder, apologizing. "For what?" he asked. He knew. Didn't he know?

"For being careless with our lives."

He got me a can of ginger ale and I tried to eat half a banana. Was this what COVID felt like? I couldn't stay upright, a hangover from the last eight hours in which I had been quite memorably deboned. I was no longer sick or well. Where was Sooki? She couldn't be alone.

After a while she drifted up to the kitchen, taking a stab at the half of banana I had abandoned. "Are you okay?" I asked. I was having trouble with my own volume now. "I was so afraid I'd killed you."

Outside the rain was dark and lashing. Sooki had brought her computer with her. She was checking e-mail or trying to make notes. "It was so important," she said, her voice pretty much vanishing in her mouth. I was trying to read her lips. I knew I should sit with her at the table but I couldn't imagine it.

"Are you not sick?"

She looked at me. "No, I'm fine. Are you sick?"

I nodded.

"Maybe it's all the chemicals I have in me already. I'm good. It's just." She stopped. There were no words because it wasn't about words.

"Was it like they said it would be, life changing? Are you not sorry you did it?" I felt like it took me two minutes to put that much together.

"I understand so many things now," she said. "All the people who love me and how hard this has been for them, the cancer. I could see them, my family and my friends. I felt their love for me. I could see what they needed and what they'd given me. I could see Ken and how he's always been there for me, how he steps back to let me shine. I could see what the cancer's given me. If it hadn't been for the cancer I never would have come here. I wouldn't have had this time with you and Karl. That's worth everything."

"So it really was what they said, a definitive spiritual experience?" She'd seen people. She felt their love and heard their voices while I was hacking up snakes in some pitch-black cauldron of lava at the center of the earth.

"Absolutely. I can't tell you how grateful I am. Did you have a hard time?"

"I had a hard time."

"What was it like?"

"Death," I said. I didn't say, *Your death.* I didn't say, *This thing you live with every minute, this heaving horse's skull, I held it for you today so that you could talk it out with the people who love you.* I had set my intention going in: I wanted to help my friend. In making the journey to Oz, she had found the strength and clarity she needed to go home again.

SOMEONE WOUND THE clock. Suddenly the second hand, so long suspended, began to tick again, pushing us forward. Sooki let my friends with the plane know that she would be there on Thursday. She had to pack her boxes the next day, Tuesday. Wednesday was chemo. She'd scarcely left the house for more than three months, and yet it was impossible to push the world back into the Mary Poppins suitcase. On her last night we sat in my office after yoga and I asked her every last question I could think of: When did she work on the documentary about George Romero and when did she marry

Ken? What was the line of children's clothing called? When was she first diagnosed with pancreatic cancer? How had she known something was wrong? All this time I'd been afraid of prying, only to discover that Sooki was happy to talk, to tell me about the bats, the sailboat to St. Barts, the desert in Tan-Tan, the surgery. She told me that part of the reason she'd been hesitant to stay with us was that she didn't want to trade on Tom's friendship with me. That she'd always been so careful not to cross any lines, not to advance herself through connections to people she'd met through him.

"Not to advance your cancer treatment? Are you serious? Can you imagine Tom sitting at home saying, 'I can't believe Sooki used my connections to get into a clinical trial in Nashville'?"

"No, of course not, I'm just telling you. I remember when you asked me months ago if he knew I was here and I panicked. I try to keep all the parts of my life separate."

We will never know all the things other people worry about.

She told me how lovely it had been to lay down the burden of her own vigilance. That at home she felt responsible for overseeing every aspect of her treatment, researching cures, double-checking medical orders—she had caught a few harrowing errors along the way, near misses—but here she knew that Johanna and Karl always had their eyes on her. She had their protection, and that knowledge had opened up so much time in the day. We talked about the nightmare of health insurance, and how the percentage of treatment costs she and Ken had to pay out of pocket had wiped out their retirement, had wiped out everything. "I should have planned better," she said.

"You should have planned for the financial fallout of having pancreatic cancer twice?"

She said yes.

How had I not asked her all these things before? She was perfectly willing to talk, she wanted to talk, and now she was leaving in the morning. Why had I been so careful?

Because I was trying to protect myself. I had been afraid of how the story would end.

On Thursday morning I started to cry while walking Sparky. It came up like one of those weird storms that had plagued us through the spring. I never cry, and yet I had plans to do nothing else for the rest of the day and maybe the rest of the week. Sooki's impending departure touched a memory I made a point of not revisiting: My sister and I flew from Tennessee to Los Angeles for one week every summer to see our father, and on the morning of the day we were going back to Tennessee I would start to cry. There was no stopping it. It would be another year before I saw my father again, an unimaginable unit of time in the life of a child. I didn't have the money or freedom or wherewithal to buy another ticket and see him sooner. We were in a pandemic, Sooki had recurrent pancreatic cancer, and so this goodbye reminded me of my father coming onto the plane with us, sitting with me and my sister, the three of us sobbing inconsolably until finally the flight attendant would tell him he had to go.

SOOKI WASHED HER sheets and towels, cleaned the bathroom, vacuumed. She lugged her suitcase out to the car without my knowing it. When she came upstairs ready to go she was wearing the black velvet coat with the peonies on it.

"You had it here all this time?" The coat wasn't the way I had remembered it. It was so much more beautiful, the overlying color of every petal, the very light pink against the blackness.

"I was saving it," she said.

How was it possible? How could anything have been saved? How could there still be so many things I didn't understand when our time was nearly over?

Karl had gone back to work by this point, but he canceled his patients in the afternoon to drive us to the hangar where my friends kept their plane. We were early, they were late. I was grateful for both of those things. I was grateful. Karl went to talk to the pilots about the plane, and Sooki and I sat in the little waiting area. We tried to be jolly and failed and cried again. Look at what a success this time had been! Her CA 19-9 was 170, down from 2100 when she'd arrived in February. Now she would go home to her husband, her children, her grandchildren, her friends. Tom and Rita were back from Australia. They had recovered. Sooki had work to do. UCLA would fold her into their trial, everything seamless. We had found each other and we would not be lost. We repeated these facts, we made them a mantra.

My friends arrived, and we waved at each other from a distance as they gathered Sooki up. Out on the tarmac, I could see her again exactly as she was, resplendent in her velvet coat, her black beret. Sooki, who was light and life and color itself. A minute later everyone was on the plane and gone.

[MAY.31.20] I've already worked out this morning. I did a Pilates DVD we never got around to. It had zero spiritual component. Your hike looks gorgeous and loaded with spiritual compo-nent. If there were too many people there, you managed to crop them out. There are suddenly people everywhere. The park was packed this morning. What will happen?

Forget about the heartfelt letters. You yourself are heartfelt, and all the love in the world has been expressed. There is no sense in putting that burden on yourself. Karl is not waiting on a thank you note, I promise. I understand the impulse but I also think we've transcended it. (I say this as someone who is spending my days trying to write about our friendship and what happened here. It's HARD. I keep throwing things out. I'll get there but it's no small task to try and sum this up.)

I sent you another book that will show up eventually, a tiny French novel I love called THE LOST ESTATE (Le grand meaulnes) by Alain-Fournier. It may resonate.

I'm around if you want to talk. Just remember, Wednesday chemo left you very sad on Friday and Saturday, so it stands to reason that Thursday chemo will break your heart on Saturday and Sunday.

All my love.

[MAY.31.20] Sooki wrote: I had the most unusual dream last night. I'm not sure I can describe it without sounding like an extension of the mushrooms, but it had that kind of depth and clarity of message for me.

There was an abstract image, and it was clearly you—not in a physical way, but as a soul. The most important human qualities were being applied to this form. They would flow on in papery layers, in a creation act. It seemed to be key to the way humans were shaped, and I was aware that this was going on for others around you. But for you, there was also a vapor that would come in and fill in any gap that was left in the process, and I realized, "Oh, this is what is special here and so essentially Ann." There was a completeness. No empty spiritual space. Everything filled in.

I'm sure these words can't adequately convey what was such a radiant message, but it stayed with me so strongly as I woke up during the night, and that's the best I can describe it. I've never experienced anything like it, or you.

Have a wonderful day today. I'll send photos from San Diego. I think we'll be back tomorrow.

LOVE

As it turned out, Sooki and I needed the same thing: to find someone who could see us as our best and most complete selves. Astonishing to come across such a friendship at this point in life. At any point in life.

CA 19-9 is 66.7 as of this moment.

Tell me how the story ends.

It doesn't.

It will.

It hasn't yet.

· Two More Things I Want to Say · about My Father

THE EDITOR

When I finished writing my first novel, *The Patron Saint of Liars*, I printed out a copy and mailed it to my father. I was twenty-seven at the time, which means my father would have been sixty. He had not yet retired from his career in the Los Angeles Police Department, and I had not yet sold a book. I knew from the short stories I had sent him in graduate school that he was a good reader with a sharp eye for typos and grammatical errors. He would let me know when a scene felt stilted or slow, or when a character did things that a real person would never do. After thirty-three years in law enforcement, many of those years spent as a detective, he was also the best fact-checker / research assistant I would ever have.

The problem with my father's editing was that he brought his own moral imperative to my work. He circled every instance of my characters' swearing and then drew an X through the offending word. No need for that.

I never believed that my father never swore. I only believed that he never swore in front of me and my sister. But after he died, several of the cards we received from the police officers he'd worked with mentioned exactly that: what a gentleman he was, how he liked a good martini, how he didn't swear. He did, however, smoke for half his life: nevertheless he told me that the characters in my book had no business smoking.

"But they *do* smoke," I said. The two offending characters were both marines in basic training: the novel's hero and a minor character who was a corporal of the guard.

"They don't need to," my father said. "It does nothing for the scene."

"They *smoke*." I felt like I was the one who'd been caught with a Camel. The fact was, I did smoke when I was twenty-seven. I smoked in my father's house when I went to visit, opening the flue in the living room fireplace and cramming myself beneath the chimney once my father and stepmother were asleep. I couldn't go outside to smoke because the burglar alarm could only be disabled from inside their bedroom.

"You're setting a bad example," my father said of the smoking marines. "Young people could be reading this book."

"But you smoked."

"I quit," he said. He had quit when I was in high school, maybe even before then.

The cigarettes stayed, but our compromise was a good one. In my version the corporal threw his butt on the ground moments before accidentally shooting the hero in the leg. Smoking and littering was simply too much for my father to bear, so he explained how the character would field-strip what was left of the offending cigarette: pulling off the paper, rolling it into a tiny ball and scattering the remaining flakes of tobacco. Like smoking, field-stripping seemed to be something a marine would do.

In truth, I rarely gave in to my father's moral code, but that code had a profound effect on me all the same. I would stand up for a character's right to smoke in one book, but have a different character put his cigarettes aside (along with his swearing and sex life) in future books. My father's insistence on wholesomeness wore at me. One of the biggest arguments we ever had concerned a scene in the memoir I wrote about my friendship with the writer Lucy Grealy. In *Truth & Beauty* I told a story about the night that Lucy and I read together in front of a packed house in Provincetown. She read an essay about masturbating for a very long time in front of a man she had met in a bar. In my book about Lucy, I wrote about how bothered I had been to hear my friend tell such an intimate story—a story I had never heard—in front of so many strangers.

"It's a terrible thing to say about her," my father told me over the phone. "You've got to take it out."

"But it's true," I said. "I didn't make it up. I can get corroboration from a hundred and fifty witnesses."

"She can't defend herself." He was right about that: Lucy couldn't defend herself. She had died, and it was her death that had led me to write about her.

"She wrote the essay, she read it out loud, and then she published it," I said. "It isn't gossip."

My father told me I should be a better friend. The story stayed in, but believe me, no one else ever masturbated in anything I wrote.

In all fairness, my father was only expressing his opinions, opinions I could have easily divined. I could have waited and just sent him the books once they were published, but he loved to see my work as stacks of paper, and I relied on his assistance. Every time we talked he asked me how close I was to finishing. He'd sit down and read whatever I sent him the minute it arrived. That immediacy meant a lot to me. It means a lot to any writer.

My father died of a neurological disorder called progressive supranuclear palsy. For four years we thought he couldn't possibly have more than a month to live, and for four years he surprised us. In that time I wrote a book of essays called *This Is the Story of a Happy Marriage*. There was plenty in that book I hadn't wanted him to see, but I thought he would die before it came out. When I realized that wouldn't be the case, I flew to California and read the book to him. His illness had made speaking difficult, and his criticism and praise were now marked by economy. "Not good," he said at the end of a couple of the essays. "Yes," he said to others. When I read him the essay about the death of my grandmother, my mother's mother whom he had dearly loved, he sat in his wheelchair and cried.

People love to ask writers about their influences. Did growing up in the South shape my work, or was it my early obsession with Saul Bellow? Did I think of myself as a Catholic writer? A women's writer? I will tell you: as a writer I am first and foremost my father's daughter. I didn't operate out of a desire to please him so much as a desire not to offend him, and the truth is that the constraints did my work little harm. I found plenty of things to write about that weren't smoking or swearing or sex. With the extra time and energy they had, my characters went out and saw the world.

Before he died, I used to wonder what it would be like to know I would never have his eyes on something I'd written. My father was still alive when I was working on *Commonwealth*, and once again I was certain I wouldn't finish it until after he had died. This time I was right.

I loved my father, and I wished for him every minute of life that his body could afford him. He didn't want to die. Still, after his death, I wrote with an openness I had not previously known. I was fifty-one years old. I wrote about California and divorce and police officers, second marriages and stepchildren. I wrote about people who were like my family and nothing like my family. It was time to pull down the fences and let my story go wherever it wanted to go. I had been a good daughter, and my father had been a good father. He had helped me in every way he knew how. I would miss his advice, even the advice that had irritated me. His death marked a passage in my growth as a writer, but if I were able to choose—the book or my father—I would have him back.

OR NOT.

It was just after New Year's in 2012 when I ran into my friend Felice at Costco. She asked me how I was doing and I told her.

"My dad is dying," I said. My sister and I, along with our husbands, had just spent Christmas in California with my father and stepmother, and it was clear that Dad's Parkinson's, diagnosed two years before, had reached a new and critical phase. My sister, stepmother and I kept slipping off to cry together, so shaken were we by the fact that he was really dying now. I stayed on an extra week to arrange for around-the-clock help. My stepmother could no longer lift him in and out of the bed by herself, on and off the toilet, in and out of the shower.

In Costco I told Felice that I would do everything I could to help my father, but that I wasn't going to be sad. "He's still alive," I said, imagining then that he might last a few months more. "I've decided to wait and feel terrible once he's dead."

"Or not," she said brightly, and gave me a hug.

Or not. Those two words followed me around for the next three years while my sister and I made our monthly alternating trips to California, as I took on all the extra work I could find to pay the crushing costs of in-home care, as I made those sad daily phone calls. When my father could no longer hold the phone, my stepmother put him on the speakerphone, and when he could barely speak, I carried on the conversation without him. Every time I visited he was a little more frozen, his muscles boiling beneath the surface of his skin. He liked to hold hands in the last months of his life, and holding his hand was like holding a linen sack full of bumblebees.

My father's medical care did not contain a single heroic measure— no feeding tube, no respirator. Some of the pills he took calmed his condition for a few hours at a time, but none of them improved or slowed the progression of his disease. But what my father's care lacked in heroic measures it made up for in bravery, especially on the part of my stepmother, who cared for him at home with unflagging love and good cheer. Even with help he was her full-time job, and I knew that without her he would have been my full-time job, or my sister's. My father, strapped into his wheelchair, never stopped demanding in his vanishing whisper that he wanted to go: to the opera, to the movies, to his weekly Rotary meeting. She brushed his hair and teeth, stretched his bent limbs, kept him clean. She cut his food into smaller and smaller bites and fed it to him slowly, a perilous task as he was prone to choking.

I had been wrong when I told Felice that I would wait until after he died to feel sad. I felt sad about my father all the time. When I closed my eyes at night I saw him lashed to a raft in a storm-tossed sea: dark rain, dark waves, my father crashing down again and again as he waited to drown. He had been with the LAPD for thirty-three years. He was the guy who took in Sirhan Sirhan the night Bobby Kennedy was assassinated. After his retirement he often spent three hours a day working out. When he got his diagnosis, first for Parkinson's and then for progressive supranuclear palsy in his late seventies, he could still do a hundred pull-ups.

In the last year of my father's life, I reread Updike's Rabbit Angstrom novels. I couldn't explain why, other than to say I craved them. I got to the end of *Rabbit at Rest* just as the plane touched down in San Diego. Things were bad with my father, and my sister and I were flying out together to say goodbye. How many times had we come to say goodbye? I closed the book and turned on my phone. I listened to a message from Karl telling me Dad had died. What I felt when I heard the news was joy.

I had told Felice that I would feel bad when my father died. "Or not," she had said.

MY FATHER'S BODY was still at the house when we arrived. My stepmother, crying in a room full of friends, said she wanted him to be there for us. My sister and I went into the bedroom together, and there he was, his head tilted back on the pillow, his eyes closed, his mouth slightly open. We kissed his lovely face and cried and held one another, and then we looked at him again. Something funny was going on. "He looks like he's about to tell a joke," I said, peering closely. My sister, who is a more tender person than I am, quicker to cry, leaned forward. "Dad," she said quietly. "Say something funny."

When we went to sit among the crying people in the other room, I was stunned by the explosion of happiness spreading through my chest. Of course I was glad for my father, the end of his suffering, his ticket off the raft, but it was more than that. I was glad for my stepmother even as she sat beside me in her fiery grief, because she was still healthy and young. In time she would go out with her friends again, take a trip, read a book, waste an afternoon looking at shoes. I felt glad for my sister and for myself, that any bit of extra time and money we had would no longer be offered up in the name of filial devotion. This wasn't about whether or not I loved my father. I did love him. He was brave and funny and smart. He could also be difficult even in the full bloom of health, and he often drove me witless, just as I could be difficult, and drive him witless. I was his daughter, after all. I was happy for all of us that this hideous struggle that had extended past the most unreasonable expectations was finally over. I was trying my best not to glow.

I stayed on in California for a while to be with my stepmother. I confided my happiness to a few friends, and for the most part they were quick to assure me that I would be grief-stricken soon enough. They meant it kindly. By using the words *death* and *joy* in the same sentence, I had gone far beyond the limits of "He's in a better place." They wanted me to know that later I would have the chance to redeem myself through suffering.

"What if you've thrown a dinner party," I said. "And at eleven o'clock your guests finally get up to leave. The dishes are still on the table, the pans are in the sink, you have to go to work in the morning, but the guests just keep standing in the open door saying good night. They tell you another story, praise your cooking, go back to look for their gloves. They do this for four years."

I've often wondered why the people who seem most certain of the existence of God are the ones who want to keep the respirator plugged in. If you were sure that God was waiting for your father, wouldn't you want him to go? Wouldn't you want him to go even if you didn't believe in God, because death is the completion of our purpose here on earth? He's finished his job and now is free to send his atoms back into the earth and sea and stars. Isn't that really kind of great?

Like most everyone else, I've had my share of grief. When my sister's husband died unexpectedly at the age of fifty-nine, I fell down the open manhole with my sister and the rest of the people who loved him. But my father? He'd been gone for such a long time. He had told us how much he loved us, and we'd told him how much we loved him, again and again and again, until there was nothing left to say.

Except for this: Dad, there is joy in the place that you left.

What the American · Academy of Arts and Letters Taught Me about Death

I went to the American Academy of Arts and Letters in 2005 because I'd won a writing prize, and with that prize came an invitation to a luncheon before the ceremony. Every honoree was allowed to bring a guest, and I invited my friend Patrick Ryan. We boarded the subway on 14th Street and took it all the way to 155th Street, he in his summer suit and me in my best dress.

I'm not a New Yorker by any stretch, and the neighborhood of Washington Heights was unfamiliar to me. The Beaux Arts building of the academy, the long, sloping hill of Trinity Cemetery, and then the view of the Hudson River made me feel like we'd gone down to catch the train in Kansas and resurfaced in Oz. Writers and artists and composers were coming towards us from every direction, people whose work we'd committed to memory and whose faces we knew on sight. The day was windy, and Patrick and I were so nervous we ducked down a few stairs on the side of the enormous building to smoke. When we finished our cigarettes we were brave again.

I have such fondness for that memory, that moment, as it would be the summer I quit smoking for good. No more cigarettes for courage while staring into an elegant cemetery after that.

I had known very little about the academy before we got there. I didn't understand anything about how the place worked. At the registration desk, I gave my name and received a program and our table number. Someone introduced me to Tony Kushner. Tony Kushner! While shaking his hand, I asked him if he had won an award as well. He told me no, he was being inducted.

"Am I being inducted?" I asked. Everyone around us laughed. Who knew I was so funny? I'd been invited to visit for the afternoon. I hadn't been invited to stay.

Patrick and I went to look for our table like a couple of middle-schoolers who find themselves in MIT's cafeteria by way of a dream. We found the table and then found our place cards. I was seated next to John Updike.

When I was young, I read the books that were available, not the books that were appropriate. I read what my mother and stepfather left lying around, which meant I read Updike. His sentences, his characters, his imperatives, filled my brain when my brain was soft and at its most impressionable. Along with Bellow and Roth, he was my influence, the person who had made me want this job in the first place, the person who (I believed) was showing me what adult life would look like, what sex and love and work would look like. He stood from the table to greet me. Of all the things I ever imagined might happen in my life, sitting next to John Updike at a luncheon in the courtyard of a Beaux Arts building beneath a white tent at a table full of flowers was not among them. Lore Segal was seated there, Calvin Trillin and Edmund White. Updike asked who I had come with, and when I told him, he winked at Patrick from across the table.

Updike could not have been kinder or more charming. In a crowd of people whom I imagined to be his friends, he was conversationally attentive to me. Still, I could feel the strain in every seam of my composure. I asked him about Bellow, who had died a few weeks before. He shrugged. He said he didn't know him well. How was that possible, when the two of them had been stacked, one on top of the other, on so many nightstands of my youth?

When I could not bear the proximity for another minute, when I feared I would grab the lapels of his light-colored suit jacket and shout *Don't you know that you are my god?*, I gave Patrick the high sign with my eyebrows. We excused ourselves separately and found our way to what appeared to be a ballroom that no one was using. Much of the art on the walls had been painted by people who were, at that exact moment, eating lunch beneath the tent. Patrick and I held hands and tried not to scream.

"*I am sitting next to John Updike!*" I scream-whispered.

"*You are sitting next to John Updike!*" he silently screamed in reply.

After lunch we were separated, sent off in two directions by staff holding clipboards: Patrick went into the auditorium, while Updike and I took our seats side by side in folding chairs on the stage. Updike was going to present my award, which consisted of a certificate and a not insignificant check. Joan Didion was there, Gordon Parks, Chuck Close, Cindy Sherman, John Guare, everyone arranged on risers like a freakishly talented grade school class waiting to have their picture taken.

And then someone took our picture.

The ceremony that followed was epically long: honors bestowed, lifetime achievement medals distributed, speeches made. The room was hot, and as time passed the luncheon receded into distant memory. From where we sat, we could watch the members of the audience falling asleep in their theater seats: family, friends, editors, agents. Every time an award was given, Updike remarked on whether or not a kiss had accompanied the handing over of the certificate and check.

"Look," he said, leaning sideways to whisper. "He kissed her."

The two hundred fifty members in the American Academy of Arts and Letters are a group composed of writers, composers, visual artists, and architects. The number stays at 250. When a member dies, potential new members are nominated and voted on. Twelve years after my visit, I received a letter informing me of my induction.

I stood in my kitchen and stared at the paper in my hand for a very long time. I was thinking of Updike. After my blunder with Tony Kushner, I had never allowed myself to wonder if I might one day be elected. But someone had died and, in doing so, had made a place for me.

THE PORTRAIT GALLERY is a large room in the Academy building where a photograph of everyone who has ever been a member is hung. Black-and-white portraits in identical narrow frames hang floor to ceiling, side to side, without an inch of space in between. The photos are arranged not in order of birth or death but in the order of induction, as if that were the moment life began. I'd walked through the gallery briefly the first time I was there and marveled at the assemblage, but when I went back in 2017, I had the time to make a real study of the place. There at the beginning in the highest corner was Samuel Clemens, then Henry James and Edward Mac-Dowell. They were among the founding members of the Academy in 1898. I walked slowly around the room, letting my gaze run up and down the walls. Again, it was an afternoon in May. Soon we would be called to a luncheon and ceremony. Those things didn't change. I hadn't had a cigarette in twelve years and was well past missing them. People wandered in and out of the gallery, some of them talking, others standing there, taking it in. W. E. B. Du Bois and John Dos Passos and Winslow Homer and Langston Hughes and Randall Jarrell and Georgia O'Keeffe and Eudora Welty, Steinbeck and Stravinsky, Thornton Wilder and E. B. White shared a defining connection: they were dead.

But then I found I. M. Pei, inducted in 1963, the year I was born. He was still alive. After more dead people I found W. S. Merwin, inducted in 1972. Alive! Then dead, dead, dead, dead—until I found George Crumb, inducted in 1975. Alive. After that, a mix: alive and alive and dead and dead and dead and alive. It went like that, broken up, almost equal for a few short minutes until finally the balance tipped and more and more people were alive, fewer were dead. There was John Updike, the great man, whose work was now irretrievably out of fashion. Was there a college student anywhere who cut her teeth on those Rabbit novels now? Probably not. Could I have wished for a better influence in my early life when I was still capable of being influenced? Never. There was Grace Paley, who died in 2007. She had been my teacher in college. Her stories full of practical activism are perfect for these times, but who's to say that anyone's getting around to them? Two more of my teachers were on the wall—Allan Gurganus and Russell Banks—still very much alive. And then at last I came to the end of my review, finding, already framed and hanging, the group of the writers who would be inducted in a matter of hours: Kay Ryan, Edward Hirsch, Amy Hempel, Ursula K. Le Guin, Colum McCann, Junot Díaz, Henri Cole, Ann Patchett.

Me. My framed black-and-white photograph so clearly in the camp of the living. The picture I'd chosen to send was joyful because joyful was how I felt when they asked for one. I'm showing all my teeth and am completely out of step with every serious and circumspect photograph surrounding me. If you were to look at all those photos without knowing who any of us were, you would point to mine and say, "That one's still alive."

But the math in this room was inescapable—two hundred fifty seats at the table, and no one gets to stay. Over time, what is considered to be the center of the exhibition will shift, and my photograph will eventually be in the middle, closer to the group that are mostly dead, and then finally enveloped into the entirely dead. Dying was the essential contract, after all. The Portrait Gallery laid it out clearly: this is where I am and this is where I'm going.

Somewhere a bell was ringing. We were being called outside to lunch. For a split second I wondered if I hadn't made a mistake by accepting the invitation, in handing over my picture. Wasn't that a laugh? It was a beautiful day, a day of celebration. We ate and then I took my place in the front of the risers with my class.

Soon after I was home, I received a small white envelope in the mail with a small white card inside.

*The officers of the American Academy of Arts and Letters note
with sorrow the death of the novelist Denis Johnson, of California,
on Wednesday, May Twenty-Fourth, Two Thousand Seventeen, at
the age of sixty-seven. Mr. Johnson was elected in Two Thousand
Fourteen.*

THE SIMPLE FORMALITY of the announcement moved me, and so I kept it. Another one came in June: A. R. Gurney was dead. In July, it was Sam Shepard.

I had a wooden box made to hold the cards. In the years since becoming a member, I've received forty of them. Ursula K. Le Guin died eight months after being inducted, her picture just a couple of frames over from mine. Philip Roth, who had been inducted in 1970, died the week after Tom Wolfe, who was inducted in 1999. The human impulse is to look for order, but there isn't any. People come and go. When you try to find your place among all the living and dead, the numbers are unmanageable, but working within a fixed group—two hundred fifty people, one building, a roomful of framed photographs—there's no fooling yourself. Is this my time? Maybe and maybe not, but my time is coming, and it should. Someone out there is waiting for my place.

John Updike died of lung cancer in Danvers, Massachusetts, on January 27, 2009, three and a half years after I first stood at the top of 155th Street and looked down the green lawn of Trinity Cemetery and out to the Hudson River, three and a half years after I sat beside him onstage. If I could stop time, it would be to read all of his books—the stories and novels and poetry and essays and criticism, the successful books and the failures, the ones I'd read before and the ones I'd never heard of. I wouldn't care what anyone had to say about them. There would be so much of life left for me if that was all I asked for.

"Oh," he had whispered after a particularly disappointing presentation of an award. "No kiss."

When my name was called, we walked down to the lectern together and he handed me the framed certificate and check, then kissed me on the cheek, the way a father kisses a daughter on her wedding day before stepping back.

That was the gift, not the award or the induction. It was the beautiful day, the view of the river, the long sloping lawn of the cemetery, the single cigarette, that kiss.

· A Day at the Beach ·

Every day we say we should go to the beach. The beach is our idea: Patty's, Georgienne's, mine. We sit around Sooki on the sofa and suggest a change of scenery. Wouldn't it be good to get out? Sooki agrees. She loves the beach. We can make it a girls' trip, a getaway. We can bundle her up and put her in the front seat, drive slow on the twisting canyon roads. We'll be careful—those roads would make anyone carsick. Even if we only went for an hour, it would be worth it. Patty says we should have a sleepover at her house, but Sooki isn't sure she could be gone overnight.

I tell her the two of us can sleep together in the big bed downstairs, so if she needs to get up in the night, I'd be there. If she needs a pill, I'd be there. Larry, a doctor friend whose helpfulness has proved indispensable, could come over in the morning and start the infusion. Infusion on the beach! It sounds like a cocktail. It is a sort of cocktail, with the potassium and magnesium, the Zofran. We could go for a night and give Sooki's husband Ken a rest. Maybe?

At the end of every day, Sooki says, "I wanted to get to the beach today." She thinks about the ocean all the time, about the ocean and the mountain trails and the birds and the bats and the skinks. Sooki is bound to the natural world, and as beautiful as her living room is—with its blue walls and white curtains and the light coming in from three sides—the chance to feel the sun on her face would be worth everything now.

The beach we have in mind is only a half-hour drive, but we might as well be planning to move her to Cap-Ferrat for the summer. How do the days get away from us? All we do is wait on phone calls from doctors. We wait on her stomach to settle and the sharp pain in her back to ease. We wait on lab results and the morning visit from Laura, the gentle home-health nurse who works the night shift on an obstetrics ward before coming over to start Sooki's line. She tells us how many babies had been born the night before. "Five!" she says when she arrives one morning. "I never sat down all night." Her husband drives her over and waits in the car because she's too tired to drive.

"Let's really go to the beach today," Georgienne says. "Once this bag is over."

Our fixation on the ocean feels both beautiful and foolish. The IV fluids nauseate Sooki, as does sitting up, standing up, speaking. Food is out of the question. But then one afternoon out of nowhere she says, "Okay, let's go."

We move quickly then. We mean to seize the day, knowing there are a million things to stop us. We put a half a scopolamine patch behind her ear and pack the hydromorphone and the bright blue plastic bags for throwing up. We pour the little bit of smoothie she tried and failed to drink for lunch in a to-go cup, and bring along the telescoping steel travel straw Georgienne gave her. Georgienne brought one for each of us. We had taken turns massaging Sooki's feet all morning, working the edema up her legs until her feet resembled feet again. These feet that had run marathons and hiked trails and carried her up and down the endless flights in hospital stairwells while she tried to raise her white count. These feet look like baby's feet now, too soft and round to think that they could hold her. We carefully stuff them into her shoes. We hold her hands going out to the car, one of us on either side.

Thirty minutes later, we're looking at waves, inhaling the fresh sea air. Time was, we thought that triumph meant beating recurrent pancreatic cancer. We weren't looking for remission but a full-on cure. Later, we thought that triumph would be hanging on a few more years. But on this day we know that triumph is making it to the beach. Sooki has accomplished this singular act of heroism, and we are overjoyed.

Sooki has her sunglasses on. Patty drags the lounge chair over and we wrap our friend in furry blankets until she looks like a tiny movie star making her transatlantic crossing incognito. Sooki's friend Jill arrives, and then Jill's husband, Sparky, and we sit in a circle around the chaise longue and make one another laugh. Sooki has told us more than once that even if she wasn't talking, she liked to hear us talking. She liked the sound of our laughter. But that isn't even why we're doing it. We're laughing because we're happy. We feel like we've gotten away with something. We managed to skip out on our sadness for a couple of hours and come to the beach, and that's the closest thing to a miracle we can drum up at this point.

This group is bound together by our desire to hold Sooki aloft, to lift her up to the sun. I'm the new friend and no one cares. They've all been so welcoming. More friends will arrive after I leave, more family, and more friends will come after that, until there are no more days. Patty's husband, John, crosses the beach with his guitar and sits in a chair at Sooki's feet, his back to the ocean. "I'm going to sing you a song," he tells her. "I've been practicing."

And then he begins to sing, *Close your eyes and I'll kiss you, tomorrow I'll miss you.*

I don't know how many times this has happened—I'm fine, and then suddenly there is such a crack in my chest that I think I will lie down in the sand and never get up. The same thought flashes around the circle, I can feel the bright needle of sorrow stitching us together, but we sing the chorus anyway because it's all we know to do.

All my loving, darling I'll be true.

Had anyone asked, I would have said that trip to the beach would be her last time out of the house. Two days later, her art show will open at the ROSEGALLERY in Santa Monica and no one thinks she can go. Sooki and Jill and I had taped a talk on Zoom a while back to play in the likely event of her absence. Arrangements are made so that Sooki can watch the whole thing from the sofa. Her two sisters are flying in from the East Coast with their ninety-five-year-old mother. Sooki's daughter and son-in-law will be there, her son and daughter-in-law, her two grandchildren. Patty brings over a sharp-looking black jumpsuit for Sooki to wear, size Impossibly Tiny, and it hangs like a shadow on the back of the living room door. Ken tries on the sport coat and the blue shirt he plans to wear to the show, and we all remark on how the shirt brings out his eyes. Sooki's eyes are closed.

But when the time comes, she's awake. She digs in deep and

finds one more vein of inner resources that has yet to be tapped. Inner resources! What could be left? For three years of illness she has mined herself: her strength and her sheer force of will, her mind over matter. She persists by borrowing from herself, borrowing reserves she does not have. Sooki pulls herself up from the sofa and puts on eye makeup. She puts on her velvet coat embroidered with peonies, and Ken drives her to the gallery along with her mother and sisters.

JILL HAD TOLD Sooki months before that she should paint a self-portrait wearing that coat, and Sooki had done it. There it is, hanging on the wall of the ROSEGALLERY when we arrive. Sooki the artist, the exquisite hipster. She's wearing her sunglasses, looking back at the viewer, while a brightly colored exotic bird flies off the edge of the canvas behind her—a piece of her own dazzling self broken loose and soaring away.

Rose, the gallery owner, has put two comfortable chairs in a corner so Sooki and her mother can sit and receive the crowds, the throngs. They accept every embrace, and stack the bouquets of flowers on the small table between them. I want to say that for two hours she seems so well that no one would know she's dying, but everyone knows. People form a line in order to declare their love to Sooki, and then they go and study her paintings, the bright orange poppies of Topanga State Park after the fire, her granddaughter Anja striding forward, her grandson Oliver reading a book. There are paintings of bats, of the Malibu coast, of two bright owls, of Ken sitting in front of their house. I have seen all of these paintings before, but seeing them together on the walls I understand the enormity of what we stand to lose: color, imagination, this singular eye.

I ask Rose if she's going to say a few words, and she tells me there are too many people. She'd never be able to get everyone to be quiet. I smile at her and raise my voice like a Catholic school principal, a mother superior. "Everyone," I call out, and immediately they settle, turning their faces towards us as one. "Pay attention. We're all here to celebrate Sooki." Quieting rooms is my party trick.

Rose says a few words, and so do I, Sooki standing between us. Then Sooki lifts up her voice while the crowd stays perfectly still, holding their collective breath to listen. She lifts her voice like the bird flying past the shoulder of her peony coat. "I can't tell you what it means for all of you to be here, and to be in my life, celebrating this moment," she says. "Celebrating the years we've had together. It's been such a special part of my life, really, from my heart, thank you." And then the people in the gallery are clapping and clapping and they will not stop. They cheer, and the cheering gets louder. Sooki, who has spent so much of her life weathering applause for other people, stands in this thrum of noise that is only for her. She puts her hand to her heart, and accepts what is given with radiance.

At the end of the night, I say goodbye to my friend. That was always our plan. I would leave after the opening, after her mother and sisters arrived. There would be a hand-off. We stand in the corner and hold each other, and then we let go. We've said goodbye forever before. We know how it's done. My friend Maile has come to the show to collect me, and I sit in her car and I cry.

AND THAT WOULD be the end of the story, except that while I'm at my stepmother's house two hours away, my travel plans change. It turns out there are a few extra days after all, precious days that no one expected, and so I go back. Sooki's sister Judy has taken their mother home to New York, but her sister Ruthie has decided to stay. As soon as I'm in the house again, I start to rub Sooki's feet. She has gotten measurably weaker in the few days I've been gone. Things have been lost even though I would have sworn there was nothing left to lose

"Let's go to the beach," Patty says on my last day. This time it's the real last day. I've been staying at Patty's.

"Really?" I say.

"Let's," Sooki says.

WE ALL KNOW what the end will be now, we've known it for a while. If an ending could be changed through strategic planning or force of will or the sheer love of life, things would go differently, but this cannot be changed. Sooki did everything that could be done. The miracle is that we make it back to the beach, Patty and Georgienne and Larry, Sparky and Jill, sweet Ruthie. We wrap Sooki up again. We sing "Harper Valley P.T.A." and make ourselves laugh. We write the important letters that need to be written and make ourselves cry. We take in the fullness of the day and the joy of being together and we are grateful for every second until it's time to go.

I say goodbye to Sooki in the driveway. "We keep doing this," I say. For once I am making an effort not to cry, or to cry less.

"Let's keep doing this," she says. "Let's do this forever."

SOOKI RAPHAEL, BORN June 13, 1955, died April 25, 2021.

Acknowledgments

The following essays were originally published in slightly different form in the following publications:

"Three Fathers," "How to Practice," and "Flight Plan" originally appeared in the *New Yorker*

"The First Thanksgiving": *New York Times*

"The Paris Tattoo": *An Innocent Abroad*, ed. Don George

"My Year of No Shopping": *New York Times*

"The Worthless Servant": *Not Less than Everything*, ed. Catherine Wolff

"To the Doghouse": *Washington Post*; *The Peanuts Papers*, ed. Andrew Blauner

"Eudora Welty, an Introduction": *The Collected Stories of Eudora Welty*, reprint ed.

"How Knitting Saved My Life. Twice": *Knitting Yarns*, ed. Ann Hood

ACKNOWLEDGMENTS

"Tavia": *Real Simple*

"A Paper Ticket is Good for One Year": *The Lonely Planet Travel Anthology*, ed. Don George

"The Moment Nothing Changed": *Wall Street Journal*

"A Talk to the Association of Graduate School Deans in the Humanities": Talk given in Nashville

"The Nightstand": The Eudora Welty Lecture

"Cover Stories": *The Dutch House* (Waterstone's special edition)

"Reading Kate DiCamillo": *New York Times*

"Sisters": *Washington Post*, May 10, 2019; *Apple, Tree*, ed. Lise Funderburg

"Two More Things I Want to Say about My Father": "The Editor," Powell's Books Blog, and "Or Not," *New York Times*

"These Precious Days": *Harper's Magazine*

About the Author

ANN PATCHETT is the author of eight novels, four works of non-fiction, and two children's books. She has been the recipient of numerous awards, including the PEN/Faulkner, the Women's Prize in the U.K., and the Book Sense Book of the Year. Her most recent novel, *The Dutch House*, was a finalist for the Pulitzer Prize. Her work has been translated into more than thirty languages. *TIME* magazine named her one of the 100 Most Influential People in the World. She lives in Nashville, Tennessee, where she is the co-owner of Parnassus Books.

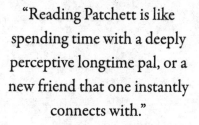